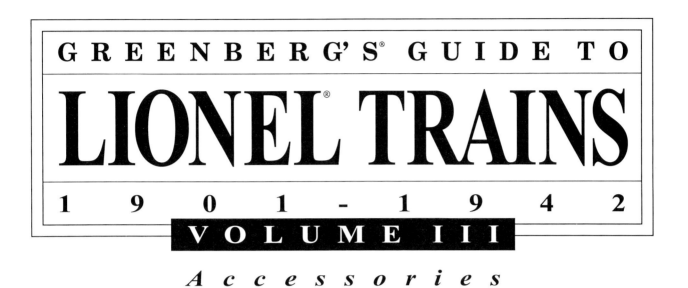

GREENBERG'S® GUIDE TO
LIONEL® TRAINS
1 9 0 1 - 1 9 4 2
VOLUME III
Accessories

Peter H. Riddle, Ph.D.

Greenberg Publishing Company, Inc.
Sykesville, Maryland

Copyright © 1993
Greenberg Publishing Company, Inc.

Greenberg Books
A Division of Kalmbach Publishing Co.
21027 Crossroads Circle
Waukesha, WI 53187
(414) 796-8776

First Edition
Originally published in hardcover, 1992
Second printing, 1992
First paperback printing, 1996

Manufactured in the United States of America

Greenberg Publishing Company, Inc., publishes the world's largest selection of Lionel, American Flyer, LGB, Marx, Ives, and other toy train publications as well as a selection of books on model and prototype railroading, dollhouse building, and collectible toys. For a complete listing of current Greenberg publications, please call 1-800-533-6644 or write to Kalmbach Publishing Co., 21027 Crossroads Circle, Waukesha, Wisconsin 53187.

Greenberg Shows, Inc., sponsors *Greenberg's Great Train, Dollhouse and Toy Shows*, the world's largest of their kind. The shows feature extravagant operating train layouts and a display of magnificent dollhouses. The shows also present a huge marketplace of model and toy trains, for HO, N, and Z Scales; Lionel O and Standard Gauges; S and 1 Gauges; plus layout accessories and railroadiana. They also offer a large selection of dollhouse miniatures and building materials, and collectible toys. Shows are scheduled along the East Coast each year from Massachusetts to Florida. For a list of our current shows, please call (410) 795-7447 or write to Greenberg Shows, Inc., 7566 Main Street, Sykesville, Maryland 21784 and request a show brochure.

Greenberg Auctions, a division of Greenberg Shows, Inc., offers nationally advertised auctions of toy trains and toys. Please contact our auction manager at (410) 795-7447 for further information.

ISBN 0-89778-432-4

Library of Congress Cataloging-in-Publication Data

Riddle, Peter.
    Greenberg's guide to Lionel trains, 1901–1942 / Peter H. Riddle—
    1st ed.
        p. cm.
    "Amplification of Bruce Greenberg's original research"—Galley.
    Contents:—v. 3. Accessories.
    ISBN 0-89778-432-4
    1. Railroads—Models.   2. Lionel Corporation.   I. Greenberg,
    Bruce C.   Guide to Lionel trains, 1901–1942.   II. Title.
    III. Title: Guide to Lionel trains, 1901–1942.
    TF197.R486 1993
    625.1'9'075—dc20
                                                    92-39687
                                                            CIP

CONTENTS

ACKNOWLEDGMENTS

The author is indebted to many talented and knowledgeable people who have contributed immeasurably to this volume. Their generosity has proven to be boundless. Some have provided access to their collections, while others have donated considerable amounts of time to reviewing this manuscript for accuracy. Others have made possible the many photographs which fill this book, and assisted in polishing the text.

The diversity of items manufactured by Lionel is so vast that no one person could assemble an accurate record without help. Our research is enhanced by the efforts of many enthusiasts who have contributed separate pieces of the mosaic of Lionel Prewar accessory production. Despite all the effort that has gone into the project so far, this book cannot be considered complete, and we eagerly solicit any and all information that may increase our knowledge. Readers who discover inaccuracies, or who possess variations not listed in these pages, are encouraged to share this information with us, so that the next edition may be more accurate.

Gay Riddle is my partner in train collecting as well as my wife, and in addition to her enthusiastic support of my efforts, has proofread every word of my manuscripts. Her keen eye for inconsistency, and her sure sense of what is both historically probable and sociologically sensible, have led me to examine carefully the conclusions reached through my studies. Almost as important is her expertise with computers, which has bailed me out of difficulties on more than one occasion.

Ron Morris possesses an exceptional memory for detail, and an almost encyclopedic knowledge of early Lionel accessories. His acute observations led the author to search out new information that avoided many possible errors. Ron also assisted in achieving greater consistency in terminology and color definition, and contributed countless details to the descriptions. His cooperation and donation of time were considerable, and his reproductions of Lionel scenic plots grace the author's layout with beauty and authenticity.

Gary Zippie opened his home to the author for a memorable three-day session of examining and photographing his extensive collection of new and nearly new boxed accessories. His donation of time and expertise shed much new light on these beautiful toys, and his steadfast preservation of them is a service to everyone in this field. His associate in the hobby, **Gary Barnett**, also provided a considerable number of his valued Lionel pieces for examination and photography at the expense of his personal time and travel, and we are very grateful. Special thanks also go to **Roger Bartelt** for allowing us to photograph his extensive collection of many late Prewar accessories.

Brad Schwab was our man behind the camera for the Zippie-Barnett shoot. It is largely through his expertise that readers may examine with exceptional clarity and in such minute detail the accessories of Lionel's Prewar period.

Through his research into and authorship of many articles and books concerning toy trains, **Dr. Bruce Greenberg** has developed a discerning grasp of virtually all areas of the subject, as well as an acuteness of perception when examining the toys themselves and the historical context in which they were made. His kindness in opening his home and collection to the author is matched only by his assistance in creating accurate descriptions of items included in this book.

Special thanks are due to **Christian F. Rohlfing**, the editor of *Greenberg's Guide To Lionel Trains, 1901-1942, Volumes I and II*. His amplification of Bruce Greenberg's original research, and his careful compilation of bits of information from so many different sources, gave the author of this book a firm foundation from which to work.

Mike Wolf of Mike's Train House and **Norman A. Thomas, Jr.** of T-Reproductions generously provided the author with information about reproduced Lionel accessories. **Stuart Armstrong** helped clarify the manufacture of bimetallic strips and design specifications of early motors, and provided other information, as did **Dave McEntarfer** and **Lt. Col. (Ret.) Michael Pandolfo**.

Carlton McKenney of Richmond, Virginia, assisted in describing prototypical sources for Lionel's power station designs. The hospitality he and his wife afforded to the author, including access to their beautiful antique Steinway piano, was greatly appreciated. **Stephen Simon** provided insights into several areas of Lionel production, and helped with descriptions of motorized accessories.

A. Gordon Thomson assisted with technical details of Lionel circuits, and also provided insights into prototype practice, based upon his forty-year career as a railway signal engineer. **Jim Flynn**, who is well known for his knowledge of Marx products, provided additional variations and updated pricing information.

Charles Weber provided such insights as the possible origins of the earliest Lionel accessories, as well as power station prototypes and other items. **Louis A. Bohn**, a Professional Engineer who has worked on other Greenberg publications, offered corrections, dimensions and comments about specifications of bulbs and other items. His corrections of nomenclature about bridge designs were especially helpful.

Of all the many hobbyists and dealers who have assisted the author in acquiring examples of accessories for study during the preparation of this book, Gordon Bosworth deserves special mention. Mr. Bosworth embodies the finest qualities to be found among train collectors: a love of these old toys that goes far beyond their monetary value, a thorough knowledge of items in his collection, a generous willingness to share that knowledge, and scrupulously fair trading practices. His beautiful two-train Magic Electrol Set No. 1061 now graces the author's layout, and its special controller provided first-hand examination of this fascinating technological accessory.

At Greenberg Publishing Company, Editor **Winston Lill, Jr.** organized the overall layout and production of this book, Managing Editor **Allan Miller** oversaw the project, Production Manager **Cindy Lee Floyd** supervised the production of the book, and Art Director **Norm Myers** designed the cover. Acquisitions Editor **Samuel Baum** provided support throughout the project. Graphic Artist **Rick Gloth** designed and pasted up the book's interior, Staff Photographer **Alan Fiterman**, took many of the photos, and Darkroom Specialist **Bill Wantz** developed many of the author's black and white photographs. **Donna Price** proofread the manuscript.

Peter H. Riddle
Kentville, Nova Scotia

FOREWORD

The products of the Lionel Corporation listed in this book include almost everything except locomotives and rolling stock made and sold between 1901 and 1942. In addition to dates of manufacture, dimensions and physical descriptions, a general guide to current values is provided for every item. These values are derived from reports obtained from reviewers, the author's personal purchases, sales and exchanges, and records of auction sales, relying heavily upon prices realized at train meets and shows where the greatest dollar volume of transactions occurs.

These values are selling prices. Should the reader attempt to sell train-related items to dealers for resale, however, it is unlikely that these values would apply. Rather, a dealer would be expected to offer between 50 and 70 percent of these values, in order to resell them at a profit. Private sales may net a higher dollar return, provided the items offered are of especial interest to a particular purchaser.

The value of an old toy train or accessory may depend upon a combination of attributes, including condition, rarity, attractiveness and intended use (operation or display). Conditions may range from Poor to New, but the majority of items from the Prewar period will be found in Good to Excellent condition, and this book provides relative values in these categories. In addition, the expected worth of properly restored pieces is included. These conditions are defined as follows:

GOOD (GD): Scratches, small dents, dirty.

EXCELLENT (EXC): No dents or rust, minute scratches only.

RESTORED (RST): Professionally refinished to appear like new, in a color closely approximat-

ing the original finish; containing all original or accurately reproduced trim and components. (The quality of restoration work varies widely; only refinishing equal to factory standards qualifies an item for the prices listed in this classification.)

Other grading categories are frequently encountered at train meets and in mail order listings. Most common are Fair, Very Good (between Good and Excellent), Like New, Mint and Factory Sealed. The latter two refer to items that are absolutely new and unused, in the original box, and the last requires that the boxes have never been opened. Some larger train meets provide examination of such pieces by means of X-ray. It should be noted that while the difference between a Good and an Excellent example of any accessory may be modest, a *very* substantial premium may be asked for any in really choice condition. The Good and Excellent classifications given in this book are intended for comparative purposes to aid the reader in evaluating these other grading descriptions.

The abbreviation **NRS** also appears following some items. This notation stands for "No Recorded Sales," and indicates that too few reports are available to allow an accurate range of values to be established.

In some instances, the value of an original Lionel item depends upon its particular components. In the majority of cases, however, the color of the finish constitutes the primary difference between variations. For example, only a few 437 Switch Signal Towers were sold with a factory-painted orange roof, and their rarity makes them more desirable and hence more valuable to a collector concerned with such variations. In the case of a restored item, however, color by itself is of no significance; a piece repainted in a color scheme that is considered rare, *even if the piece was that color before restoration*, is of no greater value than the commonest color version in restored condition.

Early Lionel equipment, made during the first two decades of the century, is especially hard to find in excellent or like new condition, and collectors consider good and very good items to be highly desirable. With all toy trains, the highest level of concern is normally given to exterior appearance, and operation is usually secondary. A well preserved piece may be regarded as Excellent and still not be working. Most train meets have test tracks available for prospective purchasers to whom function is an important consideration.

While this book will help a collector to determine whether any given price asked for a toy train accessory represents good value for the money, **there is no substitute for knowledge and experience. We strongly recommend that novice collectors obtain the assistance of friends, with substantial expertise in buying and selling trains, before making major purchases.** Many Lionel items have been reproduced in recent years, and in most cases these items are marked by the manufacturer in order to help the purchaser to ascertain that they are not original. However, such labeling is not always present, or it may be located in an inconspicuous place. In the case of scarce or especially desirable items, **extreme care should be taken to verify originality.** It is advisable to seek the opinion of experts when examining any Lionel piece that has been known to have been remanufactured by others.

The color descriptions used in this book correspond to the chart published by the Train Collectors Association.

Whereas such terms as "red" and "light red" are subject to personal interpretation, this chart provides a standard by which identification may be made with a reasonable degree of accuracy. However, the finish on old toys may be affected by any number of variables, the most common of which are fading (especially due to exposure to sunlight) and paint lot differences at the factory. Rarely does a *minor* difference in color constitute a major difference in value, unless it can be established with certainty that one variation was definitely produced in such few numbers as to constitute true scarcity. The listings also attempt to differentiate between color and material. The most common confusion exists in the use of the term "aluminum" to describe a silvery color of paint, although it may sometimes mean the type of metal of which the toy is made. This book employs the term "aluminum-painted" to describe all items to which this color paint has been applied, regardless of the component materials.

Toy trains are more than mere objects. They constitute artifacts reflective of many facets of life, shedding light upon the social, financial and psychological motives and desires of whole groups and populations. To study them is both personally rewarding and of value to the continuation and expansion of human knowledge, and the sharing of such knowledge is vital. Please join us in this effort.

For further reading, we suggest *Greenberg's Guide to Early American Trains*. Carlisle & Finch, Hafner, and Dorfan, the companies that pioneered toy train design, manufacturing and marketing are extensively covered.

ABOUT THE AUTHOR

When not prowling about auctions and train meet tables, **Peter** and **Gay Riddle** serve Acadia University in Wolfville, Nova Scotia, Canada. Pete is Full Professor and Administrative Head of the School of Music, and has been on the faculty since 1969. In addition to teaching, he oversees programs in performance, education and theoretical subjects, and is an active clinician and festival adjudicator. He is privileged to be associated with a number of public school music programs, for which he writes compositions and arrangements and assists in ensemble concert tours. His earned degrees include a Bachelor of Science, Master of Arts and Doctor of Philosophy.

Gay is Conference, Facilities and Food Services Supervisor for the University, and both of the couple's children are graduates of Acadia. Son **Kendrick** earned a degree in History and is currently employed in Vancouver, British Columbia. Daughter **Anne** is an economist and presently works in Mississauga, Ontario.

Pete's interest in trains is life long, beginning with a set of Lionels even before he was old enough to assemble the track. After many years as an HO-scale modeler, he returned to toy trains upon receipt of a very special gift: a 1917 Ives clockwork set from his wife's parents, **Gertrude** and the late **Harold M. Bull**. This beautiful and almost perfectly preserved toy rekindled a fascination that led Pete to begin assembling his extensive collection of Prewar trains, which now represents fourteen different manufacturers. He has restored many of his acquisitions to factory-fresh condition for use on his three home layouts: clockwork, O Gauge and Standard Gauge. He is the author of two previous Greenberg books, and has served the company as a reviewer and external editor since 1987.

CHAPTER I

Accessories Make the Difference

Joshua Lionel Cowen probably had a monumental cash flow problem in the years immediately following World War I. He commanded a large and efficient factory with a skilled work force capable of producing tens of thousands of train-related toys twelve months out of the year. Keeping this plant in operation meant constant capital, payroll, operating and repair expenses, but sales were largely concentrated into the two months of November and December. He needed a way to promote his products in the off months.

Perhaps no industry is more seasonal than toymaking, with its marketing strategy geared heavily toward the Christmas season, and toy trains became associated with yule celebrations early in the century. Indeed, the image of a Lionel train around the Christmas tree is one of the most pervasive symbols of American life. Lionel sold a tremendous quantity of products during the holiday season, but the factory and workers languished somewhat until it was time to gear up for the following year. While Cowen never completely solved this problem, it was not long before he hit upon at least a partial remedy to his dilemma. He began to shift his emphasis away from the idea of "toy train" and toward the concept of "model railroad."

An examination of the early Lionel catalogues reveals an overwhelming emphasis upon locomotives, rolling stock, trolleys and track products. The 1908 edition, for example, devotes only one page to accessories, limited to three stations and a tunnel. The situation had changed only marginally by 1916, when out of forty pages, only three were concerned with items of a scenic nature to accompany the trains: a station, a bridge (which was probably never made), semaphores, two lamp posts, a tunnel and a set of miniature figures. By contrast, the same catalogue is replete with dozens of trains in two gauges, showing both steam and electric-style locomotives and freight and passenger cars, as well as track and power supplies to make them run, plus a full page of trolleys. Explanatory text deals with motors and the construction of the trains themselves, but almost nothing about the few available accessories.

By contrast, the German manufacturer Märklin catalogued an almost bewildering array of stations and other buildings, lamps, signals, bridges, crossing gates and fences, plus plain and elaborate tunnels with such details as roads, bridges and even castles. That firm's 1904-1908 offerings even included a roundhouse and several sizes of turntables, and such attractive items as derricks and gantry cranes. In the United States, Ives was selling a power house in the 1912 catalogue, as well as a number of tunnels, signals, stations, lamps,

313 Bascule Bridge in a layout setting. P. Riddle Collection and photograph.

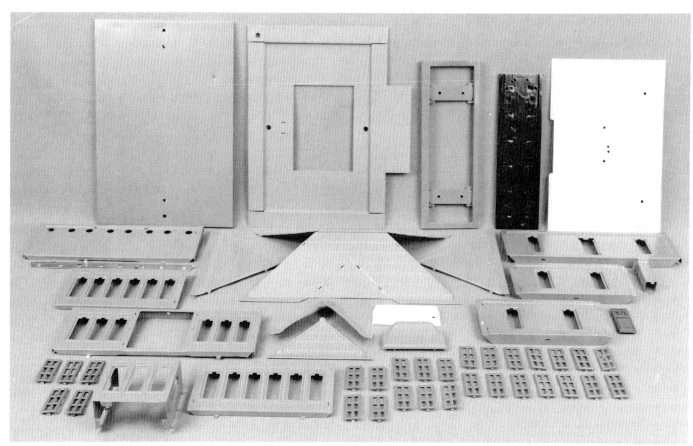

Designed to fit together like a three-dimensional jigsaw puzzle, all of the components of the 437 Switch Signal Tower connect by means of tabs and slots, with the exception of the black-painted wooden knife switch mounting panel (back row, second from right). This item fastens to the lower back wall (back row, third from right) by means of four machine screws. P. Riddle Collection and photograph.

turntables, crossing gates and bridges. These items were heavily promoted, as Ives advertised not just its trains, but an entire "Miniature Railway System."

For Lionel, the first hint of a change in emphasis came with the 1920 catalogue, and the bold invitation printed on the cover: "Own a Railroad and Operate it Yourself." This theme was echoed inside, next to an illustration dominated by a colorful station, a bridge with approach ramps, lamp and telegraph posts, a warning sign, a semaphore and a tunnel. The trains in this drawing seem almost to be an afterthought, lacking detail and overshadowed in size and color by the accessories. "Notice How Realistic the whole layout appears," the text reads. "The addition of plenty of accessories . . . adds wonderfully to the realism, and operating the trains grows more interesting and absorbing than ever."

The number of pages and the prominence given to these items, while still secondary to the trains themselves, is substantially greater than in catalogues of previous years. Especially noteworthy are "The New Lionel Steel Stations" shown in two drawings which emphasize their interior and exterior illumination and complex and attractive simulated brick and stone walls. Prior to this, the company had sold Ives' less elaborate lithographed designs and wooden stations made by the Philadelphia manufacturer Schoenhut.

Although rendered only in black and white, Lionel's two bridge and ramp designs are shown in ten separate illustrations. The semaphores are now brilliant in orange, red and green; the same page in the 1916 catalogue is in drab black and white. Even the simpler signals, posts and warning signs are bright red, yellow and green. Tunnels in three sizes are shown in color on a page all to themselves, and most important of all, "A Complete Electric Railroad" is advertised, with heavy emphasis upon the scenic accessories included with the trains.

Lionel's revised marketing strategy was becoming increasingly apparent. While the early catalogues stress the products "For Window Display and Holiday Gifts," a philosophy destined to equate toy trains with seasonal items to be packed away for most of the year, the promotion of "A Complete Miniature Railroad All Your Own" (1920 catalogue) suggests a toy worthy of permanent installation in the household, to which new items could be added at any time of the year, not just when the Christmas tree was up.

The theme expanded in 1921, and in the 1922 catalogue it burst forth in an impressive illustration of the first Lionel Scenic Railways, displayed on page 2. With their substantial tables, rugged terrain and even a brook, "fitted with a watertight container in which gold fish can be placed," these are hardly just toys.

Selling at prices from $100 to $335 in the East, and consuming floor space equivalent to large pieces of furniture, few were ever sold for home use. Dealers displayed them prominently as promotional devices, however, and they undoubtedly served to whet the appetites of both children and adults who were captivated by miniature railroading. In this manner, the Scenic Railways stimulated the sale of accessories and promoted the concept of year-round railroading.

Nor was this sales approach limited to a single catalogue page. Five "Complete Railroad Outfits" are shown on three separate pages. Although lacking a table and landscaping, these sets were packaged with stations, tunnels, signals and bridges along with both simple and elaborate train sets, priced as low as $20. Newly revised illustrations promote attractive accessories to be purchased separately for addition to existing train layouts. Significantly, the text drives home the idea of a permanent installation, by using such terms as "miniature railroad" frequently. "No miniature railroad is complete without the addition of a 'Lionel City' station," states page 32, and page 35 reads "No miniature railroad layout is complete without the addition of Lionel lamp posts." Page 37 tells us that "A miniature railroad is considerably enhanced by the addition of a set of telegraph posts."

Page 34 of the same catalogue is both curious and significant. The entire page is devoted to a set of replacement bulbs, shown in color, and a kit for installing interior lighting in passenger coaches. Although simple replacement bulbs would not seem to be glamorous items worthy of such attention, for a generation to which the convenience of electric lighting was still relatively new, the image of brightly lighted miniature trains, stations and lamp posts was almost irresistible. Lionel emphasized this attractive feature repeatedly. Miniature bulbs were neither very reliable nor long lasting in those days, and Lionel made sure that the customer knew they were always available, to keep one's railway bright.

A most important development in accessory promotion slipped in almost unnoticed, however, in a small drawing largely overshadowed by semaphores and lamp posts on a page in the 1921 catalogue. The 69 Warning Signal was Lionel's first operating accessory made for toy train use, a post fitted with a railroad crossing sign and a bell to signal the approach of the train. With it came the clever insulated track design that would activate a wide variety of ac-

tion toys through the mid-1930s. Train layouts now had not only motion and lights, but sound!

Had the company realized the sales potential of this item, no doubt the catalogue would have displayed it more prominently. In 1922 it received greater attention, with additional text in larger print. The copy indicates that Lionel had a runaway best seller on its hands: "This accessory was recently introduced by us and has proven to be one of the most popular we make." The designers were not slow to recognize the appeal of accessories that do things, and by 1923, two new concepts appeared in the line, the 76 Block Signal, with its red and green lanterns that light alternately according to the location of the train, and the 77 Crossing Gate that lowers automatically to protect a grade crossing. Both were instantly successful products.

Throughout the 1920s, Lionel's catalogues grew in size, beauty and exaggeration. "The Reason Why Lionel Trains Are Supreme" was immodestly discussed on page 3 in 1924, for example, and the catalogue featured color printing on every one of its forty-four pages. The "Complete Railroad" concept continued, but the company wisely converted the Scenic Railways from table-mounted packages to platforms with scenic components, at substantially reduced prices. Two major innovations appeared early in the decade. First, the residents of Lionelville finally received places to live; in a beautiful two-page spread in the 1923 catalogue, the company introduced its line of three different bungalow and villa designs, brightly lithographed and enameled, and glowing with interior lights. (These were actually first made available in 1922.) In 1924 the 78 Train Control Signal, "The Greatest Achievement in Miniature Electric Train Engineering," promised and

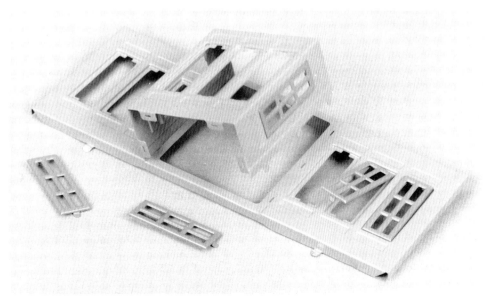

Six tabs connect the bay window to the upper front wall, which is punched out in the center to allow the bay to be lighted by the central interior bulb. Each of the window inserts has two tabs (top and bottom), and the window openings in the walls are recessed and notched to accommodate them. P. Riddle Collection and photograph.

Four tabs from the canopy hold the floor and walls of the bay window together. Top and bottom tabs hold the window frame in place. P. Riddle Collection and photograph.

delivered a reliable system for causing trains to pause briefly in front of a station, then continue down the track, completely without operator intervention.

The latter 1920s were remarkably prosperous years, and Lionel's marketing achievements funded elaborate expansions into massive and ever more elaborate train sets. By 1928 accessories and complete railroads dominated thirteen of the catalogue's forty-eight pages, and operational items (such as remote-control switches and a Standard Gauge turntable) were featured on other pages. The success of previously introduced buildings, bridges and signals led the designers to create the first of a series of huge and impressive structures for the "luxury" segment of the market. They placed their largest station on an elevated terrace over 2½ feet long, complete with six lamp standards and with a flagpole and flower urn surrounded by detailed garden plots. On page 42 the most impressive toy train bridge ever built in America made its initial appearance: a model of New York City's East River "Hellgate." Finally came an immense industrial power station capable of concealing two large transformers with room to spare, and towering 1½ feet in the air.

In 1929 Lionel produced virtually everything needed for building year-round train layouts, although none of the accessories required permanent installation. Even the largest could be set up and taken down by children for whom toy trains were a bedroom floor activity. Railroaders could buy operating railroad and

traffic signals, stations, houses, power stations and signal towers, lamp posts and telegraph poles, and bridges in three styles to span waterways both real and imaginary on layouts in homes from coast to coast. A substantial dealer network existed in the United States and Canada, with significant exports overseas, and the prospects for the company were bright, just on the eve of the Great Depression.

The early 1930s brought drastic reductions in the amount of disposable income for the average family, and toy production in the United States fell to a fraction of the volume enjoyed in the late 1920s. Although the number of new items created was similarly smaller, Lionel did continue to innovate, and a floodlight tower, freight station, water tower and merchandise containers to load into gondolas were all included in the 1931 catalogue. Sales of the more expensive items were the first to decline, and a low-priced line of Lionel-Ives products (later renamed Lionel Junior) and the subsidiary Winner Toy Corporation trains formed an increasingly important portion of the company's output. Accessories were created for this market, too, mostly confined to a lithographed station design, non-operating signals and telegraph poles, and a manual crossing gate. Nevertheless the concept of the "Complete Railroad" was also maintained; the lowest priced was a clockwork train set running on a circle of track, mounted on a landscaped base with a tunnel, bridge, house and four farm animals, all for $2.50.

Although the firm faced difficult times and near bankruptcy during those early Depression years, dedication to quality and innovative toys never disappeared. Scenery received special attention with the 1932 introduction of landscaped plots for bungalows and villas, a grove of trees and a park with a fountain, and even complete villages with houses, plantings and roads already installed. A signal bridge, roundhouse, weighing scale and high tension tower appeared, all relatively high-priced items, and a new line of Lionel City Stations was produced, modeled roughly after New York's Grand Central.

By 1937 the Lionel Corporation had succeeded in creating America's most complete line of model railroad items, and attempted to cover every possible segment of the market. While the toy-oriented part of the business was not overlooked, overtures were made to serious modelers with the introduction of the magnificent scale Hudson locomotive, designed to run on more realistic T-rail track. In response to the growing small scale market, designers were busily preparing the OO Gauge line for introduction the following year. The 1938 catalogue displays a new emphasis on realism, with the older toylike sheet metal locomotives in a minority position, being replaced by modern streamliners and die-cast engines strikingly similar to the real thing. The newest crossing gates were less than half the bulk of earlier models, and no longer towered above the trains. Trackage, especially the new

OO Gauge and solid rail O72 items, looked much more like a real right of way than the tubular sections.

Concurrent developments among the company's most creative designers were about to lead in an entirely new direction, one which would set the pattern for Postwar production. The first accessory with a moving human figure, the Automatic Gateman, had appeared in the 1935 catalogue, and was destined to become Lionel's best selling accessory for over half a century. The level of public demand was such that animation became a top priority, and the first of Lionel's motorized freight loaders debuted in 1938. The remote-control Coal Elevator was designed to be more than a stand-alone accessory. To reach full potential, it requires a spur siding, a remote-control track section and an automatic coal dump car, allowing it to move the freight from an unloading bin on one side to a storage bunker, and then deliver it to a car waiting on the opposite side. Not only was it an attractive item in itself, the Coal Elevator generated sales of switches, track and operating cars to accompany it.

Two years later a motorized Log Loader accomplished the same goals. Introduced at the same time were a magnetic crane and Lionel's only operating bridge prior to the Modern Era, the splendid Bascule Bridge. These motorized accessories more than any other promoted the concept of operation. Lionel Trains no longer traveled through static (if scenically beautiful) countrysides; now they had real purpose! By remote control, logs and coal and scrap metal could be moved from place to place with ease and precision, thanks to dump cars and an ever-improving system of automatic uncoupling.

As North American involvement in the European hostilities moved steadily closer, culminating in Canada's entry in 1939 and the attack on Pearl Harbor in 1941, companies with industrial capabilities were increasingly called upon to convert to wartime production. Lionel's experience with electrical products, especially in building small electric motors, resulted in numerous contracts with the United States Navy. The manufacture of toy trains was halted in 1942, and did not resume until the war ended in 1945. It is apparent, however, that the company did not ignore its staple product during the war years. Research and development continued, and numerous technical developments were tested and ready for production very quickly after wartime contracts lapsed.

In 1945 the Lionel Corporation moved in several new directions. The emphasis shifted almost entirely away from scenic railways to operational ones, with many new action accessories such as water towers,

The upper-story walls are joined at the corners, and also have tabs along the lower edges that project through the floor and trim rail panel. P. Riddle Collection and photograph.

The lower walls are slotted at both top and bottom. Tabs from the base project upward to hold them square, and tabs from the upper walls project downward to link the entire building together. The door is tabbed into a recessed opening, and the black-painted wooden switch panel is recessed into the open-framework rear wall. P. Riddle Collection and photograph.

freight loaders of every description, animated milk and cattle cars and eventually novelty items that bore little or no resemblance to actual railroad practice. Gone forever were the magnificent tunnels and the artfully executed scenic plots, strictly visual toys that gave way to animation and a concentration upon such features as smoke and knuckle couplers.

But for a brief period just before the War, purchasers of Lionel products had it all! For a few short years, the company offered not only trains but a whole world in miniature. Lionel Prewar accessories are beautiful, functional and a comprehensive representation of life around a railroad line, and fortunately for all of us, their quality and high production figures guarantee that we may enjoy them today, fifty and more years after they first appeared.

CONSTRUCTION TECHNIQUES

With the exception of some tunnels and landscaping items, Prewar Lionel accessories were made chiefly from metal stampings, although some have a few diecast, fiber and even wooden parts. The main construction technique employed was the tab and slot. The various steel panels that make up each accessory are either punched with narrow slots or provided with short metal extensions (tabs) to fit into corresponding slots on adjacent pieces. After insertion, the tabs were bent over at the factory to hold the panels together. This method of manufacture was quick, efficient and cost effective, since no extra hardware items (such as nuts, bolts and washers) were required. However, it makes restoration of these toys somewhat more difficult, as the tabs tend to break off when bent during disassembly, or when the toy is put back together after repair.

An examination of one of the more complex accessories, the 437 Switch Signal Tower, reveals a general pattern common to most Prewar Lionel accessory designs. This two-story structure consists of 132 separate parts: 53 metal stampings, a wooden insulator block and 78 pieces of hardware (mostly knife switch components and screws). Most of the hardware items, however, are not essential to the structure itself, but are part of the electrical components mounted on the back and used to control lights and track turnouts.

The construction tabs have rounded edges which facilitate insertion into the receiving slots. At the factory, when these tabs were bent over to hold the pieces together, they formed a tight and reliable bond between components. The steel retained most of its strength when folded over just once, although bending these tabs back again weakens them considerably. It was not intended that these toys should ever need disassembly. Any components requiring service (light bulb replacement, for example) could be accessed through a removable roof. The binding posts which were provided for connecting wires from the transformer were also bolted in place, rather than held by tabs.

Some Lionel buildings are simple rectangles, but the 437 Tower has a bay window in the front wall of the upper story. Rather than attempt to bend the wall in such a complex shape, the designers provided the bay as a separate stamping, fitted with tabs for connection to the wall and slots at the bottom where the trim pieces attach.

While a few early accessories have soldered joints, the vast majority were built using only these mechanical connections. This resulted in considerable savings, as neither solder nor heating tools were required, and tab and slot assembly proved to be much more rapid. Nor did it require a high level of skill on the part of the workers, leading to greater consistency of quality and higher production figures. By using clever design to

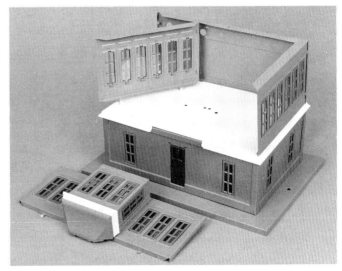

With all the window frames in place, the walls are mounted on the base and upper floor. P. Riddle Collection and photograph.

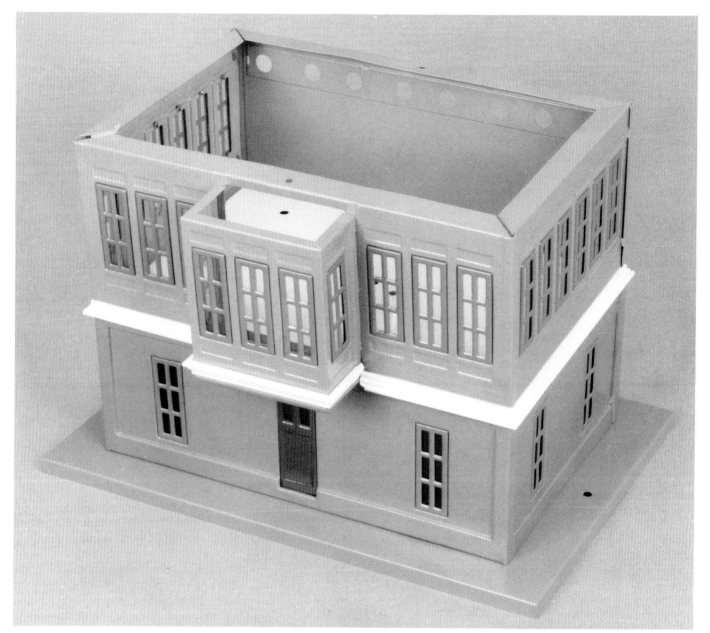

The structure is now complete except for the addition of the roof, the underside of which is recessed to fit down over the perimeter of the walls. Note that the bay window walls do not extend all the way to the top of the building. This allows clearance for the roof, which is not recessed for the bay. P. Riddle Collection and photograph.

solve manufacturing problems in advance, Lionel increased the efficiency of its assembly lines, especially important during the lean years of the Depression.

It was not unusual for Lionel designers to have the tabs perform more than one function. In the bay window design, the decorative canopy above the door in the lower wall has six tabs, two of which are inserted into that wall. The other four project upwards through corresponding slots in the bay window floor, and then into the slots in four bent sections at the base of the bay window walls. Thus the same four tabs serve to connect both the floor and the canopy.

Each of these components was pre-painted at the factory in contrasting colors before assembly. Because of the possibility of scratching the paint while

inserting the tabs, the order of assembly was very important, and some Lionel accessories could be built without surface damage only if the proper sequence was observed. For example, attempting to add the canopy alone beneath the bay after the rest of the structure is complete is virtually impossible without marring the paint on the lower wall, but if a bay/floor/canopy subassembly is attached to the building after the main walls are complete, there is little danger of scratching the paint. (Note that in these photographs, which were prepared to illustrate the attachment points of the various tabs, this sequence is not apparent.)

Each of the wall panels is bent over at right angles along both the top and bottom edges. This affords extra

Five of the six roof stampings plus the chimney are shown with the connecting tabs lined up prior to attachment. P. Riddle Collection and photograph.

Long U-shaped channels along the lower edges of the roof panels fit over the edges of the base. Note the tabs from the bottom of the chimney extending through slots in the base. P. Riddle Collection and photograph.

rigidity to the structure. The corners of two of the walls are similarly bent, with projecting tabs that enter slots in the remaining two walls. In addition to making the joint secure, this method gives the appearance of narrow columns at the corners, an architectural detail used to great visual advantage in many of Lionel's buildings.

In the two-story Switch Signal Tower, one panel does double duty as the floor for the upstairs room and as a decorative trim rail around the entire building. The stamping was shaped to simulate a molded trim rail, which also gave the panel extra strength and resistance to bending. This feature is typical of Lionel buildings, which are generally very sturdy and resistant to damage. It is not unusual to find a heavily scratched example over half a century old that has nevertheless survived considerable toy box abuse with the basic structure fully intact.

This back view of the 437 Tower shows six knife switches, plus space for three track turnout controllers. Note that a single heavy wire connects the top terminals of the knife switches, and is attached to the upper terminal nut visible at right. The lower terminal nut provides a ground for the building's interior light. P. Riddle Collection and photograph.

Like most Lionel buildings, the base of this structure is a single stamping, bent downward along all four edges and punched with tabs that project upward to hold the lower walls. A single door fits into a recessed panel in the front wall, secured by four tabs. The back wall of the first story is actually an open framework, fitted with two recessed steel panels that are tapped to receive machine screws. The wooden mounting board for the knife switches fits into this opening, and is drilled in the appropriate place for the screws that hold it to the steel supports.

The choice of wood for this component in an otherwise steel building was practical, rather than aesthetic. In all illuminated buildings, Lionel used the entire structure as an electrical ground, thus necessitating the routing of only one wire to the lamp socket. However, the six knife switches had to be insulated from this ground, and while this could have been achieved by means of fitted gaskets or fiber washers under each

switch, the designers provided natural insulation for all six by using a non-conducting wooden panel as the back wall.

When the upper floor/trim rail panel is placed over the lower walls, it fits snugly and its slots line up exactly. The tabs on the upper walls project through the floor and into the lower walls, where they are bent over. It now becomes apparent why the wooden knife switch panel was designed to be bolted in place within an open-framework wall section. The assembly line workers needed access to the interior of the building in order to bend over the tabs holding the walls together. Only after this task was accomplished was the wooden panel screwed in place. This removable panel was essential to the assembly process.

In order to simplify lamp replacement, most buildings of this type have no permanent connections for the roof. Instead, the underside of the roof is recessed to fit

Lionel's impressive 437 Switch Signal Tower. P. Riddle Collection and photograph.

into place at one time, greatly increasing the chances of marring the surface. In order to spare the workers the need for taking such care, Lionel made painting the roof the final step. (Careful examination of the roof panels revealed scratches under the paint, which probably originated with the factory assembly process.)

The back wall contains six knife switches below and a mounting bar with eight tapped holes above the trim rail. The latter provides space for operators to attach up to four of Lionel's Distant Control Switch controllers for track turnouts. This mounting bar is made of heavier gauge steel than the wall panels, to prevent the possibility of accidental bending of the structure when the controllers are operated.

At the time this accessory was built, Lionel made no motorized accessories; the first (the 97 Coal Loader) would not be offered until 1938. Therefore the knife switches were intended primarily to control lights, such as lamp posts or the interior bulbs in stations and bungalows, all of which required the same voltage. The top terminals of the switches were interconnected by a single heavy wire, which was in turn attached to a single terminal screw. An operator could therefore connect just one wire from a fixed voltage post of the transformer (commonly 12 or 14 volts) to this terminal. Any given accessory could then be wired to the opposite terminal of any one knife switch, and opening or closing that particular switch would control just that specific light. Lionel provided a comprehensive instruction sheet explaining this procedure; it was cemented to the underside of the base on the author's example.

While this did reduce the number of wires to be attached to the transformer, it still meant that up to six wires would be routed from accessories to the Switch Signal Tower. In addition, each accessory required a ground wire. If four track turnout controllers were mounted at the top, each requiring three connections, the amount of wiring was considerable, but this accessory did provide for a certain amount of order, and a neater appearance than four loose controllers scattered around the floor. The Switch Signal Tower also required a ground for its own interior light, and this was provided for by a second terminal nut on the back wooden panel.

snugly over the outer edges of the walls, tightly enough to remain secure but easy to lift off when necessary. For this reason, the paint on the walls is often abraded along the upper edges.

There are six main stampings plus a chimney which must be fitted together to form the hip-style roof. The main section forms the front and back, while each of the ends is a separate piece. A short extension capped by a sloped gable tops the bay window, and the entire assembly is fitted to a base with a recess matching the length and width of the walls. A rectangular opening in the main roof panel admits the chimney, which then fastens to the base sheet by two tabs.

When the roof was disassembled in preparation for taking the photographs for this book, it became apparent that Lionel did not pre-paint the individual parts. The interior surfaces were mostly bare metal, or had just traces of paint sprayed on them. Obviously the entire roof had been painted after being put together, and the reason for this soon became apparent.

The tab and slot method of assembly was not used to attach the roof to its base. Instead, each of the five upper pieces was bent over a full 180 degrees along the lower edges, forming a shallow channel. This channel slips over the flat edges of the roof base, holding the entire structure together. The complex angles formed by the interlocking pieces of this roof, coupled with the need for inserting the base into the long edge channels, make assembly very difficult without scratching the paint. In some cases several parts had to be slipped

This clever accessory allowed a young engineer to operate a railroad from a single location, and on permanent layouts where the wires could be hidden beneath the table, it made for efficient wiring and increased the possibility of an orderly arrangement of connections.

The construction details described above are common to all Lionel Prewar accessories prior to the use of Bakelite, the first of our modern plastic materials. The introduction of this substance led to a gradual decline in the use of sheet metal, and thus in the tab and slot method of construction. In the Postwar years, most new accessories would be built of

Various accessories in a layout setting. **C. Brasher Collection, Classic Toy Trains** *photograph.*

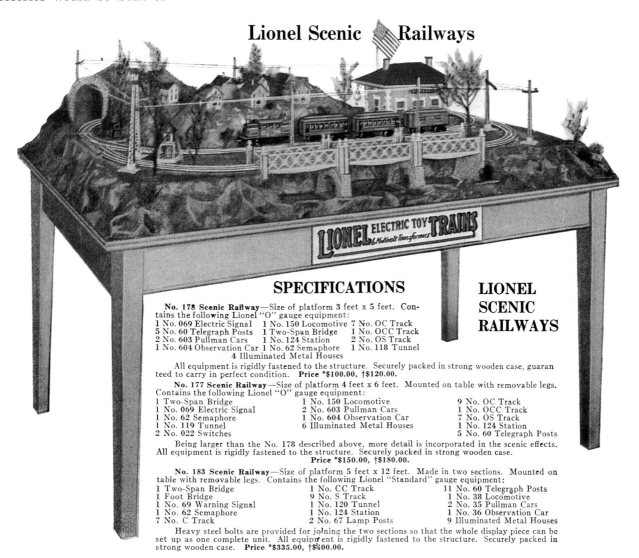

Lionel Scenic Railways

SPECIFICATIONS

LIONEL SCENIC RAILWAYS

No. 178 Scenic Railway—Size of platform 3 feet x 5 feet. Contains the following Lionel "O" gauge equipment:

1 No. 069 Electric Signal	1 No. 150 Locomotive	7 No. OC Track
5 No. 60 Telegraph Posts	1 Two-Span Bridge	1 No. OCC Track
2 No. 603 Pullman Cars	1 No. 124 Station	2 No. OS Track
1 No. 604 Observation Car	1 No. 62 Semaphore	1 No. 118 Tunnel
	4 Illuminated Metal Houses	

All equipment is rigidly fastened to the structure. Securely packed in strong wooden case, guaranteed to carry in perfect condition. **Price *$100.00, †$120.00.**

No. 177 Scenic Railway—Size of platform 4 feet x 6 feet. Mounted on table with removable legs. Contains the following Lionel "O" gauge equipment:

1 Two-Span Bridge	1 No. 150 Locomotive	9 No. OC Track
1 No. 069 Electric Signal	2 No. 603 Pullman Cars	1 No. OCC Track
1 No. 62 Semaphore	1 No. 604 Observation Car	7 No. OS Track
1 No. 119 Tunnel	6 Illuminated Metal Houses	1 No. 124 Station
2 No. 022 Switches		5 No. 60 Telegraph Posts

Being larger than the No. 178 described above, more detail is incorporated in the scenic effects. All equipment is rigidly fastened to the structure. Securely packed in strong wooden case.
Price *$150.00, †$180.00.

No. 183 Scenic Railway—Size of platform 5 feet x 12 feet. Made in two sections. Mounted on table with removable legs. Contains the following Lionel "Standard" gauge equipment:

1 Two-Span Bridge	1 No. CC Track	11 No. 60 Telegraph Posts
1 Foot Bridge	9 No. S Track	1 No. 38 Locomotive
1 No. 69 Warning Signal	1 No. 120 Tunnel	2 No. 35 Pullman Cars
1 No. 62 Semaphore	1 No. 124 Station	1 No. 36 Observation Car
7 No. C Track	2 No. 67 Lamp Posts	9 Illuminated Metal Houses

Heavy steel bolts are provided for joining the two sections so that the whole display piece can be set up as one complete unit. All equipment is rigidly fastened to the structure. Securely packed in strong wooden case. **Price *$335.00, †$400.00.**

Lionel Scenic Railway illustration, page 2 of the 1922 catalogue.

plastic, allowing greater detail than stamped steel but also having a greater inherent fragility. While Lionel's Postwar products became increasingly more realistic as a result, they lost the substantial feel of the metal buildings that dominated the line in the 1920s and 1930s. The look and style of Lionel's Prewar accessories was a direct result of the construction methods employed, and they are easily identifiable as a result.

Some of Lionel's best accessories in action. C. Brasher Collection, Classic Toy Trains *photograph.*

45 Gateman. P. Riddle Collection and photograph. Color photograph of 45 Gateman in Chapter VII on page 74.

CHAPTER II

Railroad Buildings and Industries

In the mid-1920s, buyers of toy trains were offered an increasingly wider variety of railroad-related structures with which to build a layout. Page 43 of the 1926 Lionel catalogue introduced three new dual-purpose accessories, practical designs that actually perform the functions after which they are named: the 435 and 436 Power Stations and the 437 Switch Signal Tower.

The first two buildings were designed to conceal Lionel's Multivolt transformers, while providing access to controls through the roof. The attractive little 435 Power Station has a cutout base that allows it to slip down over either of Lionel's low power transformers (models A and B). A notch in the rear provides for the emergence of the power cord and wires to be attached to track, lamps and signals. The open top is covered by a slotted skylight, which is removable to allow the operator access to the speed control lever and binding posts on top of the transformer. (Because it is not attached, this skylight is frequently missing; however, reproductions are available.)

436 Power Station. F. Wasserman Collection.

In appearance, the 435 Power Station resembles a typical low-capacity electrical generating facility in some details, while in other respects it is a substation. The rectangular structure is topped by a raised cornice surrounding a flat roof. A tall door in each end is surmounted by a brass plate inscribed "POWER STATION", and three arch-top windows are cut out in each of the longer side walls. Door and window frames in contrasting colors are mounted by tabs in the cutouts, and enclose multi-pane window and door inserts. A tapered steel smokestack rises from one corner of the roof.

Carlton McKenney of Richmond, Virginia, a long-time Dorfan collector and professional engineer, suggests that the presence of a stack supports the power station concept, as a substation would not contain a fossil-fuel burner to produce steam. "Leave off the stack," Carlton writes, "and you come close to the typical downtown indoor substation which you can still find in big cities." However, a power station would require an entrance for fuel, which is lacking on the Lionel model. Nor are the doors of the structure large enough to allow passage of transformers or generators, and there are no apparent bushing insulators to bring out the power, although Carlton suggests this would imply underground cables. At best, the Lionel design is a suggestion rather than an accurate representation, but according to Carlton, "With a stack it has to be a power station." Such stations would typically be located near a river, to provide a source of water to cool the condensers.

Although Lionel never identified a specific building as the inspiration for its power stations, a very similar structure appears in a photo on page 124 of *Metropolitan Corridors*, by John R. Stilgoe (New Haven and London, Connecticut: Yale University Press, 1983). This power plant also has arched windows and a raised cornice surrounding the upper walls, but it has four stacks on the roof instead of just one.

The walls are embossed to simulate protruding cement block columns at each corner, and embossed

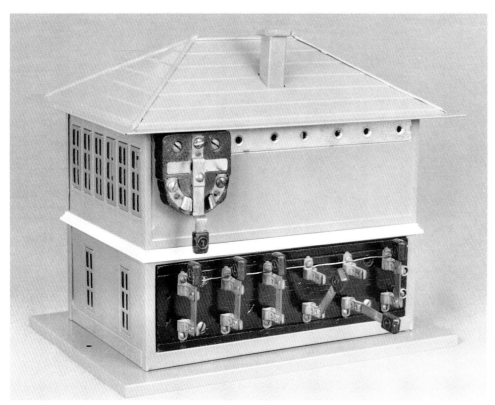

Six factory-installed knife switches and space for four turnout controllers (one is shown) make the 437 Switch Signal Tower a functional as well as decorative railroad building. P. Riddle Collection and photograph.

Although lower in price by eighty-five cents than the larger 436 model ($2.50 compared with $3.35 in the 1926 catalogue), the 435 Power Station is less common, suggesting that fewer were made and sold. This may be an indirect result of its size. The 436 model could enclose any size Lionel transformer of that period, while the 435 was limited to the two smallest. Further, it may be assumed that the larger transformers would be owned by families with larger and more expensive train sets which required higher power capacity for operation. Such families would ordinarily be more affluent, and therefore more likely to purchase accessories such as a Power Station. Transformers A and B could only be used with less expensive sets, many of whose owners would be less able to acquire costly extras. Lionel's lowest-priced train set in 1926 sold for just $5.75, and four other sets could be purchased for less than $10. A single accessory costing half the price of a complete train set would be considered a luxury item.

An impressive and functional Switch Signal Tower (No. 437) was the third innovation illustrated in the 1926 catalogue. Like the Power Stations, this relatively expensive accessory ($8.50 at time of introduction) was designed to be functional, and came with six knife switches mounted on a wooden plate recessed into the lower portion of the rear wall. These switches are fitted with screw terminals to allow connection to signals, lamps and illuminated buildings, permitting the owner to turn them on and off from one central location. On the author's example, a wire interconnects one terminal of each knife switch with a binding post, to which a single wire from the transformer can be attached. This wire may have been installed at the factory, as it appears the same age as the accessory, but it is not shown on the schematic wiring diagram. A second binding post for the ground wire provides power for the Tower's interior illumination.

A metal plate recessed into the upper rear wall is tapped with eight threaded holes and fitted with bolts which can be used to attach the control levers for Lionel's "Electrically Controlled Switches" which were also introduced in the 1926 catalogue. The term "switch" in this case refers to Standard Gauge track turnouts (see Chapter XIII) which are fitted with solenoids to move the pivoting track points and divert a

panels lie below each window. Above each of the doors are three embossed diamond-shaped decorations. The cornice is similarly embossed with a single recessed panel on each side. The base is a separate metal stamping, and creates a platform that surrounds the building. Over the years the various components were enameled in a variety of colors, and at least eight different combinations have been identified.

Similar in appearance but bigger and differing in details, the 436 Power Station was designed to enclose Lionel's larger multivolt transformers (models T, C and K). The sides are very similar to the 435, with three arch-top windows above three embossed panels, and the ends are likewise fitted with doors that have brass or nickel plates above them. In addition to the usual "POWER STATION" plates, a few examples have been found lettered "EDISON SERVICE". (Catalogue illustrations commonly show "LIONEL" plates on both the 435 and 436, but no examples have been found and it is presumed they were never made this way.)

The larger building is also fitted with three tall rectangular windows in the upper portion of each end wall, constructed in two parts of tabbed-on frames and multi-pane inserts in contrasting colors. The cornices have three recessed panels on each side instead of one. Seven color combinations have been identified. Neither Power Station is fitted with interior illumination, as the space was meant to be filled with a transformer.

train to an alternate section of trackage. Thus the 437 Switch Signal Tower allows central control not only of lights and signals, but also of the routes a train might take over a layout.

This building is a reasonably accurate representation of an interlocking tower; Lionel claimed in the catalogue description that it was "built absolutely to scale." In prototype practice, the term "interlocking" refers to a system of mechanical levers or electrical relays that prevent signal operators from setting turnouts or signals in such a manner as to allow two or more trains to converge on the same line of track. According to John R. Stilgoe in *Metropolitan Corridors*, such safety-conscious systems were like crude, large-scale computers, designed to eliminate the possibility of derailments or collisions caused by human error.

A very similar structure, the "HUNT" tower at Huntington, Pennsylvania, was pictured in the January 1992 issue of *Railpace*; this photo is reproduced here with permission, courtesy of Mr. Gordon Lloyd.

The construction of the 437 Switch Signal Tower is quite complex, and must have required considerable assembly time. A total of 132 separate parts were used to make up the author's example. An explanation of the construction techniques employed appears in Chapter I. The building alone contains fifty-three metal stampings, all fastened together by means of tabs and slots. A wooden block mounts on the back wall to support six four-piece knife switches interconnected by a single heavy wire, and a light bracket and socket

437 Switch Signal Tower. R. Bartelt Collection, A. Fiterman photograph.

provides for interior illumination. Four washers, six nuts and forty machine screws connect this hardware together, both mechanically and electrically.

A low, wide base supports four lower walls that make up a rectangular structure, into three sides of which are installed a total of six tall six-paned windows (two per side). A central door with two upper window panes is centered in the long front wall. The back wall contains the knife switches. This lower story is topped

HUNT Tower. G. Lloyd photograph.

by a flat panel that extends slightly beyond the walls, forming a decorative molding. On the long side above the door, a rectangular extension protrudes to support an upper bay window. Below this protrusion is a separate trim piece forming a canopy over the door and painted a contrasting color.

The upper story is elaborately embossed with rectangular panels both above and below the many tall windows that encircle three sides and the bay window. Five windows are fitted into each end, plus three on either side of the bay for a total of six on the long wall. The bay itself has three in the front and one in each side. The lower back wall is plain except for the wooden switch-mount panel. An intricate six-piece hip roof with an extension over the bay fits over the top edges of the tower, and has a chimney centered just behind the peak. On the underside of the base on some examples, Lionel cemented a detailed instruction sheet, complete with illustrated wiring diagrams for connecting a transformer to the Switch Signal Tower and thence to the

840 Power Station. G. Zippie Collection, B. Schwab photograph.

The 200 Turntable mechanism consists of a hand-turned knob mounted on a shaft, a pair of reduction gears and a shaft-mounted worm gear. The latter meshes with a large-diameter disk with gear teeth around its perimeter. This gear was made from insulating fiber, as it also serves to support a ring made of thin brass that touches brass contacts on the base and distributes power between all of the third rails on the base and rotating table. P. Riddle Collection and photograph.

200 Turntable and 444 Roundhouse in a layout setting. C. Brasher Collection, Classic Toy Trains *photograph.*

track and accessories. When used in this manner, the 437 Switch Signal Tower was both decorative and functional in the manner of the prototype.

An earlier representation of a Signal Tower preceded the 437 model, although it was much smaller and had no function other than decoration. The 092 design first appeared in the 1923 catalogue at $2.10. This diminutive two-story rectangular building rests on a low base and is topped by a roof reminiscent of an oriental pagoda. The catalogue shows it with a chimney, although no examples have been authenticated. The chimney disappeared in the 1926 catalogue. (The later 438 Elevated Signal Tower uses the same building and roof, and *is* fitted with a chimney; since the roofs are interchangeable, some 092 towers may be found with chimneys, but these are not believed to be factory production.)

The end walls are each fitted with three upper windows having two over-and-under panes (simulating standard double-hung sashes). The lower portions of these walls are plain except for an embossed panel forming a decorative arch. The front wall contains six upper windows, and a lower embossed arch panel with three solid door inserts, stamped to simulate wooden panels. The back wall is similar, but lacks the doors. The various components were enameled in several colors, and five different combinations have been identified. A bulb in a socket fastened to a floor-mounted bracket provides interior illumination.

In 1927 the company adapted the 092 structure to create the low-priced functional 438 Signal Tower, by adding two knife switches to the rear wall and mounting it on an elevated structure. At $4.25 in the catalogue, this model cost

just half of the big 437's price, but provided a limited amount of operational control from a central point. Some 438 models were manufactured without the knife switches, however, and also lack mounting holes for them, which suggests that components intended for production of the 092 model may have been substituted.

The building is identical in construction to the 092 except for the addition of a chimney centered behind the peak of the pagoda-style roof. (Interestingly, the 1926 catalogue illustration does not show this addition, while the 092 was shown initially with a chimney it never had. The 1928 catalogue correctly depicts the chimney on the 438.) It rests upon a tower made to represent structural steel, fastened to a thick base simulating reinforced concrete. A brass or red-painted ladder extends from this base to the floor of the building in line with the central door. A brass or nickel plate is tabbed to the front of the base, while in the back two binding posts provide power for the interior light. In the 1927 catalogue, a railing is drawn around the floor of the structure, but it was never made this way and the illustration was corrected the following year.

Small interlocking towers of the type represented by Lionel's 438 were built all over North America. Especially in more northern climates, the lower portion of the structure was usually enclosed, as shown in a photo of a New York Central tower on page 155 of John R. Stilgoe's aforementioned *Metropolitan Corridors*. The upper portion of this structure, with its peaked roof and tall rectangular windows, is remarkably like Lionel's.

The last in this series of functional buildings was introduced in 1928, the huge and magnificent 840 Power Station, designed to hold two of Lionel's largest transformers. The entire back page of the catalogue was devoted to announcing this accessory. It was priced to sell at $20, a considerable sum to be spent on a toy even in the prosperous days of the latter 1920s.

A trapezoidal base with a separate central floor panel supports a simulated masonry building, the lower level of which is encircled with large rectangular

441 Weighing Scale, front view. B. Greenberg Collection, A. Fiterman photograph.

multi-paned windows. These windows are of complex design, representing two over-and-under central panes, six sidelights and four small transom panes on each. The central area of the building is empty, while the two outer wings of this level contain space for one transformer each, below a flat roof cut out for access and covered by skylights larger than those used on the 436 Power Station. On each side and just below the roof cornice is placed a brass plate lettered in black "No. 840 LIONEL" above "POWER STATION". Removable steps fit into slots at the front and rear of the base. An unusual door- window insert mounts in the wall just above these steps, and incorporates sidelights and a transom similar to the window treatment.

The smaller but still massive upper-story structure is square and fits between the two skylights. It consists of four walls, a flat roof forming a trim rail, and a high cornice atop and encircling the roof. Twenty-seven very tall, narrow windows encircle three sides (nine per side), while six knife switches are mounted on the fourth side. The switches may be located adjacent to one of the skylights or on the back or front, depending upon which way the factory oriented the upper story on the main structure during assembly. On the roof are mounted a water tower and three tall tapered stacks, over which fits a huge sign spelling out "LIONEL" in separate cutout letters. Unlike the two smaller Power Stations, the 840 has interior illumination, provided by a bulb in a lamp bracket that is

dissimilar to those used in all other Lionel accessories. According to Ron Morris, this is actually an automotive lamp.

Despite its obvious attractiveness, this immense accessory did not sell in great numbers, probably for two main reasons. The high initial cost would have put it out of the reach of most families, and its size (it consumed about four square feet of floor space) made it suitable only for large homes with room enough for a large and preferably permanent layout. Excellent reproductions have been manufactured by T-Reproductions and Mike's Train House.

Two train yard accessories are closely related and meant to be used together, although they did not appear in the same year. The 200 Turntable was introduced in 1928 and the 444 Roundhouse in 1932. The former was produced for Standard Gauge only, and consists of a circular stamped-steel base cut out in the center, within which a smaller steel circle rotates by means of a hand-turned wheel and gear mechanism.

Three rails equivalent to a single section of straight Standard Gauge track are fastened to this inner circle, and when rotated they line up with any of eight short track sections spaced equidistant around the perimeter of the outer base. These short sections are fitted with track pins for connection to sidings which then radiate outward like the spokes of a wheel. The middle rails on the base are wired together to ensure power will reach each siding. The middle rail on the rotating disk

441 Weighing Scale, back view. B. Greenberg Collection, A. Fiterman photograph.

Several different 93 Water Towers: 93(A), 93(F), 93(B) and 93(E). R. Bartelt Collection, A. Fiterman photograph.

receives power from a flat brass ring that rubs against a series of brass studs inside the base.

Alternatively these turntable lead tracks can be attached to the trackage inside 444 Roundhouse sections. These buildings were designed to fit side by side to form a multi-stall roundhouse which would partially encircle the turntable, and Lionel manufactured a special clip (No. 444-18) to hold them together. The geometry is such that the angle of the tracks projecting from the turntable align correctly with the 444 stalls, four or five of which make an impressive display. However, the high cost of this toy (it was introduced in the Depression year of 1932 at $12.50) suggests that few children would have been lucky enough to own multiple sections.

An interesting anomaly surrounds this combination of toys. A turntable is intended to rotate steam locomotives and their tenders, as these units do not normally operate in reverse in regular service. However, both the Turntable and the Roundhouse are too short to accommodate even the smallest Standard Gauge Lionel steamer. They can handle the smaller box cab electric locomotives, but in prototype practice these engines could and did operate with ease in either direction, and never required turning. It is likely that only on Lionel railroads did box cab locomotives ever experience rotation on a turntable with any regularity.

Construction of the 444 Roundhouse is relatively simple when compared with other large Lionel structures. A wedge-shaped steel base supporting a special 20-inch section of straight Standard Gauge track is tabbed to flat walls enclosed within plain upright side and corner posts. The side facing the turntable is lower than the back part of the building, and has a flat sloping roof. Rectangular six-paned windows and solid doors encircle the lower story. Rising above the back section is a second story containing almost square four-paned windows on all sides, surmounted by a flat roof with two skylights. Rounded finials are mounted above the six corner posts, four around the raised story and two at the front of the sloping roof. The metal components are stamped "Made in Italy" and the interior is lighted.

An interesting but relatively scarce accessory, the 441 Weighing Scale, was introduced along with the Roundhouse in 1932. At $10, it represented a substantial investment and sold in small numbers. With it, a railroader could actually measure the weight of rolling stock by means of a balance beam and a set of round brass weights that stacked on a platform suspended from the beam. (The use of past tense is deliberate here. Both the balance beam and the platform mechanism were formed of impure zinc castings, and virtually all known examples have either broken or swollen so as to be inoperable today.)

438 Signal Tower. R. Bartelt Collection, A. Fiterman photograph.

A long steel base supports short sections of Standard Gauge track at each end, tilted upward at a gentle angle to match the level of the central section which forms the weighing platform. This platform, containing a section of track, is suspended upon a mechanism which transmits the downward pressure of a piece of rolling stock to the balance beam. The number of weights needed to achieve balance at the beam's other end indicate the relative mass of the car on the platform.

A small steel shed with six sides, three windows and a flat roof encloses the balance beam, which is accessible through doors in the straight side opposite the track. Two binding posts adjacent to one of the angled sides power the track on the platform, and a brass plate identifies the accessory with "RAILROAD TRACK" above "NO. — SCALES — 441" above "THE LIONEL

CORPORATION — N.Y." in red lettering. Because the weights and their support were unattached to the scale, it is very unusual to find this accessory complete with all of its component parts today.

Lionel's chief competitor, American Flyer, produced both large and small water towers before the Second World War, the former having a solenoid-operated spout that could be lowered over a tender by remote control. By contrast, Lionel offered only one model of this essential railroad structure during the prewar years, the diminutive and very inexpensive 93 Water Tower. It first appeared in the 1931 catalogue at seventy-five cents, increasing to $1.25 in 1942 just before the company stopped toy production in order to contribute to the war effort.

Seven variations in appearance are known, distinguished by color combinations of the components and presence or absence of a red-lettered "LIONEL TRAINS" decal above the spout. The steel base is square, and four simulated structural steel girders taper inward to support a circular collar into which the small round tank fits. A domed roof is tabbed to the top of the tank, and a round pipe extends downward from the bottom to the middle of the base, centered between the girders. A U-shaped bracket supports a hollow formed spout which may be raised or lowered by hand.

The 93 Water Tower is attractive if not exciting, but it appears unrealistically small even beside O Gauge trains, and could not be used satisfactorily with Standard Gauge. It was not until the introduction of the massive 38 Operating Water Tower in 1946 that Lionel produced a convincing and truly interesting model of this necessary piece of train yard equipment.

Following are descriptions of known variations of railroad building and industry accessories produced by Lionel between 1923 and 1942.

GD   EXC   RST

092 ILLUMINATED SIGNAL TOWER (1923-27): Identical to 438 Signal Tower without elevated tower and chimney, interior light, rubber-stamped in black "No. 092 SIGNAL TOWER / MADE BY / THE LIONEL CORPORATION" on underside, base measures 4⅛" x 2¹³⁄₁₆", roof measures 5⅜" x 4⅛", 4¾" high. D. Ely and C. Rohlfing comments.

(A) Mohave base, terra cotta walls, pea green roof, maroon doors, cream windows. P. Riddle Collection.

60   135   60

(B) Yellowish State brown base, terra cotta walls, pea green roof, brown doors with black lines, cream windows. S. Blotner Collection. **60   135   60**

(C) Yellowish State brown base, terra cotta walls, dark pea green roof, red doors, ivory windows. C. Rohlfing Collection. **60   135   60**

(D) Mohave base, white walls, red roof, red doors, pea green windows. **75   150   60**

(E) Same as (A), but with wood-grained doors. **60   135   60**

GD EXC RST

93 WATER TOWER (1931-42, Postwar): 8⅜″ high.
(A) 1931-34, maroon base, burnt orange tower, pea green tank and pipe, brass spout (same colors used for Ives tank), no decal. C. Rohlfing Collection.

20 45 25

(B) 1935-41, vermilion base, aluminum-painted tower, tank, and pipe, black spout, silver decal outlined in black with red "LIONEL / TRAINS". C. Rohlfing Collection. **25 50 25**

(C) Same as (B), but maroon base. M. Ocilka Collection. **20 45 25**

(D) 1941-42, vermilion base, green legs, tank and pipe, black spout, light red lettering on decal "LIONEL / TRAINS". D. Ely Collection. **20 45 25**

(E) 1942, same as (B), but tower, tank and pipe painted 92 gray. C. Rohlfing and J. Flynn Collections. **20 45 25**

(F) Same as (B), but tower and tank painted 92 gray. P. Riddle Collection. **20 45 25**

(G) Same as (B), but tower only painted 92 gray. **20 45 25**

(H) 1931-32, made for Ives. **20 45 25**

200 TURNTABLE (1928-33): Standard Gauge only, central disk containing section of straight track rotates by means of hand-turned brass wheel and gear mechanism, to align with any of eight short tracks fitted with track pins to connect to sidings; 17″ diameter; reproduced by T-Reproductions and Mike's Train House.

(A) Pea green base, mojave rotating disk. D. Ely Collection. **100 175 100**

(B) Pea green base, red rotating disk. P. Riddle Collection. **100 175 100**

(C) Pea green base, black rotating disk. Confirmation requested **NRS**

(D) Black base, red rotating disk. Confirmation requested. **NRS**

(E) 1986-87, reproduction by T-Reproductions, die-stamped on base "T / R", "T / R-NAT", or "T-Reproductions"; 1987 price $75. **— 100 —**

(F) 1988, reproduction by Mike's Train House; issue price $75. **— 100 —**

435 POWER STATION (1926-38): Base 7½″ x 6″, building 5¾″ x 4½″ x 5″ high, brass plates over doors read "POWER STATION", fits over A or B Transformer; reproduced by Mike's Train House.

(A) Gray base, mustard walls, terra cotta roof cornices, green skylight, dark green door and window frames, wood-grained doors, pea green windows, mojave chimney base, red chimney. **125 225 110**

(B) Gray base, terra cotta walls, mustard roof cornices, green skylight, dark green door and window frames, maroon doors, pea green windows, mojave chimney base, dark red chimney (could have come with very scarce "EDISON SERVICE" plate over door instead of usual "POWER STATION" plate). D. Ely comment, confirmation requested. **NRS**

(C) Gray base, ivory walls, cream roof cornices, green skylight, dark green door and window frames, red doors, orange windows, mohave chimney base, dark red chimney. D. Ely Collection. **125 225 110**

(D) Gray base, terra cotta walls, light cream roof cornices, green skylight, green window frames, mojave chimney base, red chimney. **125 225 110**

(E) 45N green base, cream walls, State brown (mustard) roof cornices, red skylight, red door and window frames, white windows and doors, red chimney base, aluminum-painted chimney, black-lettered brass "POWER STATION" plate over door. Weisblum Collection. **125 225 110**

(F) Gray base, ivory walls, terra cotta roof cornices, pea green skylight, dark green door frame, pea green window frames, red chimney. D. Ely Collection. **125 225 110**

(G) Same as (E), but nickel "POWER STATION" plate. D. Ely Collection. **125 225 110**

(H) Gray base, cream walls, terra cotta roof cornices, light green skylight and window frames, dark green door frames, red doors, orange windows, olive green chimney base, red chimney, no brass plate over door. D. Anderson Collection. **125 225 110**

(I) Same as (E), but nickel plates. **125 225 110**

(K) 1987, reproduction by Mike's Train House; issue price $75. **— 100 —**

(L) 1929-30, made for Ives under catalogue No. 253. **125 250 110**

(M) 1931-32, made for Ives under catalogue No. 1876. **125 250 110**

436 POWER STATION (1926-37): Similar to 435 Power Station, but modestly larger, base 9⅛″ x 7⅝″, building 7″ x 5½″ x 5⅞″ high to cornice, with black-lettered "POWER STATION" plates over doors, underside of base black rubber-stamped "NO. 436 POWER STATION / MADE BY / THE LIONEL CORPORATION / NEW YORK", fits over C, K or T Transformer; reproduced by Mike's Train House.

(A) Gray base, terra cotta walls, yellow roof cornices, light green skylight, dark green door and window frames, maroon doors, light green windows, dark gray chimney base, bright red chimney, brass plates. D. Ely comment. **125 225 110**

(B) Gray base, terra cotta walls, cream roof cornices, pea green skylight, medium green door frames, pea green window frames, red doors, orange windows, mojave chimney base, red chimney, brass plates. **125 225 110**

(C) Gray base, terra cotta walls, light cream roof cornices, pea green skylight, medium green door frames, pea green window frames, red doors, cream windows, mojave chimney base, red chimney, brass plates. P. Riddle Collection. **125 225 110**

GD   EXC   RST

(D) Gray base, terra cotta walls, light cream roof cornices, pea green skylight, dark green door and window frames, maroon doors, pea green windows, dark mojave chimney base, red chimney, brass plates lettered "EDISON SERVICE", very scarce. D. Ely comment. Weisblum Collection.   **250   400   250**
(E) 45N green base, cream walls, mustard roof cornices, red skylight, red door and window frames, white doors and windows, red chimney base, aluminum chimney, brass plates, block rubber-stamping on underside of base in five lines: "NO. 436 POWER STATION / MADE BY / THE LIONEL CORPORATION / NEW YORK / U.S. OF AMERICA". Riley and Koff Collections.   **125   225   110**
(F) Same as (E), but nickel plates. D. Ely Collection.   **125   225   110**
(G) Gray base, terra cotta walls, cream roof cornices, pea green skylight, dark green door and window frames, red doors, orange windows, mojave chimney base, red chimney, brass plates. C. Rohlfing Collection.   **125   225   110**
(H) 1987, reproduction by Mike's Train House; issue price $75.   **—   100   —**
(I) 1930, made for Ives under catalogue No. 254.   **125   225   110**

437 SWITCH SIGNAL TOWER (1926-37): 10¼" x 8⅜" x 8⅞" high, interior light, with knife switches and switch controller brackets on rear. Reproductions have been made by T-Reproductions, Mike's Train House and Lionel Trains, Inc.

(A) Mojave base, burnt orange lower walls, ivory band between floors, mustard (buff) upper walls, pea green roof, red door, peacock windows, vermilion trim under dormer, red chimney. D. Ely Collection.
                                          200   375   190
(B) Same as (A), but terra cotta lower walls. P. Riddle Collection.   **200   375   190**
(C) Mojave base, terra cotta lower wall, ivory band between floors, upper cream walls, peacock roof, red door, orange windows, lithographed brick chimney. D. Ely Collection.   **200   375   190**
(D) Mojave base, burnt orange lower wall, white band between floors, light mustard upper walls, pea green roof, maroon door, peacock windows, vermilion trim under dormer, red chimney. S. Blotner Collection.
                                          200   375   190
(E) Red base, yellow lower and upper walls, brown band between floors, orange roof, red door, green windows, cream chimney. Very rare.   **NRS**
(F) 1986-87, reproduction by T-Reproductions, die-stamped on base "T / R", "T / R-NAT" or "T-Reproductions"; 1987 price $125.   **—   175   —**
(G) 1987, reproduction by Mike's Train House.
                                          —   175   —
(H) 1991, reproduction by Lionel Trains, Inc., catalogue No. 13804, embossed "LTI" or "Lionel Trains, Inc."   **—   200   —**

438 SIGNAL TOWER (1927-39): Base 6" x 4¾" x 12" high, sheet steel construction except brass roof, switches on back except for 1927, possibly modeled after Pennsylvania Railroad prototypes. Reproductions have been made by T-Reproductions and Mike's Train House.

(A) 1927, mojave base, pea green tower, cream upper base, orange walls, red roof and doors, white windows, lithographed brick chimney, brass ladders and number plate on base, no switches on back. D. Ely comment, P. Riddle Collection.   **200   400   165**
(B) Same as (A), but with knife switches and cream chimney. D. Ely Collection.   **150   275   135**
(C) Gray base, aluminum-painted tower, gray upper base, ivory walls, red roof and doors, red windows, ivory chimney, red ladders, and nickel number plate on base.   **200   375   135**
(D) Black base, aluminum-painted tower, black upper base, white walls, red roof and doors, red windows and ladder, white chimney, nickel plate on base. D. Ely Collection.   **200   375   135**
(E) 1986-87, reproduction by T-Reproductions, die-stamped on base "T/R", "T / R-NAT" or "T-Reproductions"; 1987 price $100.   **—   150   —**
(F) 1987, reproduction by Mike's Train House.
                                          —   150   —
(G) 1930, made for Ives under catalogue No. 255.   **150   300   140**
(H) 1931-32, made for Ives under catalogue No. 1867.   **125   250   110**

441 WEIGHING STATION (1932-36): Standard Gauge only, green base, cream walls, maroon crackle finish roof, terra cotta window frames, brass plate painted red, lettered "RAILROAD TRACK NO. 441 THE LIONEL CORP.", with die-cast scale and brass weights, double doors on back, interior light, 29½" long, 4¾" high, 9½" wide. G. Zippie Collection.
                                          400   800   350

444 ROUNDHOUSE (1932-35): A very large building, 24" wide in back and 8¾" wide in front, designed so that a number of sections could be put together (Lionel recommended four); terra cotta sides, cream trim bands, pea green roof, two green skylights, maroon windows, interior light. Reproductions have been made by T-Reproductions and Mike's Train House. Price for one section.

(A) Lionel original.   **1400   2500   1200**
(B) 1986-87, reproduction by T-Reproductions, die-stamped on base "T / R", "T / R-NAT" or "T-Reproductions"; 1987 price $195.   **—   300   —**
(C) 1988, reproduction by Mike's Train House; issue price $195.   **—   300   —**

444-18 CLIP (1933): Used for securing roundhouse sections together.   **NRS**

840 INDUSTRIAL POWER STATION (1928-40): Largest single-unit accessory ever built by Lionel,

26" wide, 21½" deep, and 18" high. Prices quoted require all accessories listed below. Replacement grates, steps, and smokestack units with signs have been made and not marked; reproduced by T-Reproductions and Mike's Train House; substantial premium for original box.

(A) Green base, two sets of cream steps mounted on base, dark mojave floor attached to building which fits into green base, cream walls, many multi-paned green windows, orange bands around building at first- and second-floor levels, orange roof, two orange skylights (one for each wing), three smokestacks in one unit with sign reading "LIONEL" fastened across them, red sheet metal water tower, side panel with six knife switches, interior light with large socket bulb, designed to enclose two large transformers.   **1600   3000   1500**

(B) White walls, red roof and trim, different green base. Very rare.   **NRS**

(C) 1985-86, reproduction by T-Reproductions, die-stamped on base "T / R", "T / R-NAT" or "T-Reproductions"; issue price $295.   **—   450   —**

(D) 1986, reproduction by Mike's Train House; issue price $345.   **—   450   —**

CHAPTER III

The Wonderful Bimetallic Strip

The Greatest Achievement in Miniature Electric Train Engineering was announced on page 38 of the 1924 Lionel catalogue. In the center of the page is a huge picture of the 78 Automatic Train Control Block Signal, the first of a series of clever accessories that must have seemed like magic to young railroaders of the 1920s. It can be wired to the track in such a manner as to cause the train to stop, pause for an interval of up to half a minute, and then resume its travels, simultaneously changing the signal from red to green and back again. The mechanism that powers it is a simple and reliable one, similar to a device already present in any home equipped with an automatic furnace, clothes washer or dryer, or dishwasher.

The temperature in homes heated by gas or oil burners (and in some major appliances) is regulated automatically by a simple device called a thermostat, which senses the degree of heat in the air and turns on the furnace when it drops below a preset level. The heat-sensing device is an old and simple one called a bimetallic strip (Figure 3-A). This device consists of two strips of metal which are fused together. Stuart Armstrong of Los Altos, California,

suggests they are joined by the cold-rolling process. These strips are not made of the same substance, but rather are two different materials with differing rates of thermal expansion. In other words, when the temperature rises, one strip expands *by growing longer* at a faster rate than the other. This causes the bimetallic strip to bend (Figure 3-B).

Such a strip is used to make an electrical contact inside a thermostat. When the temperature in a home is cool, the strip is in a position similar to Figure 3-C, and electric current passes through the contact and causes the furnace to operate. When the air heats up, the strip expands and bends (Figure 3-D), breaking the contact and cutting off power to the furnace motor, which then shuts off. As the air inside the house gradually cools again, the strip bends back to close the contact, turning on the furnace once more. This cycle repeats endlessly, keeping the temperature at an even level.

The desired temperature can be preset by the thermostat adjustment lever, which alters the position of the electrical contacts. With the contacts close together, the strip will activate the furnace at a higher temperature, and the house will stay warmer. With the contacts further apart, the strip must cool off by a greater amount for the contacts to close, allowing the house to be cooler too.

Lionel adapted this gadget as a means for causing bulbs to blink, and to route power to sections of track automatically. The method used to heat the bimetallic strip was a coil of thin resistance wire, made of a material that impedes the flow of electricity. This

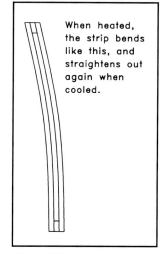

When heated, the strip bends like this, and straightens out again when cooled.

Figure 3-B

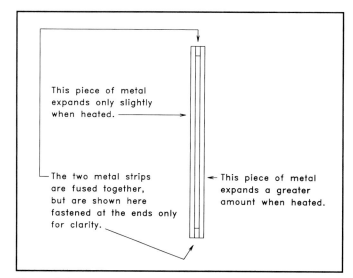

This piece of metal expands only slightly when heated.

The two metal strips are fused together, but are shown here fastened at the ends only for clarity.

This piece of metal expands a greater amount when heated.

Figure 3-A

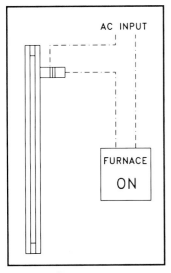

Figure 3-C

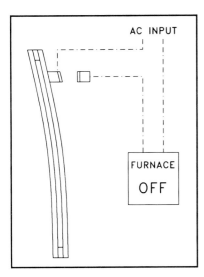

Figure 3-D

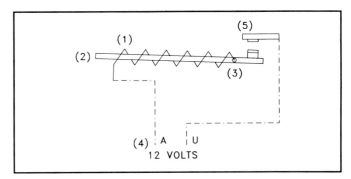

Figure 3-F: Lionel bimetallic strip circuit, open.

causes friction among the electrons of the wire, which in turn produces heat.

In the most common adaptation (Figure 3-E), a coil of resistance wire (1) is wrapped around a piece of insulating material which covers the bimetallic strip (2). One end of the resistance wire is connected to the strip at (3), while the other end is attached to "hot" post A of the transformer (4). Ground post U of the transformer connects to the contact (5). When the transformer is turned on, power flows from post A through the resistance wire and then to the ground through the point where the strip touches the contact (5). It heats up, causing the strip to bend away from the contact and breaking the flow of electricity (Figure 3-F).

As soon as the contact opens, the strip begins to cool off and bends back, finally touching the contact again and restoring electrical current, which heats up the strip again and breaks the circuit. This on-off cycle keeps repeating as long as the transformer is turned on and power reaches the resistance wire.

The simplest application of this device occurs in the 83 and 87 Railroad Crossing Signals (see Chapter IV), each of which contains a single blinking bulb, illustrated in Figure 3-G. In addition to the connections of the resistance wire, a bulb is wired to the hot post (A) and to the end of the bimetallic strip, which grounds it to post U through the contact at (5). When power is

Bimetallic strip from 83 Traffic Signal. P. Riddle Collection and photograph.

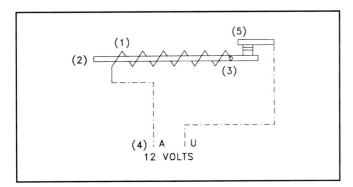

Figure 3-E: Lionel bimetallic strip circuit, closed.

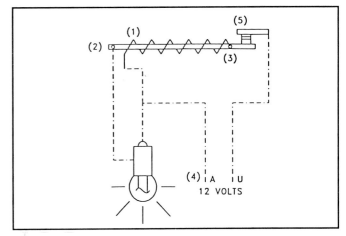

Figure 3-G: 83 Signal circuit, closed.

applied, the bulb lights and the resistance wire begins to heat up. As soon as the strip bends away from the contact, the ground is broken and the bulb goes out. The strip cools, the contact closes, the bulb lights, the wire heats, the contact opens, the bulb goes out, and so on as long as the current flows, causing a steady blinking action.

This circuit is highly dependent upon the amount of voltage applied to the resistance wire. High voltage causes the strip to heat faster, and breaks the contact quickly. Therefore the bulb is on for a very short time, and off longer. Low voltage makes the bulb glow less brightly, but allows it to stay lighted longer, as the strip heats more slowly. Experimentation with the balance between the amount of voltage and the relative brightness of the bulb can produce a stable and even rate of blinking. Lionel instruction sheets specified 12 volts as the proper connection, although under some circumstances better results may be obtained by using an 8-volt bulb and correspondingly less power.

A slightly more sophisticated circuit involving two bulbs was created for the 79 Flashing Signal first offered in 1928 (see Chapter IV), in which two red lights suspended from a crossbar flash on and off alternately. The wiring was designed to shunt current from one bulb to the other as the bimetallic strip alternately opens and closes the circuit. Achieving an even rate

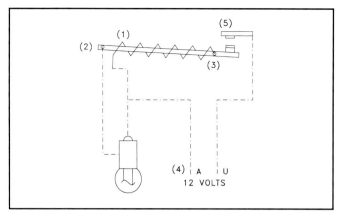

Figure 3-H: 83 Signal circuit, open.

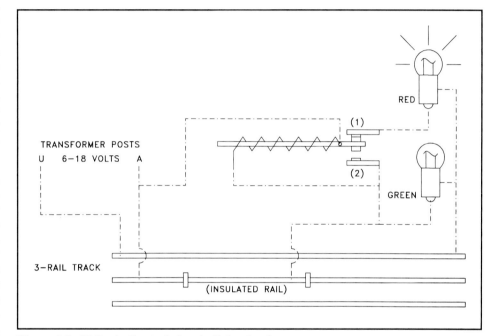

Figure 3-I: 78 Train Control circuit, lighted red.

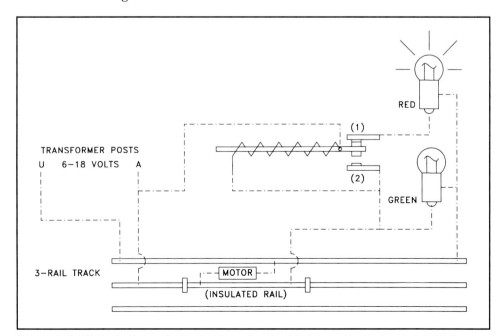

Figure 3-J: 78 Train Control circuit, lighted red, with locomotive in insulated block.

of flash is tricky, and depends upon the load rating of each bulb and the amount of voltage applied. Even when fixed voltage posts are used, the rate of flash may be affected by the varying load placed upon the transformer as the trains slow down and speed up and other accessories such as crossing gates operate. (On his Standard Gauge layout, the author powers a 79 Flashing Signal with its own transformer, a very small Postwar model of 35 watts, which keeps the volume of current constant.)

An even more complex circuit was applied to the 78 Train Control Signal. This device is interconnected with the track, and therefore operates only when a train is running, as diagramed in Figure 3-I. When wired as shown, power reaches the red bulb through the contact (1) touched by the end of the bimetallic strip. Because this is a direct connection, and electricity always follows the path of least resistance, no current passes through the resistance wire.

A special length of track called a "block" is insulated by placing fiber pins in the middle rail at each end; Lionel recommended using three track sections to make up this block. When the locomotive enters this area it stops, since no current is flowing directly to the middle rail (Figure 3-J). However, a separate wire is connected from the dead middle rail to a second contact (2) in the signal, and also to the green bulb. When the locomotive enters the dead block, a trickle of current passes from the ground rail through the motor to the insulated rail, then to the second contact (2) to which the resistance wire is connected. The red bulb goes out as this trickle current heats the wire, and the bimetallic strip begins to bend, breaking away from contact (1) and touching contact (2). This sends power from hot post A through the bimetallic strip to light the green bulb and energize the insulated middle rail (Figure 3-K). The train starts and goes on its way. With current no longer routed through the resistance wire, the strip begins to cool, and the light changes back from green to red. Contact is broken and the middle rail of the block no longer receives current, so the train will stop again the next time it comes around.

The same system was applied to the 82 Automatic Train Control Semaphore (Chapter IV), except that instead of alternately lighting two different bulbs, the circuit raises and lowers the semaphore arm by means of a solenoid. The arm contains two celluloid disks, one red and one green, that line up with one constantly lighted bulb. Red appears when the train stops, and green shows when the signal allows it to proceed again. The operation of solenoid-activated accessories is explained in Chapter VI.

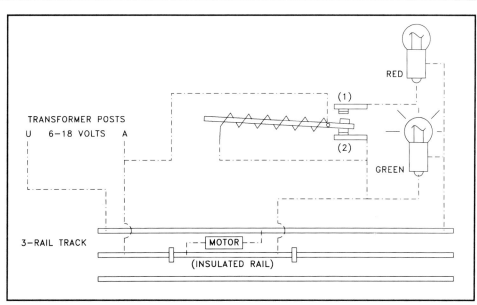

Figure 3-K: 78 Train Control circuit, lighted green.

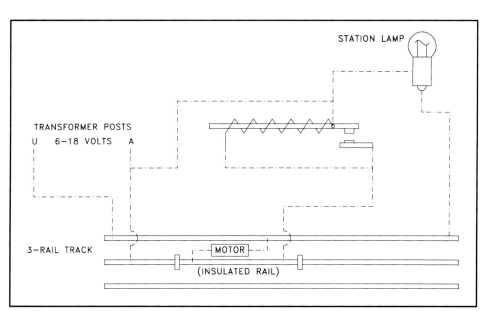

Figure 3-L: Train-stop station circuit.

The 78 Train Control Signal more closely resembles a huge traffic light than a railroad block signal. A. Gordon Thompson, a railway signal engineer of forty years' experience, reports no prototype that resembles this model. In 1932 Lionel replaced it with the 99 Train Control Block Signal (see Chapter IV), a three-light device that is grossly oversized but looks more like modern prototypes. It functions in the same manner as the 78, but has a yellow bulb located in the center position. The circuit was designed to light the yellow bulb when no train is in the insulated block, the red light when a train stops there, and the green light when the train resumes travel. A special section of track with one insulated outside rail was originally required to make the circuit operate, but this was later replaced by a special pressure-operated switch called a "contactor" that functions in response to the weight of the train. Applications of insulated track sections and contactors are discussed in Chapters IV and VI. This signal has a lever which allows the operator to vary the length of time the train pauses. It works much the same as a household thermostat adjustment lever.

Since the most logical place for a train to stop is in front of a depot, Lionel placed its Automatic Train Control system in revised versions of the five largest stations beginning in 1935, and assigned them catalogue numbers 137, 136, 134, 115 and 116, in order of increasing size. Descriptions of these buildings may be found in Chapter V. The circuit (Figure 3-L) is essentially the same as in the 78 Signal, but without

the two colored bulbs. Instead, a single clear bulb illuminates the interior of the station, and brightens noticeably when a locomotive stops in the insulated block, only to dim again when the train starts up.

Lionel made great use of the bimetallic strip, both to provide blinking warning lights and to stop and start the trains without human intervention. The Automatic Train Control enjoyed an especially long production life, beginning in 1924 with the 78 Signal and extending through 1955 in the plastic Postwar 132 Passenger Station. The fascination these accessories excite did much to promote the sale of Lionel trains, and to stimulate the development of child engineers into adult scale model railroaders.

CHAPTER IV

Warning Signals and Automatic Train Control

In 1921 the Lionel Corporation first introduced the concept that was to set the company apart from its competitors, giving it a head start over all other American producers of toy trains, and a substantial advantage in the marketplace. The 69 Warning Bell was the first of a long line of accessories that did things, either automatically when the trains went by or at the touch of a remote-control button. Such toys carried Lionel a giant step forward, from trains that simply went round and round to aural and animated special effects that gave the trains a realistic environment in which to operate.

It is probably safe to say that most children like to make noise (and that most parents would rather they did not). It was likely no accident that J. L. Cowen's first automatic accessory was a noisemaker, the 69 Warning Bell introduced in 1921. It was an immediate sales success, and was soon followed by a series of lighted and animated railroad signals actuated by the passage of trains on the track.

The concept seems to be a simple one in this day of digital electronics, but in 1921 the development of a foolproof method for triggering such automatic devices was a significant advance. The Warning Bell is a railroad crossing sign mounted on a post, with a ringing apparatus not unlike a doorbell fastened behind the sign. Lionel needed some sort of automatic switch — a means whereby the bell would ring only when a train approached, and stopped ringing when it had passed by.

An electrical switch is a device that either prohibits ("off") or allows ("on") the passage of electricity. A common knife or toggle switch could have been used to activate the bell, but that would have required the intervention of the operator, and Lionel wanted the trains themselves to initiate the noise. The solution was a simple and ingenious device that utilized the electrical circuit of the trains themselves.

The normal section of electric train track has three rails mounted on metal ties. The two outer rails touch these ties directly, and any electric current that passes through one of them will be transferred to the other through the ties. The center rail, however, is insulated from each of the ties by small folds of nonconductive

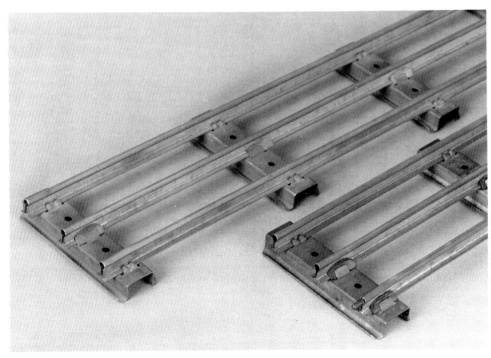

At left is an ordinary section of Lionel track, with the outer rails touching the metal ties and the center rail insulated from them. At right is a special section with one of the outer rails also insulated from the ties; note the fiber insulators on the middle and right-hand rails on this section. P. Riddle Collection and photograph.

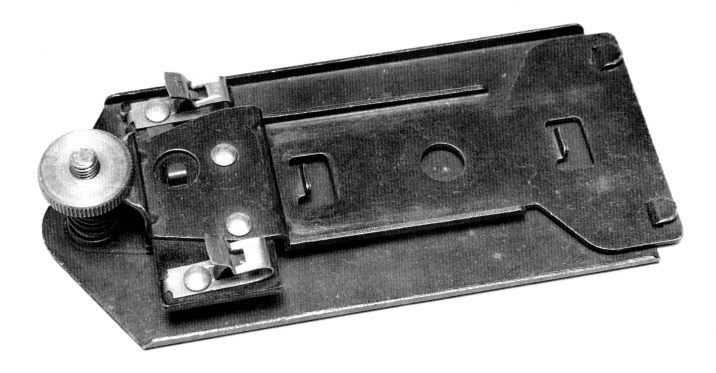

41 Contactor. B. Greenberg Collection, A. Fiterman photograph.

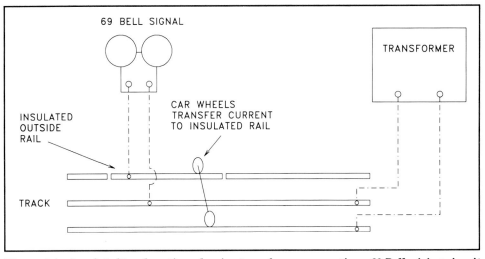

Figure 4-A: Insulated track section, showing transformer connections, 69 Bell wiring circuit and Lockon.

material, seen on the left section of track in the photograph. This material prevents the flow of electricity to the ties. Any electric circuit requires two connections in order to function, a "hot" wire and a "ground" wire. Therefore wires from two posts of a transformer must be connected to the track, one to the middle rail (hot) and one to either of the outer rails (ground). Because the outer rails are connected through the metal ties, both become electrical grounds.

The middle rail supplies current to a locomotive motor through a pickup roller mounted on the underside. To use the simplest analogy, current passes through the roller to the motor to make it work, then exits through the wheels to the outer (ground) rails. If

there were no ground, the circuit would be incomplete, and the motor would not run. However, it is not necessary for both of the outer rails to serve as grounds; one is sufficient.

Lionel created a special track section in which one of the outer rails was insulated, as well as the middle one, shown at right in the photo. To further isolate it from adjoining sections of track, a nonconductive track pin was designed to be placed in each end of the rail, also shown in the photo. When this track section is inserted in a layout, the trains continue to function normally, as the circuit to run their motors is still complete through the uninsulated ground rail on the other side. However, an important change takes place when a train enters this section.

The wheels of a locomotive or car are not insulated from each other, and when these wheels touch the uninsulated ground rail, they transfer the ground to the insulated rail on the other side. Whenever a train is on that section of track, both outer rails are grounded, but when the train leaves, the insulated outer rail is once again isolated. This is the heart of the automatic accessory switch, diagramed in Figure 4-A. The concept is further explored in Chapter VI.

66 Semaphore. F. Wasserman Collection.

Lionel provided this special track section with connections for two wires, similar to the Lockon (a gadget that "locks on" to the middle and one outer rail) by which wires are attached to the track from the transformer to make the trains run. However, on this special section the Lockon is attached to the side of the track with the insulated outer rail. In practice, the 69 Warning Bell is connected by two wires to the two terminals of this Lockon, and therefore to the middle rail and the insulated outer rail of the track section.

With the transformer on and the trains running, the bell can receive current through the hot wire from the middle rail, but since the outer rail to which it is attached is not grounded, the circuit is incomplete and the bell is silent. However, when a train reaches the insulated track section, the wheels carry the ground from the opposite outer rail to the insulated one, which completes the circuit and causes the bell to ring. By placing the track slightly ahead of the Warning Bell, a young engineer can have the bell ring automatically as the train is approaching, and stop ringing as soon as it passes by.

Since the Warning Bell was sold for use with both Standard and O Gauge trains, Lionel made special insulated track sections in both sizes, and distinguished between their usage in the catalogue by assigning the number "69" to the Warning Bell that came with Standard Gauge track, and "069" to the version with O Gauge track. This numbering system was applied to all dual-purpose accessories, such as the 77 and 077 Crossing Gates, 78 and 078 Train Control Signals, and others. The accessories themselves were otherwise identical.

The company provided instructions on a heavy paper label that was placed between the rails of the track when it was packaged. On one O Gauge version, the label reads "Use this special section of OSS track with 068 Warning Signal, 076 Block Signal, 077 Crossing Gate, 080 Electric Semaphore and 099 Position Light Signal. Do not connect other accessories to this section or make current connections to it. The red fiber pins in the envelope packed with this track must be inserted in the ends of the outside insulated rail. Patented. Manufactured exclusively by the Lionel Corporation, New York." According to Ron Morris, the patent for this device (1,636,416) was granted to L. Gessford Handy on July 19, 1927. It was also copied by American Flyer, against whom Lionel successfully brought suit for patent infringement in 1932. Ives used a similar system, but since Lionel had acquired that company by 1930, no claim of infringement was pursued. Dorfan also advertised an insulated track system, but it is not known whether it was ever produced.

A. Gordon Thompson provided the author with some insight into the prototypical origin of the insulated rail. He writes that the "concept came from the railroads. Single rail track circuits are quite common, particularly in subway systems. Operation, however, is reversed to make the circuit fail-safe. The relay device is made to be de-energized when the circuit is occupied by the train."

At Lionel, some extra expense was involved in marketing two versions of each operating accessory, since they required different identification plates and different packaging and labels for the Standard and O Gauge versions. In addition, although the catalogues explained the differences clearly, they may have caused some confusion for customers. In 1936 Lionel introduced a new method of automatic operation, the under-tie 41 Contactor. This device is a form of switch that fits under a section of either Standard or O Gauge track, with a spring that keeps it in the up (off) position. When a train approaches and its weight presses

Two 69 and one 69N Warning Bells. G. Zippie Collection, B. Schwab photograph.

down on the track, the switch closes and electricity flows to the accessory.

This device is somewhat easier to wire than the insulated track section, as either the hot or the ground wire may be routed through the Contactor. However, its operation is less positive. It contains an adjustment knob with a spring to regulate the amount of weight needed to close the switch, but still keep it open when the track alone is pressing on it. The variation in weight between locomotives and cars sometimes causes erratic operation, as the latter may not be heavy enough to close the switch. Also, on a permanent layout, the track cannot be fastened down where Contactors are located, since the track must be free to move up and down. They are also affected by vibration, and must be adjusted frequently, whereas the insulated track sections need no attention in order to function reliably.

Catalogue numbers were altered when the Contactor was introduced, and accessories no longer came with a section of track. The distinction between Standard and O Gauge versions was therefore eliminated, and the letter "N" was added to the basic number. The 80 and 080 Semaphores became 80N, the 99 and 099 Train Control Block Signals became 99N, and the numbers of other accessories were similarly altered (although not all at once; the 45 Gateman did not become 45N until 1937, for example). The 440/0440 Signal Bridges were also renumbered 440N, but according to Ron Morris, this reflected the use of the UTC Universal Lockon, as a contactor is not required for its operation. These changes simplified Lionel's inventory, packaging and labeling chores, and made purchasing an item slightly less confusing. Chapter VI discusses the 41 Contactor and similar devices in detail.

Following are descriptions of known variations of lighted and operating warning signals and train control

076 Block Signal. G. Zippie Collection, B. Schwab photograph.

accessories produced by Lionel through 1942. Sets which include several accessories must include the original box as noted. Otherwise it is impossible to ascertain whether the components were in fact sold as a set. In all cases, the presence of the original box commands a premium.

62 SEMAPHORE (1920-32): Square steel base, tapered open girder post topped by brass finial (same as 60 Telegraph Post and 68 Warning Signal), red hand-operated semaphore arm decorated with simulated red, yellow and green light disks, control lever in base, unlighted, 8¾" high. In addition to the colors listed below, yellow and red 62 Semaphores have been reported, which according to James Flynn were made for Hafner.

	GD	EXC	RST
(A) Olive green base and pole.	15	35	15
(B) Dark green base, yellow pole.	15	35	15
(C) Apple green base and pole.	15	35	15
(D) Pea green base and pole.	15	35	15

The following Semaphores, numbered 63-66, were described in the catalogues through 1921 as having a cast-steel base, which is shown as octagonal. However, Ron Morris contends that they were probably made only with two-piece sheet steel rectangular bases and relay boxes. This is supported by information contained in Train Collectors Association publications. Reader confirmation is requested.

63 SEMAPHORE (1915-21): Black two-piece stamped-steel base and relay box (described as cast-steel in catalogues), orange rolled-steel pole topped with wood finial (often missing; cast reproductions available), single hand-operated red and black steel arm (later versions with embossed reinforcing on edge, some with V-shaped notch in end), two colored celluloid disks in arm, dark green ladder, control lever in base, unlighted, 14" high.   20   40   20

078 Train Control Signal. P. Riddle Collection and photograph.

078 Train Control Signal, back view. P. Riddle Collection and photograph.

Back View of three different Train Control Block Signals. B. Greenberg Collection, A. Fiterman photograph.

76 Warning Bell and Shack. G. Barnett Collection, B. Schwab photograph.

GD EXC RST

64 SEMAPHORE (1915-21): Black two-piece stamped-steel base and relay box (described as cast steel in catalogues), orange rolled-steel pole topped with wood finial (often missing; cast reproductions available), upper hand-operated red and black steel arm (later versions with embossed reinforcing on edge, some with V-shaped notch in end), lower hand-operated green and black steel arm (later versions with embossed reinforcing on edge but no V-shaped notch in end), two colored celluloid disks in each arm, dark green ladder, two control levers in base, unlighted, 14" high.

25   50   25

65 SEMAPHORE (1915-26): Black two-piece stamped-steel base and relay box (described as cast steel in catalogues), orange rolled-steel pole topped with wood finial (often missing; cast reproductions available), single hand-operated red and black steel arm (later versions with embossed reinforcing on edge, some with V-shaped notch in end), two colored celluloid disks in arm, dark green ladder, control lever in base, lighted, lamp socket mounted on pole behind arm, bulb with enameled steel lantern cover, 14" high.

25   50   25

66 SEMAPHORE (1915-26): Black two-piece stamped-steel base and relay box (described as cast steel in catalogues), orange rolled-steel pole topped with wood finial (often missing; cast reproductions available), upper hand-operated red and black steel arm (later versions with embossed reinforcing on edge, some with V-shaped notch in end), lower hand-operated green and black steel arm (later versions with embossed reinforcing on edge but no V-shaped notch in end), two colored celluloid disks in each arm, dark green ladder, two control levers in base, lighted, two lamp sockets mounted on pole behind arm, two bulbs with enameled steel lantern covers, 14" high.

30   60   30

69 ELECTRIC WARNING BELL SIGNAL (1921-35): Standard Gauge.

069 ELECTRIC WARNING BELL SIGNAL (1921-35): O Gauge.

69N ELECTRIC WARNING BELL SIGNAL (1936-42): Both Gauges. Lionel's first track-activated accessory; square steel base, tapered open girder post topped by brass or nickel finial, diamond-shaped sign lettered "RAILROAD CROSSING" across center and "LOOK OUT / FOR LOCOMOTIVE" around border, one (1921-26) or two (1927-42) bells mounted behind sign and rung by make-and-break momentary circuit, some marked "Germany", 8½" high; packed with appropriate section of straight track with one insulated outer rail and Lockon (69 and 069) or pressure-activated contactor switch (69N). Other color

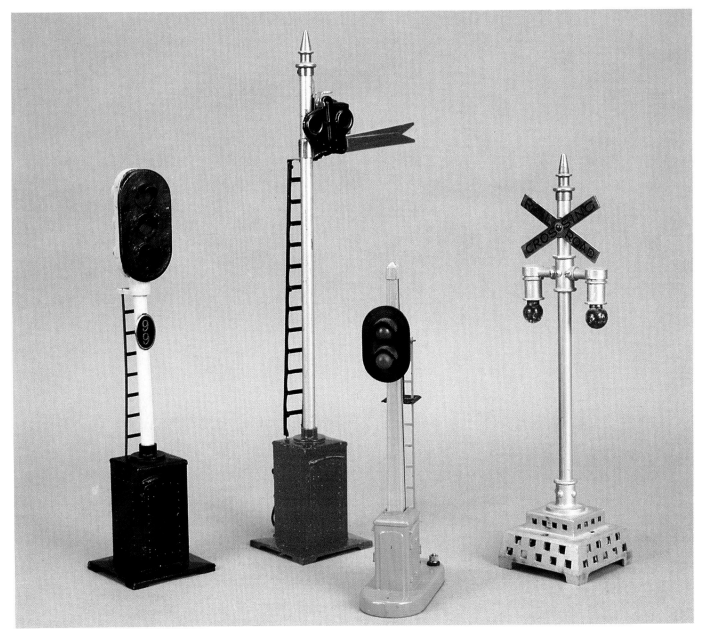

Left to right: 99 Block Signal, 80 Semaphore, 153 Block Signal, 79 Crossing Signal. G. Barnett Collection, B. Schwab photograph.

GD EXC RST

variations than those listed below are expected to be found, and reader assistance is requested to identify them.

(A) White base and pole, brass sign with red lettering, no rubber stamping on base, two shallow rounded bells (one with small half-moon opening). D. Ely Collection.   **20   35   20**

(B) Same as (A), but thicker lettering on diamond. Confirmation requested. C. Weber Collection.   **20   35   20**

(C) Cream base and pole, brass finial, brass sign with red lettering, round nickel bells. J. Flynn Collection.   **20   35   20**

GD EXC RST

(D) Maroon base and pole, brass finial, brass sign with red-etched outline paralleling inside and outside edges, red lettering with very small serifs, black rubber-stamped on bottom in two lines "LIONEL / #069", round nickel bells, left bell with small half-moon opening, adjusting screw, rectangular box on base with P-shaped slot for use with 62 Semaphore. Herzog Collection.   **20   35   20**

(E) Maroon base and pole, brass finial, brass sign with black small serif lettering, rubber-stamped "LIONEL / 69" on underside of base, round bells, no P-shaped slot. D. Ely Collection.   **20   35   20**

83 and 87 Traffic Signals. G. Zippie Collection, B. Schwab photograph.

GD EXC RST

(F) Bright red base and pole, brass finial, brass sign with black small serif lettering, no lettering on base, round bells, no P-shaped slot. D. Ely Collection.

20 35 20

(G) Maroon base and pole, brass finial, brass sign with black-etched line outlining inside and outside edges, heavy black-etched serif lettering, rubber-stamped on underside of base "LIONEL / #069", bell mechanism missing, but probably had washtub-shaped bells. Herzog Collection.

20 35 20

(H) Same as (G), but thinner black lettering, washtub-shaped bells, six holes in base. C. Weber Collection.

20 35 20

(I) Dark olive green (same as 33 Locomotive) base and pole, brass finial, washtub-shaped bells, brass sign with black-etched line outlining inside and outside edges, heavy black-etched serif lettering, rubber-stamped on underside of base "LIONEL / #069". P. Riddle Collection.

20 35 20

(J) Same as (I), but rubber-stamped on base "LIONEL / 69". C. Rohlfing, S. Blotner, D. Ely, and H. Edmunds Collections.

20 35 20

(K) Light olive base and pole, brass finial, brass sign with thick black lettering, washtub-shaped bells, two

GD EXC RST

holes in base, rubber-stamped "LIONEL / 69". C. Weber Collection.

20 35 20

(L) Light red (same as late 517 Caboose) base and pole, nickel or aluminum sign with black outlining, black sans-serif lettering "RAILROAD CROSSING" with highly stylized "R"s and "S"s, washtub-shaped bells, no rubber-stamping on bottom, mechanism mounted on front, box marked "69N"; late production. W. Harrison and D. Ely Collections.

25 45 20

(M) Green base, yellow pole, reportedly 1924-26. Further information and confirmation requested. L. Bohn comment.

NRS

(N) Flat white base and pole, brass sign with thin red serif lettering, no rubber-stamping on base, large single bell with ringer coming out the side of the control box instead of the top, triangle on control coil cover lettered "1872 / EDWARDS". C. Weber Collection.

35 55 20

(O) 1932, made for Ives under catalogue Nos. 1883 (Wide Gauge) and 1884 (O Gauge).

35 75 20

75 LOW BRIDGE SIGNAL (1921): No known examples, probably not manufactured.

76 BLOCK SIGNAL (1923-28): Standard Gauge.

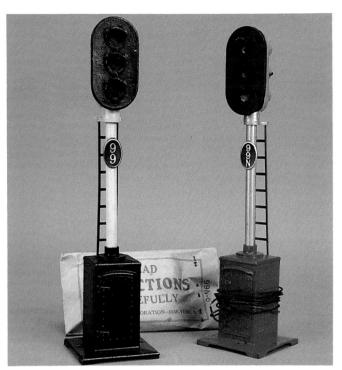

99 (left) and 99N Block Signals. G. Zippie Collection, B. Schwab photograph.

GD EXC RST

076 BLOCK SIGNAL (1923-28): O Gauge. Square steel base, tapered open girder post topped by brass finial, two nickel lamp bases with lantern-type lamp housings (similar to 65 Semaphore), one with four red celluloid lenses, one with four green celluloid lenses, three screw terminals on base usually identified with rubber-stamped lettering "A", "B", and "B", 8¾" high. Each "B" terminal is connected to one lamp while the "A" is a ground common to the frame and both lamps; packed with two special track sections with one insulated outside rail each and two special lockons, one for each track section and labeled "A" and "B" to correspond to the signal's terminals, providing power from the outside rails only when train enters that particular section. The center-rail connection provides power. When a train enters one of the special track sections, the bulb wired to that section is grounded through the wheels and lights. It was intended that the two track sections would be located one full train length apart so that the red and green bulbs would light consecutively.

(A) White base and pole, black lamp housings, rubber-stamped "LIONEL / #76" on underside of base, "A B C" printed in block letters on top of base in black. G. Koff Collection.   **20   40   20**

(B) White base and pole, mojave lamp housings, rubber-stamped "LIONEL / #076" on underside of base. W. Harrison Collection.   **20   40   20**

(C) Mojave base and pole, black lamp housings, rubber-stamped on underside of base "LIONEL / #76". W. Adkins Collection.   **20   40   20**

GD EXC RST

(D) Mojave base and pole, mojave lamp housings, rubber-stamped "LIONEL / #076" on underside of base. G. Koff Collection.   **20   40   20**

(E) Olive green base and pole, nickel lamp housings. Confirmation requested.   **NRS**

76 WARNING BELL AND SHACK (1939-42): Steel construction, rectangular red base with two screw terminals, rectangular white building (same as 45 Gateman), peaked Hiawatha orange roof (same as 45 Gateman but without chimney), aluminum-painted post with black simulated bell, brass warning sign (same as 45 Gateman, earliest production only) lettered "LOOK OUT / FOR THE LOCOMOTIVE", or white die-cast crossbuck sign lettered in black "RAIL ROAD / ROSSING", solenoid-actuated bell mechanism with large silver-dollar-sized bell housing mounted on black metal frame inside shack, silver label on toolbox lid in blue sans-serif lettering, "No. 76 WARNING BELL / AND SHACK / MADE IN THE U.S. OF AMERICA / THE LIONEL CORP. NEW YORK", 7" by 5¾" by 4¾" high; packed with pressure-operated contactor switch instead of insulated track section. The mechanism is described in Chapter VI.

(A) Brass warning sign. Oswald Collection.
                                                90   175   90

(B) Die-cast warning sign. C. Rohlfing and Oswald Collections.   **80   150   80**

78 TRAIN CONTROL BLOCK SIGNAL (1924-32): Standard Gauge.

078 TRAIN CONTROL BLOCK SIGNAL (1924-32): O Gauge. Die-cast combination square base and rectangular relay box, embossed on front with riveted door and hinge detail, embossed on sides with rivets, most embossed on one side "MADE BY / THE / LIONEL CORP. / NEW YORK / PATENTED",

440 Signal Bridge and 440C Panel. G. Zippie Collection, B. Schwab photograph.

Left to right: 069(D); 069(L); 154(B). R. Bartelt Collection, A. Fiterman photograph.

GD   EXC   RST

open on back and fitted with fiber (early) or Bakelite (late) panel held by two screws, embossed or engraved "No78 / FOR / LIONEL STANDARD / TRACK" or "No 078 / FOR / 'O' GAUGE TRACK", the "o" in "No" raised and underscored, wires labeled "1 2 3" emerging through three holes at upper right, control lever projecting at lower right, rolled-steel pole topped by platform with four trapezoidal cutouts in bottom, ladder fitted between relay box and platform, die-cast signal head resembling old-fashioned traffic light fitted into platform and held by two screws, three sides each with two round openings fitted with one red and one green steel ring and celluloid disk, train-stop circuit, 10¼″ high. The mechanism is described in Chapter III, and was patented by Willie Boemper, #1,237,287 (Ron Morris comment). Castings are subject to deterioration, but reproductions are available. All described variations were made as model "78" for Standard Gauge track; (A), (B), (D) and (E) have been found with "078" lettering.

GD   EXC   RST

(A) Maroon base, terra cotta pole, white signal head, dark green ladder, lettered "78" on panel control at back of base. D. Ely Collection.   **40   85   40**

(B) Orange base, cream pole, white signal head, dark green ladder, lettered "078" on back of base. G. Koff Collection.   **40   85   40**

(C) Orange base, dark cream pole, white signal head, pea green ladder. C. Rohlfing Collection.

40   85   40

(D) Maroon base, mojave pole, white signal head, dark green ladder, "PATENTED" missing from embossed box. C. Rohlfing Collection.   **40   85   40**

(E) Same as (D), except base is embossed "MADE BY / THE / LIONEL CORP. / NEW YORK / PATENTED / AUG. 21, 1917", engraved maroon fiber back plate. C. Rohlfing Collection.   **40   85   40**

(F) 1926-29, made for American Flyer Manufacturing Co. as catalogue No. 2033.   **NRS**

(G) 1932, made for Ives under catalogue Nos. 1907 (O Gauge) and 1908 (Wide Gauge).   **40   95   40**

79 FLASHING HIGHWAY SIGNAL (1928-40): Trapezoidal die-cast base topped by rectangular box

GD   EXC   RST

GD   EXC   RST

and circular fitting for pole, punched with nine large square holes per side on trapezoid and four small square holes per side on rectangle, rolled-steel pole topped by brass or nickel finial, elaborate die-cast crossarm with two suspended sockets and two red bulbs hanging down, brass or nickel crossbuck lettered in black "RAIL ROAD / CROSSING" fastened by screw to pole above crossarm, non-flashing red bulb in base, bimetallic strip mechanism in base to flash upper lights alternately (described in Chapter III), 11½" high. Castings are subject to deterioration, but reproductions are available.

(A) White base and pole, gold-painted crossarm, brass sign and finial, light green highlights in sides of base. D. Ely Collection.   40   85   40

(B) Same as (A), but cream base and pole, no green highlights. P. Riddle and C. Rohlfing Collections.
          40   85   40

(C) Same as (A), but cream base and mojave pole. D. Ely Collection.   40   85   40

(D) Aluminum-painted base and pole, gold-painted crossarm, brass sign and finial. D. Ely Collection.
          40   85   40

(E) Same as (D), but aluminum-painted crossarm, brass sign nickeled on front, nickel finial. D. Ely Collection.   40   85   40

(F) Same as (E), but sign is all nickel. D. Ely and C. Rohlfing Collections.   40   85   40

(G) Ivory base, pole and crossarm, brass sign nickeled in front only, nickel finial. D. Ely Collection.
          40   85   40

(H) 1929-30, made for Ives without light in base under catalogue No. 349.   40   125   40

(E) 1931-32, made for Ives under catalogue No. 1880.
          40   125   40

80 SEMAPHORE (1926-35): Standard Gauge.

080 SEMAPHORE (1926-35): O Gauge. Die-cast combination square base and rectangular relay box, embossed on front with riveted door and hinge detail,

440N Signal Bridge and 440C Panel. G. Zippie Collection, B. Schwab photograph.

GD EXC RST

embossed on sides with rivets (similar to 78 Train Control Signal), open on back and fitted with fiber (early) or Bakelite (late) panel held by two screws, wires emerging through three holes, rolled-steel pole with brass or nickel finial, steel bracket mounted on pole near top holding socket with bulb, base for lantern and steel lantern cover with hole for light to shine through, ladder fitted between relay box and bracket, black and red semaphore arm with one red and one green celluloid disk, solenoid-actuated mechanism (described in Chapter VI), 15″ high; packed with appropriate section of straight track with one insulated outer rail and lock-on. Castings are subject to deterioration, but reproductions are available.

(A) Terra cotta base, mojave pole, dark pea green ladder. D. Ely Collection. **40 85 40**

(B) Dark green base, orange pole, green ladder. D. Ely Collection. **40 85 40**

(C) Orange base, mojave pole, dark green ladder. J. Thomson Collection. **40 85 40**

(D) Black base, mojave pole, dark green ladder. **40 85 40**

(E) Light red base, aluminum-painted pole, orange ladder, nickel finial; similar to colors of 80N but not so labeled. Confirmation requested. **NRS**

(F) 1932, made for Ives under catalogue Nos. 1903 (Wide Gauge) and 1904 (O Gauge). **60 125 40**

80N SEMAPHORE (1936-42): Standard or O Gauge, same as 80, light red base, aluminum-painted pole, black ladder, nickel finial; packed with pressure-operated contactor switch instead of insulated track section. J. Flynn, D. Ely, and S. Blotner Collections.
40 85 40

82 TRAIN CONTROL SEMAPHORE (1927-35): Standard Gauge.

082 TRAIN CONTROL SEMAPHORE (1927-35): O Gauge. Die-cast combination square base and rectangular relay box topped with second smaller box, embossed on front with riveted door and hinge detail, embossed on sides with rivets (similar to but taller than 78 Train Control Signal), open on back and fitted with fiber (early) or Bakelite (late) panel held by two screws, wires emerging through three holes, rolled-steel pole with brass or nickel finial, plate numbered "82" for Standard Gauge or "082" for O Gauge, steel bracket mounted on pole near top holding socket with bulb, base for lantern and steel lantern cover with hole for light to shine through, ladder fitted between box and bracket, black and red semaphore arm with one red and one green celluloid disk, train-stop circuit, 14¾″ high; packed with appropriate section of straight track with one insulated outer rail and lockon. The mechanism is described in Chapter III. Castings, especially those painted peacock, are subject to deterioration, but reproductions are available.

GD EXC RST

(A) Peacock base, cream pole, orange ladder, brass finial, brass plate numbered "82" on pole. D. Ely, L. Bohn, and J. Flynn Collections. **45 90 45**

(B) Same as (A), but with nickel finial and number plate. L. Bohn Collection. **45 90 45**

(C) 45N green base, aluminum-painted pole, black ladder, nickel trim. **45 90 45**

82N SEMAPHORE (1936-42): Standard or O Gauge, same as 82, 45N green base, aluminum-painted pole, black ladder, nickel finial; packed with pressure-operated contactor switch instead of insulated track section. J. Flynn and S. Blotner Collections.
45 90 45

83 TRAFFIC AND CROSSING SIGNAL (1927-42): Die-cast combination trapezoidal base and rectangular box embossed with raised panels and rivets on four sides, three sides rubber-stamped in black "CAUTION / DRIVE / SLOWLY", fourth side embossed "MADE BY / THE / LIONEL / CORPORATION / NEW YORK", circular opening in top, socket and bulb mounted in center, removable signal head shaped like diver's helmet with circular openings fitted with metal-rimmed red celluloid disks, bulb blinks by means of bimetallic strip (described in Chapter III), 6¼″ high. Castings are subject to deterioration, but reproductions are available.

(A) 1927-34, mojave base, cream box, white head. P. Riddle Collection. **40 80 40**

(B) Red base, cream box, mojave head. D. Ely Collection. **40 80 40**

(C) 1935-42, light red base, cream box, white head. D. Ely Collection. **40 80 40**

(D) 1931-32, made for Ives under catalogue No. 1881. **70 150 70**

(E) 1929-30, made for Ives but with shorter center section under catalogue No. 350. **100 250 100**

84 SEMAPHORE (1927-32): Standard Gauge.

084 SEMAPHORE (1927-32): O Gauge. Most with dark green die-cast combination square base and rectangular relay box, embossed on front with riveted door and hinge detail, embossed on sides with rivets (similar to 78 Train Control Signal), open on back and fitted with fiber (early) or Bakelite (late) panel held by two screws, two terminals or three wires emerging through holes at right, control lever projecting through slot at upper center, cream rolled-steel pole with brass finial, steel bracket mounted on pole near top holding socket with bulb, base for lantern and steel lantern cover with hole for light to shine through, orange or pea green ladder fitted between relay box and bracket, black and red semaphore arm with one red and one green celluloid disk, hand-operated mechanism, three-wire versions may be connected to an insulated track block to stop train when in red-lighted position (simplified manual version of train control), 15″ high. Castings are subject to deterioration, but reproductions are available.

GD   EXC   RST

(A) Two terminals on back for electrical connection, no manual train-stop circuit.   40   85   40
(B) Three wires on back for electrical connection, including manual train-stop circuit.   40   85   40
(C) Same, but orange pole, peacock ladder. R. Morris Collection.   40   85   40
(D) Same as (C), but maroon base. R. Morris Collection.   40   85   40

87 RAILROAD CROSSING SIGNAL (1927-42): Die-cast trapezoidal base (similar to 83), rectangular box embossed with raised panels and rivets on four sides, three sides rubber- stamped in black "CAUTION / DRIVE / SLOWLY", fourth side embossed "MADE BY / THE / LIONEL / CORPORATION / NEW YORK", circular opening in top, socket and bulb mounted in center, removable drum-shaped signal head fitted with two celluloid disks lettered in black circular pattern "RAILROAD / CROSSING" around red or orange bull's-eye in center (some with black "eyebrow" near top; Ron Morris comment), bulb blinks by means of bimetallic strip (described in Chapter III), 6¾" high. Castings are subject to deterioration, but reproductions are available.

(A) 1927-34, orange base and box, ivory head.   40   80   40
(B) Dark green base, Stephen Girard green box, white head, red bull's eyes. D. Ely Collection.   40   80   40
(C) Light tan base, orange box, ivory head. Clement Collection.   40   80   40
(D) Mojave base, orange box, white head, orange bull's eyes. D. Ely Collection.   40   80   40
(E) Mojave base, orange box, ivory head, light orange bull's eyes with black crescent. C. Rohlfing Collection.   40   80   40
(F) Dark green base, cream box, white head, red bull's eyes. D. Ely Collection.   40   80   40
(G) Same as (F), but one light orange bull's eye and one red bull's eye, no crescents. C. Rohlfing Collection.   40   80   40

99 TRAIN CONTROL BLOCK SIGNAL (1932-35): Standard Gauge.

099 TRAIN CONTROL BLOCK SIGNAL (1932-35): O Gauge. Die-cast combination square base and rectangular relay box, embossed on front with riveted door and hinge detail, embossed on sides with rivets (similar to 78 Train Control Signal, but modified with two holes for ladder), open on back and fitted with fiber panel held by two screws, four wires emerging from holes at corners, curved slot with train control adjustment lever projecting, rolled-steel pole, black die-cast target head with openings fitted with red, clear and green celluloid disks, red or black ladder, brass plate numbered "99" or "099" in vertical arrangement, train-stop circuit, 12" high; packed with appropriate section of straight track with one insulated outer rail and lockon. A yellow 433Y bulb (Lionel No. 29-3, no longer manufactured)

mounts behind the clear celluloid disk in the center. The instruction sheet specifies "Lionel No. 29 special yellow bulb. No other bulb will operate in this train control." Ron Morris reports a 1447 bulb, painted yellow, will operate in this accessory. The mechanism is described in Chapter III. Castings are subject to deterioration, but reproductions are available.

(A) 1932-34, black base and ladder, cream pole. D. Ely Collection.   45   90   45
(B) 1935, red base and ladder, cream pole. D. Ely Collection.   45   90   45
(C) Black base and ladder, mojave pole.   45   90   45

99N TRAIN CONTROL BLOCK SIGNAL (1936-42): Standard or O Gauge, same as 99, light red base and ladder, aluminum-painted pole, black target head, nickel plate numbered "99N" in vertical arrangement, Bakelite back panel embossed "AUTOMATIC / TRAIN CONTROL / THE LIONEL CORP. / N.Y.", connections labeled "1 2 3 4" and plate labeled "SLOW FAST CONT." below semi-circular slot for control lever, 12" high; packed with pressure-operated contactor switch instead of insulated track section.

(A) Vermilion base and ladder, C. Weber Collection.   45   90   45
(B) Same as (A), but light red base and ladder. C. Rohlfing Collection.   45   90   45

153 AUTOMATIC BLOCK SIGNAL (1940-42, Postwar): 45N green die-cast combination elliptical base and rectangular relay box, embossed on sides with door and hinge detail, solid tapered-steel pole with brass or nickel finial, black die-cast target head with two openings for red and green bulbs, slotted two-step platform behind target head, orange ladder, 9" high; packed with pressure-operated single-pole, double-throw 153C contactor switch. All Prewar versions have a resistor in the base to allow use of 6-8 volt screw-base bulbs; all Postwar versions have aluminum-painted poles, darker green base after 1947 and 14-volt bayonet-base bulbs without the resistor after 1949.

(A) 1940-41, aluminum-painted pole.   15   30   15
(B) 1942, 92 gray pole and brass finial. Much harder to find than version (A). R. LaVoie comment.   20   45   15

154 AUTOMATIC HIGHWAY SIGNAL (1940-42, Postwar): Die- cast combination elliptical base and trapezoidal box, solid tapered-steel pole with finial (similar to 153), black crossarm with two light sockets holding two red bulbs and central sign lettered in white "STOP" vertically, white crossbuck sign with black lettering "RAIL ROAD / CROSSING" above crossarm; packed with 154C contactor to make bulbs flash alternately. All Postwar versions have aluminum poles and raised embossed lettering on either white or black crossbuck.

GD EXC RST

GD EXC RST

(A) 1940-41, aluminum-painted pole and nickel finial. C. Rohlfing Collection. **15 25 10**

(B) 1942, 92 gray pole and finial. C. Rohlfing Collection. **15 25 10**

(C) Hiawatha orange base, aluminum-painted pole, nickel finial. **25 50 10**

193 AUTOMATIC ACCESSORY SET (1927-29): O Gauge, contains 069 Warning Bell, 076 Block Signal, 077 Crossing Gate, 078 Train Control Signal, 080 Semaphore, five sections OSS track, in original box. **200 425 175**

194 AUTOMATIC ACCESSORY SET (1927-29): Standard Gauge, contains 69 Warning Bell, 76 Block Signal, 77 Crossing Gate, 78 Train Control Signal, 80 Semaphore, five sections SS track, in original box. **200 425 175**

440 SIGNAL BRIDGE (1932-35): Standard Gauge.

0440 SIGNAL BRIDGE (1932-35): O Gauge. Two combination elliptical die-cast bases with trapezoidal and rectangular boxes, large steel girder bridge consisting of one upper horizontal and two supporting vertical trusses (spanning two Standard Gauge tracks), two black circular die-cast signal heads (each with five bulbs) mounted on bridge walkway platform, three paired handrails across top walkway, brass and black plate lettered "NO. 440 (or 0440) POSITION LIGHT / SIGNAL BRIDGE / LIONEL CORPORATION", 20½" wide by 14" high. The signal heads appear to have five lights, arranged in horizontal and vertical lines of three. Two bulbs (the outer ones in either the horizontal or the vertical row) are lighted at one time on each signal head, by means of single-pole, double-throw lever switches on 440C Panel Board (included). The central position is lighted by the outer bulbs, simulating a three-light row; Ron Morris comment. Wiring may be connected to an insulated track block to stop train when lighted in horizontal position (simplified manual version of train control). Bases and signal heads are subject to deterioration.

(A) Terra cotta bases, mojave bridge, maroon walkway, brass handrail and rail supports; reproduced by Lionel Trains, Inc. G. Zippie Collection. **150 300 150**

(B) Red bases, aluminum-painted bridge, red walkway, nickel handrail and rail supports. **150 300 150**

(C) 1989, reproduction by Lionel Trains, Inc., catalogue number 51900, embossed "LTI" or "Lionel Trains, Inc." **— 300 —**

440C PANEL BOARD (1932-42): Included with 440 / 0440 / 440N Signal Bridge, red rectangular frame with curved shoulders at base (similar to 439 Panel Board described in Chapter XII), stamped-steel construction, black simulated marble composition panel board fitted with four brass or nickel knife switches with black Bakelite handles embossed "L" on each side, two central track control levers for operating Signal Bridge, two simulated meters with brass or nickel rims, arched sheet steel extension at top of frame with hooded central socket and bulb, flanked by plates lettered "LIONEL" at left and "PANEL BOARD / NO. 440C" at right, plate near bottom of base lettered "MADE BY / THE LIONEL CORPORATION / NEW YORK", 7 3⁄16" wide, 8 3⁄16" high; reproduced by Lionel Trains, Inc.

(A) Red, glossy and coarse crackle finish. Ron Morris comment. **50 100 50**

(B) Red, matte and fine crackle finish. G. Zippie Collection. **50 100 50**

(C) Light red. G. Zippie Collection. **50 100 50**

(D) 92 gray. Ron Morris comment. **50 100 50**

440N SIGNAL BRIDGE (1936-42): Standard or O Gauge, same as 440.

(A) Red bases, aluminum-painted bridge, red walkway, nickel handrail and rail supports, nickel and black plate lettered "NO. 440N POSITION LIGHT / SIGNAL BRIDGE / LIONEL CORPORATION". G. Zippie Collection. **150 300 150**

(B) 1942, same as (B), but 92 gray bridge. J. Flynn observation. **150 300 150**

1569 LIONEL JUNIOR ACCESSORY SET (1933-37): Contains four 1571 Telegraph Posts, 1572 Semaphore, 1573 Warning Signal, 1574 Clock, 1575 Crossing Gate, in original box.

(A) Black bases. D. Ely Collection. **40 75 35**

(B) Red bases. D. Ely Collection. **40 75 35**

(C) 1931-32, made for Ives. **40 80 35**

1572 SEMAPHORE (1933-37): Square steel base, tapered solid post, two cream hand-operated semaphore arms with V-shaped notches in ends, decorated with red V-shaped stripe and simulated red and green light disks, unlighted, 7" high; part of 1569 Lionel Junior Accessory Set.

(A) Pea green post, light red base. **5 10 5**

(B) Gray post, black base. **5 10 5**

(C) Gray post, pea green upper base, light red lower base. J. Flynn Collection. **5 10 5**

(D) 1931-32, made for Ives. **5 10 5**

CHAPTER V

Railway Stations and Related Accessories

After the locomotives and cars themselves, no components are more fundamental to the concept of a model railroad than passenger and freight stations. These buildings give the trains a purpose, providing both a starting point and a destination for their travels, and help to spark the imagination with images of boarding passengers and delivered merchandise.

The first Lionel stations appear on pages 16 and 17 in the 1906 catalogue, and are believed to have been of German manufacture. Toys of all sorts were imported from that country prior to World War I, and generally dominated the American market because of their high quality and low prices. Model 24 represents a typical passenger depot, and from the illustration in the catalogue, its appearance does not strongly suggest its European origins, but the No. 25 is clearly continental, containing decorative details reminiscent of Märklin or Bing products of that period.

The 24 Railway Station is a rectangular metal structure mounted on a low raised base, and has a V-shaped bay window on one long side, flanked by doors with ornate cast frames. The frame design is echoed in the two windows on the bay, but the end walls are windowless. The siding simulates large bricks, and the roof is a peaked design with a gable over the bay within which is stamped "OCEANSIDE". A central chimney and two flanking spires decorate the roof.

As shown in the catalogue, the other station (No. 25) is an open platform, consisting of two rectangular bases that can be placed on either side of the track. One side is very plain, having two sections of open-grill fence with a gap between. The catalogue mentions a "safety gate," but none appears in the drawing. The opposite side has a large semicircular roof with two up-tilted awnings, supported by four poles at the corners. A miniature figure wearing a bowler hat is pictured sitting on a bench in the center of the platform.

These two models were advertised for only two years, and in the revised 1908 catalogue Lionel pictured three stations (Nos. 27, 28 and 121) that were supplied by the Ives Corporation. The author surmises that the lack of original Lionel station designs was the result of J. L. Cowen's interest being focused primarily upon the trains themselves and their mechanical components. His most noteworthy innovations tended to be those associated with electric power, and not until the 1920 catalogue did his company announce its first station produced by Lionel designers and craftsmen. All three Ives designs were shown in the catalogue through 1912, and listed without pictures in 1913 and 1914.

Early 121 Station. G. Claytor Collection.

48W Station. G. Barnett Collection, B. Schwab photograph.

The smallest example (No. 121) is brightly colored with complex lithography, and has a hip roof with a fancy ridge platform and a central chimney. It lacks a bay window, having instead a small central window between two open doors on the long wall. End walls feature two windows each. This is the only station that appears in the 1915 catalogue, the others having been discontinued after 1914, and is similar to Ives' own model 113.

Longer by 7 inches, Lionel model 27 (Ives 116) has a V-shaped bay flanked by both doors and windows, and the bay has two windows of its own. Three chimneys adorn the roof, and on the back wall a central window replaces the bay. Two of these models combined with Ives' impressive leaded glass dome were listed in the catalogue as model 28, to create an imposing depot with track running through the center.

Sales of Ives stations by Lionel apparently ended in 1917. The author speculates that Lionel may have been planning production of its own design that year, as the catalogue pictures a model not unlike the later 124 (except for the roof design), and describes it as being "constructed of sheet steel" and "hand enameled." There is good reason to believe that competition between the two companies made joint marketing of stations uncomfortable for both of them. While in the earliest years of the century, the well-established Ives firm was the preeminent American toy train manufacturer; Lionel soon came to be seen as a substantial threat to the Bridgeport firm's position of leadership. Prior to 1910, for example, Ives built only clockwork-powered trains, but the rapid rise in popularity of Lionel's electric-powered models forced them to create a competing line in that year. Lionel advertising also became more aggressive, and targeted Ives in particular with unflattering catalogue depictions of Ives' supposedly "inferior" quality and durability. In a letter to the author, Stuart Armstrong further suggests that Ives may have had difficulty in obtaining raw materials during the First World War, and that these shortages may also have contributed to the decision by Lionel to discontinue sale of Ives stations.

In the publication *Lionel Trains, Standard of the World, 1900-1943, Second Edition*, the Train Collectors Association states that from 1917 until 1920 Lionel sold a single station design, the 121, which was a composition board (not steel) structure supplied by the American firm of Schoenhut, located in Philadelphia, Pennsylvania. (This highly successful toymaker had built a substantial reputation upon its line of miniature pianos, some of which were floor models so large as to allow a child to sit before them to perform.)

The Schoenhut station's composition sides are embossed to represent masonry blocks. A central frame in the long side encloses a swinging door, and the two flanking windows are fitted with glass. The peaked roof has a chimney near one end, and various colors were used in decoration.

By 1920 it appears that J. L. Cowen had begun to realize the potential for accessories to broaden both the appeal and the year-round sales potential of his toy inventory. As the catalogues became larger and more colorful, the number of pages devoted to accessories increased, and such items as stations, signals and lamp posts were displayed as prominently as the trains. "The New Lionel Steel Stations" were shown on two pages, and one illustration calls special attention to the interior and exterior lighting fixtures.

In creating his own stamped-steel "Lionel City" station in 1920, Cowen borrowed heavily from the appearance of the Schoenhut product, and the 121 catalogue number was retained. Dimensions are virtually the same. This design was made until the Second World War under five different catalogue numbers (121, 122, 123, 124, 134), and differs in appearance from the Schoenhut model mainly in the hip roof design and paired chimneys. It was made with and without interior lighting, and the No. 124 and 134 versions have two ornate lamp brackets fitted under the eaves at two corners. Each long side has a central door and two windows, and a single window appears in each end.

J. L. Cowen understood well the need to offer products in all price ranges. Two additional and smaller station designs appeared in the 1923 catalogue. The mid-size 125 and 126 "Lionelville" models (later renumbered 136) are several inches smaller in all dimensions than the 121 type, with the window and door treatment exactly reversed. Two huge doors appear in each long side, with a central ticket window on the front, and a door appears in each end, flanked by two small windows set high in the wall. Two more of these windows are placed between the doors on the back wall. The hip roof has two curved-top dormers and two chimneys, and the station was sold both with (126) and without (125) interior illumination.

Smallest was the 127 "Lioneltown" (later renumbered 137), intended for use with O Gauge trains only. A simple rectangle with a peaked roof and single chimney near one end, this model has a central door and two windows in each long side and two small windows in each end, plus a round vent under the eaves. The walls suggest clapboard siding.

A beautiful station accessory was offered in 1928, and sold for three years in combination with the 124 "Lionel City" as catalogue No. 128 or separately as the No. 129 Station Platform, for use with the 121, 122 or 124 stations. The catalogue description introduced the word "terrace" in 1931 when the 112-type station was substituted, and it is by this name to which the unit is most frequently referred. At over 2½ feet long, this formidable platform features a broad staircase leading up to a high base with semicircular ends which enclose landscaped flower beds, a flagpole and an ornamental urn. An open latticework fence with seven posts supporting three torchlike lamp fixtures and four round

113 and 115 Stations. G. Zippie Collection, B. Schwab photograph.

Early (right) and late 124 Stations. G. Zippie Collection, B. Schwab photograph.

globes encloses the outer portion of each end. The center of the platform is slightly depressed to allow the station to fit securely.

The largest of Lionel's prewar stations debuted in the 1931 catalogue, a massive building nearly 20 inches long and reminiscent of the spacious urban terminals that once formed the focus of downtown areas in most major American cities. The 114 "Lionel City" is suitable for either Standard or O Gauge layouts, thanks to clever proportioning of the doors and windows, and its steel construction imitates typical masonry construction of the early twentieth century, with a stone block and column design topped by projecting cornices and a flat roof with two skylights.

Four tall doors are centered on each of the long walls, below a three-piece ornamental grill surrounding a clock face. Arched window cutouts higher up on the wall are fitted with fine mesh grillwork. To the right and left of the doors rise a total of four eighteen-pane windows, above each of which is another elliptical window divided into nine segments. The end walls each have three tall window inserts, the central one having thirty separate panes while the other two have twelve panes each. On one long side of the station, a pair of torchlike lighting brackets flank the doors, and another pair of bulbs light the interior.

A smaller building with identical construction details, the 113 "Lionel City" station, has shorter front and back walls with only one window unit on each side of the main doors, and has a single bulb inside. Otherwise it was made from the same components as the 114. When sold without the exterior lighting brackets beside the doors, it was numbered 112. The base of this sta-

tion was only slightly larger than the 121 type, and beginning in 1931 it replaced the older design in combination with the 129 Terrace as catalogue No. 128.

It has been suggested that New York City's Grand Central Station served as the model for these large "Lionel City" designs, but they are not really similar. A photo of the facade of Grand Central in *Metropolitan Corridors* by John R. Stilgoe suggests only the vaguest likeness. However, stations like Lionel's do exist; for example, the Grand Trunk Central station in Ottawa, Ontario, Canada, has the tall windows, central clock and columns that characterize the 114 design, incorporated in a similar rectangular structure. A photo appears on page 64 of *An Illustrated History of Canadian Railways*, by Nick and Helma Mika with Donald M. Wilson (Belleville, Ontario: Mika Publishing Company, 1986).

By 1937 all of Lionel's stations were converted to operating accessories, with the advent of the train-stop circuit (see Chapters III and IV) which allowed the trains to pause briefly by automatic action. The three smaller stations received slightly revised catalogue numbers, with the middle digit being raised by one. The 124 became 134, 126 became 136 and 127 became 137. The large "Lionel City" designs were renumbered from 112 to 117, 113 to 115, and 114 to 116. All stations were now produced in lighted versions only, as the lamp was wired into the train-stop device.

With the onset of the Great Depression, Lionel recognized the need for more economical toys in its inventory, and developed the Winner Toy Corporation to market these low-priced items. It has been suggested that the Winner name was introduced in order to maintain an image of prestige for the Lionel trademark. After two years the Winner division was renamed "Lionel-Ives" and later "Lionel Jr." A small lithographed station was developed for this line, and fitted with a transformer (models 1012, 1017, 1027, 1028 and 1029) to power the tiny trains with which it was packaged. The basic boxlike structure is highly detailed with colorful and ornate windows and doors, and features simulated foundation planting and a peaked roof detailed to represent tiles. It also came without the transformer (1012K, 1560) and beginning in 1937 was fitted with a Lionel whistle (48W).

The choice of lithography for this station, as well as for the lowest-priced trains, is significant. Prior to the Depression, all Lionel finishes were enameled, and the firm looked with disdain upon the lithographed products of Ives and American Flyer. With clever advertising and blatant exaggeration, Lionel promoted enameled trains as superior, although they clearly lacked such fine details as rivets, hinges and especially the colorful road name logos that made Ives and Flyer toys seem more realistic. Lionel succeeded in convincing the buying public that painted trains were better; they were certainly brighter and therefore probably more attractive in catalogues and on the toy shelves of department stores. To the toy buyer of the 1920s, realism was a secondary consideration.

However, economic realities of the early 1930s forced the company to seek the most cost-effective manufacturing techniques, and lithography was substantially less expensive than painting. In a dramatic reversal, perhaps somewhat easier for management to swallow after the failure of the Ives Corporation, Lionel embraced the lithographic process at which it had once sneered. J. L. Cowen was apparently shrewd enough never to allow principle to stand in the way of profit.

Freight stations received much less attention; Lionel produced only one design before World War II. The big 155 Freight Shed first appeared in the 1930 catalogue sandwiched in between the big 219 Derrick, the LCL Merchandise Containers and the 218 Operating Dump Car. This handsome model has a high raised base, three posts supporting a peaked roof and two bulbs lighting the platform. It was introduced at the same time as a set of freight accessories, a baggage cart, dump truck and a pair of hand baggage trucks, each of which was available separately. The 155 model was suitable only for Standard Gauge, as the platform was too high to line up properly with O Gauge cars.

In 1939 the 156 Station Platform was introduced, a smaller model not unlike the 155, but not designated a freight station. It has a Bakelite base and roof and three die-cast poles. Lionel described it in the 1939 catalogue as being "useful for intermediate station stops." Its design makes it appropriate for use as either a passenger or freight platform. Two picket fences between the poles display lithographed steel

advertising signs, and a pair of bulbs under the roof provide illumination. This model was intended strictly for O Gauge, as Lionel was winding down all Standard Gauge production by that date, and is very close to scale in its dimensions. The company also produced a few small and economical accessories to add to the play value of the trains, including tool sets, barrels and miniature people.

Following are descriptions of known variations of railroad stations and related accessories produced by Lionel through 1942. Sets which include several accessories must include the original box as noted. Otherwise it is impossible to ascertain whether the components were in fact sold as a set.

GD EXC RST

24 RAILWAY STATION (1906-07): Dark red base, ivory simulated brick sides, black simulated brick foundation, two maroon doors flank projecting maroon bay window on one side, gable above bay lettered "OCEANSIDE", red and black roof, ivory chimney, 11″ wide, 7½″ deep, 8″ high, believed to be of German manufacture. **NRS**

25 OPEN RAILWAY STATION (1906-7): Two sections, one with fence only for one side of track, other with four pillars and roof for other side of track, one miniature figure, 11″ wide, 11″ long, 8″ high, believed to be of German manufacture. **NRS**

27 STATION (1908-14): Lithographed, four windows and two doors on one side, projecting ticket-telegraph office and two doors and three windows on other side, catalogued as 21″ wide, 9″ deep, 10″ high, very similar to and may be the same as Ives 116 station (although the Ives model is 18½″ wide and 8″ deep). **NRS**

28 STATION (1908-14): Two 27 stations, leaded glass dome on triangular supports spanning tracks, catalogued as 18½″ wide, 22½″ long and 11″ high (same as Ives 123 Double Station with glass dome). The illustrations in the Ives 1910 catalogue are very similar to those shown in the Lionel catalogues for 1909-12. **NRS**

32 MINIATURE FIGURES (1909-18): One dozen molded composition human figures, in seated position and with holes to fit over pins in trolley or Pullman cars, various colors. **50 100 50**

48W WHISTLE STATION (1937-42): Lithographed walls with "LIONEL" above windows on both ends, lithographed removable roof, painted base with two terminal posts at one end, press-down momentary-contact switch projects from building at opposite end, contains whistle without DC relay, walls trimmed to leave ³⁄₁₆″ gap under eaves to allow sound to be heard, 5½″ wide, 3¾″ deep, 3¾″ high.

(A) Cream-yellow walls with lithographed details (blue and white windows, brown doors, foundation plants), two-tone red lithographed simulated shingle

128 Terrace and Station (124). P. Riddle Collection and photograph.

GD EXC RST

roof, vermilion base. G. Barnett and C. Rohlfing Collections. **20 40 20**

(B) Same as (A), but orange lithographed roof, possibly a Winner station roof placed on late 48W. Additional confirmation requested. J. Gillander Collection.

20 40 20

112 STATION (1931-34): Steel walls embossed to simulate stone, columns at corners and flanking doors, flat base, flat roof with ledge and cornices, skylight, four movable doors on front and rear, rectangular multi-paned windows surrounding lower story, elliptical multi-pane windows on front and rear second story, three-section arch-shaped window grills centered on second story of all four walls, "LIONEL CITY" embossed over doors, embossed or-

GD EXC RST

namental clocks with celluloid faces above doors, interior light, 13¾" wide, 9½" deep, 8½" high.

(A) Terra cotta base, 1685 cream walls, pea green roof, skylight and window inserts, maroon doors, brass clock inserts. D. Ely Collection. **100 200 90**

(B) Mohave base, ivory walls, apple green roof and window inserts, pea green skylight, maroon doors, brass clock inserts. **100 200 90**

(C) Terra cotta base, 129 beige walls, apple green roof and window inserts, apple green or pea green skylight, maroon doors, brass clock inserts. **100 200 90**

(D) Light red base, roof, skylight, window inserts and doors, ivory walls, white metal clock inserts.

110 225 90

113 STATION (1931-34): Same as 112, but with gold-painted outside light fixtures for upright tulip-shaped bulbs mounted on columns flanking doors on one side, skylight reported either pea green or apple green (cannot be verified, as they are not fastened to the building and are easily switched). G. Zippie Collection.

125 250 120

114 STATION (1931-34): Same type construction as 112, but with longer front and back walls extended with one extra column and window on each side of doors, two skylights either pea green or apple green (see note under 113), two light fixtures flanking doors on one side, two interior lights, 19½" wide, 9¼" deep, 8½" high.

(A) Terra cotta base, 1685 cream walls, pea green roof, skylight, and window inserts, maroon doors, brass clock inserts. D. Ely Collection. **600 1200 600**

127 (left) and 137 Stations. G. Zippie Collection, B. Schwab photograph.

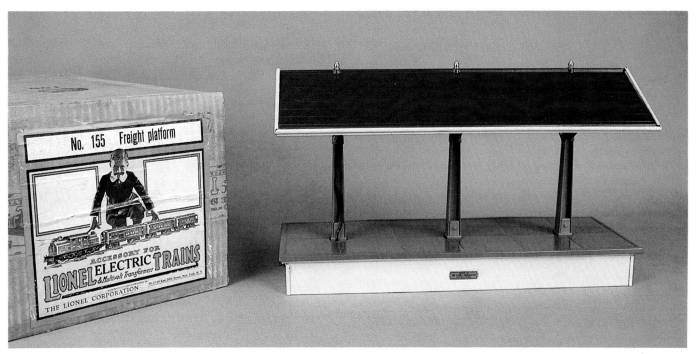

155 Freight Station, early colors. G. Zippie Collection, B. Schwab photograph.

GD EXC RST

(B) Mohave base, ivory sides, apple green roof, skylights and window inserts, maroon doors, brass clock inserts.   **600 1200 600**

(C) Terra cotta base, 129 beige walls, apple green roof and window inserts, apple green or pea green skylight, maroon doors, brass clock inserts.   **600 1200 600**

115 STATION (1935-42, Postwar): Same construction as 112, two light fixtures flanking doors on one side, interior light, train-stop circuit, 13¾" wide, 9¼" deep, 8½" high; reproduced by Lionel Trains, Inc.

(A) Early, mohave base, dark cream walls, pea green trim. Confirmation requested.   **NRS**

(B) Vermilion base, roof, skylight, window inserts and doors, ivory walls, aluminum-painted light fixtures. G. Zippie Collection.   **125 250 110**

(C) Same as (B), but light red instead of vermilion base, roof, and trim. D. Ely Collection.

125 250 110

(D) 1988, reproduction by Lionel Trains, Inc., catalogue number 13800, embossed "LTI" or "Lionel Trains, Inc."   **— 200 —**

116 STATION (1935-42): Same as 114, but with train-stop circuit; reproduced by T-Reproductions.

(A) 1935-36, mohave base, cream walls, pea green trim.   **600 1200 600**

(B) 1936-42, red base, beige (almost white) walls, red trim.   **600 1200 600**

(C) 1984-87, reproduction by T-Reproductions, die-stamped on base "T / R", "T / R-NAT", or "T-Reproductions"; 1987 price $295.   **— 450 —**

GD EXC RST

117 STATION (1935-42): Same as 115, but no exterior light fixtures. P. Riddle Collection.

140 300 135

121 STATION (1908-17): Lithographed base, walls, roof and chimney, two doors flanking central window on front and rear, lettered "TICKET OFFICE" above door, similar to Ives 113 (which was lettered "TELEGRAPH / OFFICE"), 14" wide, 10" deep, 9" high, Ives manufacture.   **NRS**

121 STATION (1917-20): Wood and composition board, sides embossed to represent masonry blocks, movable door, windows fitted with real glass, peaked roof with chimney near one end, multicolored details, 13½" wide, 9" deep, 13" high, made for Lionel by Schoenhut. Very rare.   **250 500 —**

156 Station Platform. G. Barnett Collection, B. Schwab photograph.

163 Station Set. G. Zippie Collection, B. Schwab photograph.

GD EXC RST

121X STATION (1917-19): Same as 121, but lighted, made for Lionel by Schoenhut. Very rare.

                    250   500   —

121 STATION (1920-26): Steel construction, embossed simulated brick walls, serif-lettered brass signs, hanging sign lettered "LIONEL CITY", sign on door lettered "WAITING / ROOM", no interior light or hole for light bracket, internal roof supports on later model only, 13½" wide, 9" deep, 13" high; first original Lionel station design.

(A) Light gray base, semi-dull State brown walls, cream trim, pea green roof, door and windows. R. Graves Collection. **100 195 100**
(B) Same as (A), but speckled base and wood-grained doors. **100 195 100**

122 STATION (1920-31): Same as 121, but interior light.

(A) Light gray base, semi-dull State brown walls, cream trim, pea green roof, door and windows.
                    100 195 100

GD EXC RST

(B) Gray-speckled base, salmon walls, cream-buff building and window trim, pea green roof, green window frames, wood-grained doors. **100 195 100**
(C) 1929-30, brass plate from Ives tenders on edge of roof, lettered "THE IVES RAILWAY LINES", made for Ives as catalogue No. 230. **150 300 150**
(D) 1931-32, same as (C), but with hanging sign lettered "IVES CITY". **90 200 90**

123 STATION (1920-23): Same as 121, but with 110-volt bulb to plug in directly to household current. The catalogue description emphasized the brighter illumination and independence from the transformer or reducer used to run the trains, suggesting that this version was recommended for owners with low-capacity power supplies. **100 195 100**

124 STATION (1920-30, 1933-36): Same as 121, but with interior light and two hanging light fixtures at corners under eaves, shown in 1920-25 catalogues with wires passing through rubber grommet high on one wall and large door frame lettered "WAITING / ROOM", hanging sign lettered "LIONEL CITY", brass light fixtures (confirmed by L. Bohn); shown in 1926-27 catalogues with wires fastened to binding posts and smaller door frame with brass sign lettered "WAITING ROOM" above door, nickel light fixtures; shown in 1928-30 and 1933-34 catalogues with cardstock arrival signs, and shown in 1935-36 catalogues in somewhat different colors. H. Edmunds comments.

(A) Dark gray base, terra cotta walls, cream trim, pea green roof and windows, red doors, brass light fixtures, black cardstock arrival signs. G. Zippie Collection.
                    100 195 100
(B) Same as (A), except tan base. **100 195 100**

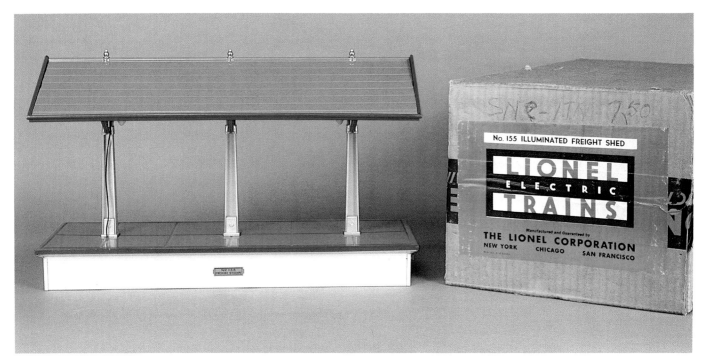

155 Freight Shed, late colors. G. Zippie Collection, B. Schwab photograph.

Late and early 156 Station platforms. R. Bartelt Collection, A. Fiterman photograph.

GD   EXC   RST

(C) 1935, same as (A), except pea green base, red roof, cream trim. G. Zippie Collection.   **125   250   100**
(D) Same as (A), but pea green doors, cast-metal lights, no cardstock arrival signs. E. Hundertmark Collection.   **100   195   100**
(E) Same as (A), but nickel light fixtures. D. Ely Collection.   **100   195   100**
(F) Same as (E), but speckled tan base. P. Riddle Collection.   **100   195   100**
(G) Reproduction by Pride Lines.   **NEW   195**

125 STATION (1923-25): Dark mojave base, lithographed red brick walls and two chimneys, pea green roof with two arched dormers, two sets of mohave or maroon arched doors on front and back, mohave door on each end, dark green door frames, arched brass ticket window between doors on one side only, other window inserts white, brass sign lettered "LIONELVILLE" above arched window, "EXPRESS" on left end door, "BAGGAGE" on right end door, not lighted, 10" wide, 7" deep, 7¼" high.

205 LCL Containers. G. Zippie Collection, B. Schwab photograph.

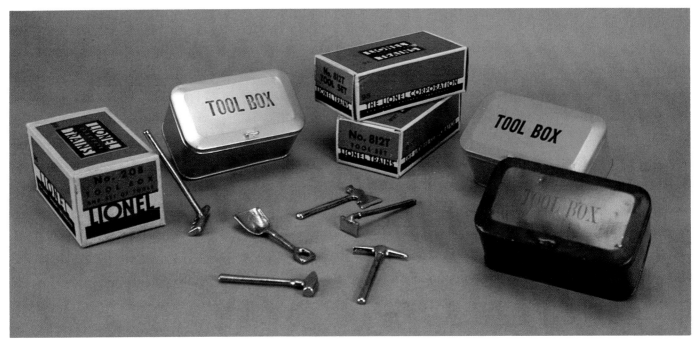

208 and 812T Tool Sets, showing early (overstamped) and late 812T boxes. G. Barnett and G. Zippie Collections, B. Schwab photograph.

GD EXC RST

GD EXC RST

Prior to about 1930, Lionel lithographed buildings were varnished. **110 200 100**

126 STATION (1923-36): Same as 125, but with interior light, lithographed or enameled walls; enameled version reproduced by Lionel Trains, Inc.

(A) Dark gray base, lithographed bright red brick walls, pea green roof, dark green door frames, mojave front and rear doors, maroon end doors,

brass ticket window, white window inserts, brass plates, lithographed red brick chimneys. G. Koff Collection. **95 190 95**
(B) Light gray base, orange-red lithographed brick front and back walls, lithographed bright red end walls, pea green roof, dark green door frames, Stephen Girard green front and rear doors, maroon end doors, brass ticket window, white window inserts, brass plates, lithographed red brick chimneys, interior lamp with

209 Barrel Set. G. Zippie Collection, B. Schwab photograph.

1012 Winner Station, shown with the No. 1000 train set with which it came. G. Riddle Collection, P. Riddle photograph.

GD	EXC	RST

brass shade and ground screw terminal mounted on steel spreader bar. G. Koff Collection.

| | 95 | 190 | 95 |

(C) Red-enameled sides. Reader confirmation and information requested. **NRS**

(D) Mojave base, crackle red-enameled walls, pea green roof, ivory door frames, pea green doors, brass ticket window, ivory window inserts, brass plates with "EXPRESS" and "BAGGAGE" in reverse positions, lithographed red brick chimneys, interior lamp with brass shade and two terminals mounted on steel spreader bar. G. Koff Collection. **95 190 95**

(E) Same as (D), but white window inserts.

95 190 95

(F) Same as (D), but pea green window inserts. P. Riddle Collection. **95 190 95**

(G) Green base, mustard-enameled walls, light red roof, white door frames, light red doors and ticket window, white window inserts, brass plates, mustard-enameled chimneys. **95 190 95**

(H) 1930, maroon walls and roof, white door frams, green doors, brass plate lettered "THE IVES RAILWAY LINES", made for Ives as catalogue No. 226.

150 300 150

(I) 1989, reproduction by Lionel Trains, Inc., catalogue number 13801, embossed "LTI" or "Lionel Trains, Inc."

— 100 —

127 STATION (1923-36): Walls embossed to represent clapboard siding, one chimney on each side of roof peak at opposite ends, two arched windows flanking door on front and rear, two rectangular windows in each end, round vent window under each gable, brass or nickel sign lettered "LIONELTOWN" at top of each door frame, interior light, 8½" wide, 4¼" deep, 5" high, intended for O Gauge

GD	EXC	RST

only. Many combinations of different colored components have been reported.

(A) Dark gray base, mustard walls, maroon roof, dark green door and window frames, wood-grained doors, Stephen Girard green window inserts and vent windows, brass plates, lithographed red brick chimneys, lighted. **65 125 60**

(B) Cream base, white walls, red roof, 45N green door and window frames, yellow doors and window inserts, nickel plates, white chimneys, underside of base rubber-stamped "No. 127 STATION / MADE BY / THE LIONEL CORPORATION / NEW YORK / U.S. OF AMERICA". D. Ely Collection. **75 140 60**

(C) Gray base, ivory sides, red roof, dark green door and window frames, maroon doors, peacock window inserts, brass plates, lithographed red brick chimneys, no rubber stamping on base. D. Ely Collection.

75 140 60

(D) Mojave base, white walls, red roof, pea green window and door frames, red doors, cream window inserts, brass plate lettered "LIONELTOWN" over one door and "LIONEL LINES" over the other, cream chimneys, rubber-stamped in black sans-serif letters "No. 127 STATION / MADE BY / THE LIONEL CORPORATION / NEW YORK". D. Ely Collection. **NRS**

(E) Mustard base, cream walls, red roof, peacock door and window frames, red doors, light yellow window inserts, brass plates, lithographed red brick chimneys, brass light fixture with adjacent terminal post with brass nut for the "hot" wire and screw fastened to the lamp support bracket for the ground wire. R. Griesbeck Collection. **75 140 60**

(F) Same as (A), but dark ivory walls.

65 125 60

GD EXC RST

(G) Same as (A), but apple green window inserts and vent windows. **65 125 60**

(H) Same as (G), but peacock vent windows. **65 125 60**

(I) Same as (D), but white walls, peacock door and window frames, yellow window inserts, two "LIONEL-TOWN" plates. **75 140 60**

(J) Same as (D), but maroon doors, peacock door and window frames, two "LIONELTOWN" plates. **75 140 60**

(K) Same as (E), but light mojave base, cream window inserts, yellow chimneys. **75 140 60**

(L) Same as (E), but mojave base, yellow chimneys. **75 140 60**

(M) Same as (E), but white walls, green door and window frames, yellow doors and window inserts, white chimneys. **75 140 60**

(N) Same as (M), but light mojave base. **75 140 60**

(O) Same as (D), but peacock window and door frames, cream windows and doors. G. Zippie Collection. **75 140 60**

(P) 1929-30, made for Ives under catalogue No. 225, brass plate over door lettered "IVES R.R." **75 150 75**

(Q) 1931-32, made for Ives under catalogue No. 1872. **40 90 40**

128 STATION AND TERRACE (1928-42): Combination set consisting of 129 Terrace and one 124, 113 or 115 Stations.

(A) 1928-30, 124 Station and Terrace. **750 1450 750**

(B) 1931-34, 113 Station and Terrace. **750 1450 750**

(C) 1935-42, 115 Station and Terrace. **750 1450 750**

129 TERRACE (1928-42): Raised steel platform, semicircular ends with decorative fences and railings, broad six-step stairway, three electric lamp posts with frosted round or tulip-shaped bulbs and

550 Figure set. G. Zippie Collection, B. Schwab photograph.

GD EXC RST

four decorative balls on each fence railing, half-circle grass plot with urn and flower bed set in indentation and encircled by one fence, similar plot with flagpole and flag within the other fence, central area sized for placement of large station, 31½" long, 18" wide. Excellent condition requires presence of all landscaping; reproduced by T-Reproductions.

(A) Early, light mojave base, pea green fences, white railings, gold-painted lamp posts, brass flagpole pedestal, terra cotta flower urn, green undersides on grass plots. P. Riddle Collection. **600 1200 600**

(B) Late, light cream base and railings, red fences, aluminum-painted lamp posts, nickel flagpole pedestal, terra cotta flower urn, light 45N green undersides on grass plots. D. Ely Collection. **600 1200 600**

(C) 1986-87, reproduction by T-Reproductions, die-stamped on base "T / R", "T / R-NAT", or "T-Reproductions"; 1987 price $295. **— 450 —**

(D) 1986-87, 129-B reproduction by T-Reproductions, die-stamped on base "T / R", "T / R-NAT", or "T-Reproductions", enlarged version to accommodate 116 Station, 37½" long, never manufactured by Lionel in this size; 1987 price $350. **— 450 —**

134 STATION (1937-42): Same as 124, but in different colors and with train-stop circuit, 13½" high, 9" deep, 13" high.

(A) 45N green base, tan walls, red roof, ivory window frames and trim, white doors and window inserts, nickel signs and exterior light fixtures, ivory chimneys, black paper simulated chalkboards lettered "ARRIVAL". D. Ely Collection. **150 300 140**

(B) Same as (A), but aluminum-painted exterior light fixtures. Further confirmation requested. H. Edmunds Collection. **150 300 140**

136 STATION (1937-42): Same as 126, but in different colors and with train-stop circuit, 10" wide, 7" deep, 7¼" high.

(A) 45N green base, cream walls, red roof, white door frames and window inserts, red doors and ticket window, brass plates lettered "BAGGAGE" at left end, "EXPRESS" at right end and "LIONELVILLE" on front, cream chimneys, three terminals mounted on base. Hahn and G. Koff Collections. **95 190 95**

(B) Same as (A), but nickel plates. P. Riddle Collection. **95 190 95**

(C) Same as (A), but mustard walls and chimneys, aluminum signs lettered "LIONELVILLE" in red, "BAGGAGE" and "EXPRESS" in black. R. Shanfeld Collection. **95 190 95**

(D) Same as (A), but dark cream walls and chimneys, vermilion doors, windows and roof, nickel plates, one terminal post never wired, underside of base rubber-stamped "No. (126) 136 STATION" with "126" crossed out and "136" stamped above it. C. Weber Collection. **95 190 95**

GD EXC RST

137 STATION (1937-42, Postwar): Same as 127, but in different colors and with train-stop circuit, 8½" wide, 4¼" deep, 5" high. Postwar sales were probably leftover stock, not new production.

(A) Tan base, ivory walls, vermilion roof, pea green door and window frames, cream doors and window inserts, nickel plates, ivory chimney. P. Riddle Collection.

75   140   75

(B) Same as (A), but dark cream base, light red roof, 45N green door and window frames, underside of base rubber-stamped in black block lettering "NO. 137 STATION / MADE BY / THE LIONEL CORPORATION / NEW YORK / U.S. OF AMERICA". C. Rohlfing Collection.

75   140   75

(C) Same as (A), but white walls and chimney, yellow windows and doors. G. Zippie Collection.

75   140   75

155 FREIGHT SHED (1930-42): Raised steel base with embossed floor, three die-cast support poles, peaked roof with three finials above pole positions, two hanging light fixtures under roof, identification plate on base, 18" long, 8¼" wide, and 11" high. Reproduced by Mike's Train House.

(A) 1930-39, yellow base, terra cotta floor, pea green posts, maroon roof with yellow underside, brass finials, brass plate lettered "MADE BY / THE LIONEL CORPORATION / NEW YORK". G. Zippie Collection.

150   300   140

(B) 1940-42, white base, red floor, aluminum posts and finials, gray roof trimmed in red, brass plate lettered "No. 155 / FREIGHT STATION". G. Zippie Collection.

175   350   140

(C) Same as (B), but nickel plate. 175   350   140

(D) Same as (C), but 92 gray posts, black finials.

175   350   140

(E) 1986, reproduction by Mike's Train House; issue price $125.   —   150   —

(F) 1931-32, made for Ives under catalogue No. 1875.

175   350   140

156 STATION PLATFORM (1939-42, Postwar): Bakelite base and peaked roof, three die-cast support poles, two finials above outer pole positions, two light sockets under roof, black simulated wrought-iron fence with or without lithographed steel advertising signs, 12" long, 3¼" wide, 5⅛" high.

(A) 1939-41, 45N green base, aluminum-painted poles, vermilion roof, nickel finials, black plastic fence with four lithographed signs. 45   90   40

(B) 1942, 45N green base, 92 gray posts, vermilion roof, black finials, black plastic fence with four lithographed signs. 45   90   40

(C) Same as (A), but light red roof. C. Rohlfing Collection.

45   90   40

(D) Same as (B), but light red roof. J. Flynn comment.

45   90   40

GD EXC RST

(E) Same as (B), but light red roof and nickel finials. C. Rohlfing Collection. 45   90   40

157 HAND TRUCK (1930-32, in sets through 1942): Die-cast, black wheels and skids, 3¾" long, part of 163 Freight Accessory Set. L. Bohn comment.

(A) Red. D. Ely Collection. 20   35   15

(B) Vermilion. D. Ely Collection. 20   35   15

158 STATION SET (1940-42): Two 156 Platforms and one 136 Station in original box. 200 375 200

161 BAGGAGE TRUCK (1930-32, in sets through 1942): Steel, black wheels, black or nickel couplers, 4½" long, part of 163 Freight Accessory Set. L. Bohn comment.

(A) Pea green. D. Ely and J. Flynn Collections.

30   60   25

(B) 45N green. D. Ely and J. Flynn Collections.

30   60   25

162 DUMP TRUCK (1930-32, in sets through 1942): Steel, black wheels, black or nickel couplers, 4½" long, part of 163 Freight Accessory Set. L. Bohn comment.

(A) Terra cotta truck with peacock bin. J. Flynn Collection. 30   60   25

(B) Orange truck with blue bin. D. Ely and J. Flynn Collections. 30   60   25

(C) Yellow truck with blue bin. J. Flynn and D. Ely Collections. 30   60   25

(D) Red truck with gray bin. Confirmation requested.

NRS

163 FREIGHT ACCESSORY SET (1930-32): Contains two 157 Hand Trucks, one 162 Dump Truck, and one 161 Baggage Truck, in original yellow box with white end label printed in black describing box contents and orange end label. Reproduced by Mike's Train House. G. Zippie, H. Brandt and R. Shanfeld Collections.

(A) Original Lionel production. 125 250 110

(B) 1986, reproduction by Mike's Train House; issue price $49.95.   —   75   —

196 ACCESSORY SET (1927): Contains one 127 Station, two 58 Lamp Posts, six 60 Telegraph Poles, one 62 Semaphore, one 68 Warning Signal, in original box. 200 375 125

205 MERCHANDISE CONTAINERS (1930-38): Three dark green steel LCL (Less than Carload Lot) boxes with hinged doors, lifting chains, brass identification plate lettered "LIONEL / RAILWAY EXPRESS" above doors, paper label printed "The L.C.L. Corporation / Merchandise Container / Patented" inserted in door, bottom stamped "No 205 FREIGHT CONTAINER / MADE BY / THE LIONEL CORPORATION / NEW YORK" with no period after the abbreviation for "number", 3½" wide, 3" deep, 4" high; reproduced by Lyle Cain. G. Zippie Collection.

(A) Original Lionel product. 150 275 125

GD EXC RST

(B) Reproduction by Lyle Cain.   **NEW 200**

208 TOOL SET (1928-32 in work train sets only, then also separately through 1942): Contains six nickel-plated cast-iron tools chosen from among axe, hammer, hatchet, hoe, pick, pincers, rake, shovel and sledge, early versions with wooden handles, in enameled metal chest with handle. Reproductions have been made by Mike's Train House.

(A) Early, gray chest, brass handle, gold rubber-stamped lettering "TOOL BOX". D. Ely and J. Flynn Collections.   **45 100 40**
(B) Later, aluminum-painted chest, nickel handle, black rubber stamping slightly smaller than (A). G. Zippie, D. Ely and J. Flynn Collections.
    45 100 40
(C) Same as (A), but black rubber stamping. G. Zippie Collection.   **45 100 40**
(D) Late, 92 gray chest, nickel handle, black rubber stamping. G. Zippie Collection.   **45 100 40**
(E) 1986, reproduction by Mike's Train House; issue price $25.   **— 35 —**

209 BARRELS (1930-32 in work train sets only, then also separately through 1942): Standard Gauge, four hollow wooden barrels divided to open at the center, ribbed, 2⅛″ high; premium for original box.

(A) 1930-34, bowed-side wooden barrels. G. Zippie, D. Ely and L. Bohn Collections.   **10 20 10**
(B) 1935-42, straight side wooden barrels simulating steel drums, although catalogued as "barrels." G. Zippie, D. Ely and L. Bohn Collections.   **10 20 10**

0209 BARRELS (1930-42, Postwar): O Gauge, six hollow wooden barrels, divided to open in middle, straight sides simulating steel drums, although catalogued as "barrels," 1⅜″ high; premium for original box. Postwar versions are solid and do not open. L. Bohn comment.   **8 15 8**

550 MINIATURE RAILROAD FIGURES (1932-36): Six hollow cast figures of 551 Engineer, 552 Conductor, 553 Porter with detachable footstool, 554 Male Passenger, 555 Female Passenger, 556 Red Cap with removable luggage, marked on base with subcontractor's name "J. HILL & CO., ENGLAND", each 3″ high, in original box. Reproductions have been made from composition board in Japan and from solid cast metal by several manufacturers. Die and paint colors used vary with years of production. J. Flynn, L. Bohn and D. Ely comments, G. Zippie Collection.

(A) Original Lionel production.   **125 225 110**
(B) 1986, reproduction by Mike's Train House; issue price $29.95.   **— 35 —**

551 ENGINEER (1932 separately, 1932-36 in 550 set): Cast figure, medium or dark blue clothing, aluminum-painted oil can, 3″ high. **15 30 10**

GD EXC RST

552 CONDUCTOR (1932 separately, 1932-36 in 550 set): Cast figure, black clothing, 3″ high.
    15 30 10

553 PORTER (1932 separately, 1932-36 in 550 set): Cast figure, dark blue clothing, removable yellow footstool, 3″ high.   **15 30 10**

554 MALE PASSENGER (1932 separately, 1932-36 in 550 set): Cast figure, dark brown or mojave clothing, 3″ high.   **15 30 10**

555 FEMALE PASSENGER (1932 separately, 1932-36 in 550 set): Cast figure, gray, pea green, dark red, State brown or dark brown clothing, 3″ high.   **15 30 10**

556 RED CAP (1932 separately, 1932-36 in 550 set): Cast figure, dark blue clothing, red hat, removable luggage, 3″ high.   **15 30 10**

812T TOOL SET (1930-41): Pick, shovel and spade, Standard Gauge size but sold only with O Gauge work train sets 193W, 197W, 240E, 277W, 293W, 769W and 789W.

(A) Early, packaged in 81 Rheostat box with label stamped "812T" on end. G. Zippie and G. Barnett Collections.   **35 75 30**
(B) Late, packaged in orange and blue late 1930s-era box, sold new by Madison Hardware in the late 1970s. C. Rohlfing Collection.   **20 35 20**

1012 WINNER STATION (1931-33): Same design as 48W, lithographed, green base, cream walls, removable orange roof, enclosed transformer, black cloth-covered two-wire line cord with Bakelite plug, 5½″ wide, 3¾″ deep, 3¾″ high.

(A) Probably 1931, lithographed "1012" on end inside border above sign lettered "WINNERTOWN" inside border, two binding posts with wire leading inside, 7½-volt output, no variable voltage control rheostat, base embossed "WINNER TRANSFORMER / MADE BY / WINNER TOY CORPORATION / NEW YORK, N.Y.", transformer coil tabbed in place. C. Weber Collection.   **20 45 —**
(B) Probably 1932, same as (A), but no number on end, no embossing on base, three binding posts labeled "COMMON", "GV", and "7½ v", reported in boxed set listed as 1012. C. Weber and L. Bohn Collections.
    20 45 —
(C) 1932, same as (B), but binding posts unlabeled, came with set No. 1000. G. Riddle Collection.
    20 45 —

1012K WINNER STATION (1932-33): Same as 1012, but without transformer. **15 30 —**

1017 WINNER STATION (1932-33): Same design as 1012, lithographed, green base, cream sides, removable orange roof, lithographed sign lettered "STATION" inside border and without number on end, base not embossed, two binding posts, right post connected to transformer by metal strap, rheostat lever

GD EXC RST

in slot above posts, transformer coil tabbed in place. C. Weber Collection. **20 45 —**

1027 LIONEL JUNIOR TRANSFORMER STATION (1933-34): Same as 1017, but yellow sides, orange or red roof, transformer coil screwed to base, slots for coil tab present but not used. C. Weber Collection. Reader information is requested concerning differentiation of unmarked Winner items from unmarked Lionel-Ives and Lionel Junior items.

20 45 —

GD EXC RST

1028 LIONEL JUNIOR TRANSFORMER STATION (1935): Same as 1027. **20 45 —**

1029 LIONEL JUNIOR TRANSFORMER STATION (1936): Same as 1027. **20 45 —**

1560 LIONEL JUNIOR STATION (1933-37): Same as 1012K, sold with clockwork (wind-up) sets, some bases embossed like 1012(A); holes for binding posts, tab holes for coil and rheostat handle slot not used. C. Weber Collection. **15 30 —**

CHAPTER VI

The Solenoid: Automatic Action

There are two main methods for creating automatic action in a toy train accessory, and the choice of which one to use in any given unit depends upon the type of motion desired. The first method, and also the more expensive, is to employ a motor, which can produce either rotary or linear motion depending upon the type of linkage to which it is attached. In addition, a motor can supply continuous action, as in the case of the drive mechanism in a locomotive which causes the wheels to turn.

The second method, called a solenoid, is much less expensive, but it is also much more limited. It is used primarily for linear motion over a short distance, such as to create the up and down motion of a crossing gate. It is powered by electro-magnetism, and is capable of a fairly strong thrust. Lionel used this device to move such items as semaphore arms, the busy 45 Gateman, and various kinds of automatic dump cars. The first application was the 77 Automatic Crossing Gate, introduced in the 1923 catalogue.

A solenoid is a spool-shaped device with a hollow core, wrapped with many turns of wire and having a rod (sometimes called a slug) inserted loosely in the center. When an electric current passes through the wire, it creates a magnetic field in the spool which draws the rod into the center of the spool. This motion is surprisingly powerful, and can be used to push the moving parts of accessories. The rod will remain in the new position as long as current is present in the coil, and also thereafter if nothing causes it to move back.

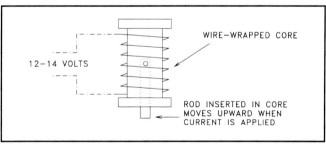

Figure 6-A: Solenoid parts and wiring diagram.

Solenoid and crank attached to 77 Crossing Gate, also showing counterweight fitted into end of gate arm. *P. Riddle Collection and photograph.*

Typical solenoid from a toy train accessory, showing coil of wire and moving rod in the center of the spool, in this case fitted with a return spring and mounting plates. P. Riddle Collection and photograph.

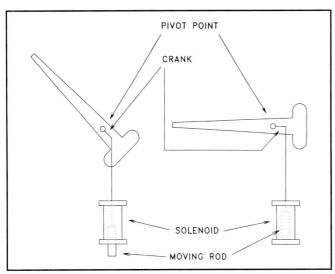

Figure 6-B: Gate arm in raised position, showing solenoid rod inside core; gate arm in lowered position, showing solenoid rod extending out of core.

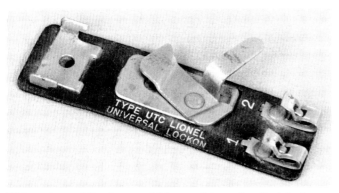

This universal Lockon could be used to make electrical connection to either Standard Gauge or O Gauge track, depending upon which way the lever was turned. P. Riddle Collection and photograph.

NORMAL TRACK SECTION: MIDDLE RAIL INSULATED
Metal Tie Clamped To Rail   Fibre Strip Insulates Rail
Metal Tie Clamped To Rail

MIDDLE AND ONE OUTSIDE RAIL INSULATED
Metal Tie Clamped To Rail   Fibre Strip Insulates Rail

Figure 6-C: Normal track section and insulated track section showing one isolated running rail.

Therefore accessories often have a spring to return them to the original position when the current is turned off. Alternatively, the weight of the moving part may be enough to cause the rod to drop back within the coil.

In the 77 Crossing Gate, the solenoid rod is connected to a simple crank that forms the pivoting axle of the gate arm. When current is applied to the coil, the rod moves into the coil in an upward direction and forces the crank to turn, which lowers the gate. The rear end of the gate is fitted with two counterweights, so that when the current is turned off, the arm rises again by gravity, and the solenoid rod descends once again out of the core.

Ron Morris has identified three variations on the 77 Crossing Gate mechanism, one with a two-piece moving rod (early), one with a one-piece rod and a long link to the gate crank (later, c. 1928-1932), and a final version (1933 and later) with a one-piece rod and a shorter link. (The author is indebted to Mr. Morris for his assistance in describing these mechanisms.)

Each of Lionel's solenoid-actuated accessories operate in a similar manner, as their motions are simple and linear. Semaphore arms move downward when rotated by a crank similar to the one in the crossing gate. The 45 Gateman comes out of his shack when pushed by the force of magnetism that moves the solenoid rod. And in the more complex accessories, such as the 164 Log Loader (described in Chapter X), a solenoid is used to lower two upright stakes and allow the logs to roll into a waiting car. A similar mechanism moves the points in remote-control track turnouts (switches).

Lighted and operating signals and semaphores were packaged with a section of track in the appropriate gauge containing one insulated outside rail which caused the accessory to function. Catalogue numbers with the prefix "0" (e.g., 082) came with O Gauge track and lockon; without the "0" (e.g., 82) a piece of Standard Gauge track was included, along with the correct-sized Lockon (or in some cases Lockons). Beginning in 1936 Lionel replaced the insulated track system with pressure-operated contactor switches that fit beneath the ties. Accessories were then designated "N" (e.g., 82N) signifying suitability for either gauge, and came packaged with a Lockon that attached to either size of track and a Contactor, if needed.

As shown in the photo, a track Lockon has two clips to which wires may be attached. The left-hand clip (usually numbered "1") connects with the middle rail of the track, while the right-hand clip ("2") attaches to one of the running rails. These devices are normally used to transmit power from the transformer to the track, but when used in conjunction with an insulated track section, they could be used to hook up accessories.

The insulated rail method of triggering accessories was both simple and positive. In a normal track section, the middle rail is insulated from the ties by fiber strips, but the two outer rails (upon which the train wheels ride) are fastened directly to the ties and therefore are connected together electrically. One wire from the transformer is attached to the middle rail through a Lockon, and current passes to the locomotives and lighted cars through their pickup rollers that ride on this rail. The other transformer wire is connected by the Lockon to either of the outer rails, and therefore to both of them, as they are attached to the metal ties. This second wire completes the electrical circuit through the car and locomotive wheels.

An insulated track section also has one of the outer rails equipped with fiber strips separating it from the ties. In addition, fiber track pins are inserted in both ends of this rail, to isolate it from adjoining sections of track. This rail is therefore electrically "dead," but the trains still receive power through the middle rail and the other outer rail. Such a track also has its own Lockon, fastened to the side with the insulated rail. Any accessory connected to this lockon receives power through the middle rail connection, but no current can flow because the other wire attaches to the "dead" outer rail, and therefore the circuit is not complete and the accessory does not operate.

As soon as a train enters the insulated track section, however, its wheels touch both of the outer rails. Current now passes from the "live" outer rail through the wheels and axles to the "dead" rail. This completes the circuit to the accessory and triggers its solenoid. The concept is further explored in Chapter IV, under the discussion of the 69 Warning Bell.

Lionel abandoned the insulated rail in 1936, and introduced a pressure-activated switch, the 41 Contactor, that serves the same purpose. A cost saving was realized, as it was no longer necessary to include a track section with each accessory. Nor was it necessary to package two different versions of each accessory, one for each gauge of track, and these dual-purpose items were now catalogued with the suffix "N" attached to

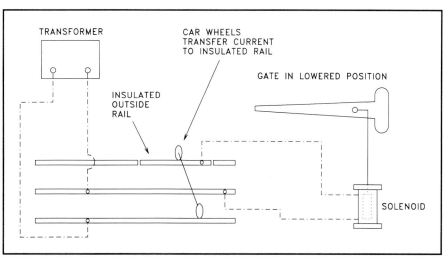

Figure 6-D: 77 Crossing Gate connected to insulated track section, in lowered position with solenoid operating when the wheels of a train touch the insulated rail.

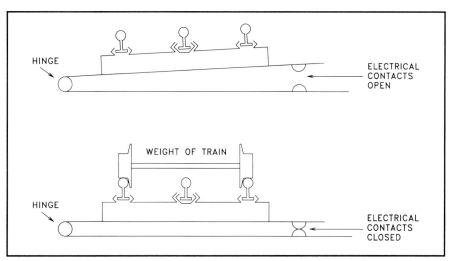

Figure 6-E: 41 Contactor in open and closed positions. The electrical contacts are insulated from each other.

their numbers. For example, the 77 and 077 Crossing Gates were replaced by model 77N.

The 41 Contactor is made up of a pair of simple metal plates, hinged at one end and fitted with two electrical contacts, one on the upper plate and one on the lower. It is placed beneath one tie of a piece of track (either O Gauge or Standard Gauge), and the two contacts are kept apart by an adjustable spring. When a train approaches, its weight counteracts the spring tension and presses the Contactor down, causing current to flow through the two contacts. An accessory wired through this Contactor will operate whenever a train of sufficient weight is present. This device is called a "single-pole, single-throw" switch or "SPST", having only one input connection (or pole) and one option, either on or off.

In actual practice, this device is less positive than the insulated track section. Since it depends upon

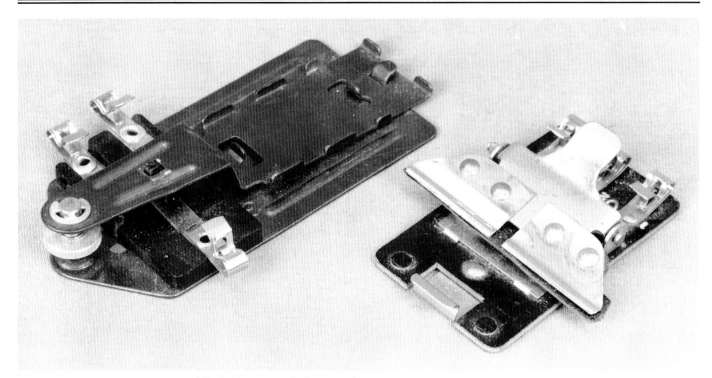

153C and 154C Contactors. P. Riddle Collection and photograph.

pressure to operate, the spring must be adjusted so that the weight of the track alone does not close the contacts. With Standard Gauge and the heavier types of O Gauge trains, it operates satisfactorily, but the lighter O Gauge cars (807 freights and 529-type passenger cars, for example) do not always provide sufficient mass to close the contacts. In addition, the adjustment spring is subject to movement by vibration from the trains, and needs frequent attention. For builders of permanent layouts, the 41 Contactor is also less than convenient, as track must be free to move up and down when the trains pass, and cannot be fastened down tightly to the table. (Lionel continued the use of contactors after the Second World War, and the problems associated with their use increased as cars were made increasingly lighter through the use of plastics. Finally the more positive insulated track method was reintroduced when Super O track was created in 1957.)

A more versatile 153C contactor provides two-way switching control. This device has a second set of electrical contacts, so that when no train is present and the hinged top plate is in the "up" position, power flows through one set only. When the train passes over and presses it down, that contact is broken but another one is established. The simplest application of this device is with the 153 Block Signal. The green bulb of the signal is wired through the upper set of contacts, and is lighted when no train is present; the red bulb is wired

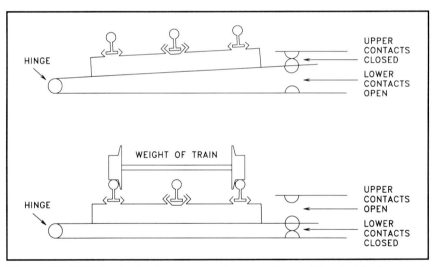

Figure 6-F: 153C Contactor in open and closed positions. The electrical contacts are insulated from each other.

through the lower set, and is off. When the weight of cars presses down on the switch, the green bulb turns off and the red one lights instead. The 153C is called a "single-pole, double-throw" switch or "SPDT", having one input connection (pole) but two optional destinations (throws, or contacts) which may be selected.

A third type is the 154C, used to flash the bulbs in a 154 Automatic Highway Signal in an alternating pattern. The mechanism is not operated by weight, but instead functions in a manner similar to an insulated track section. When the 154C Contactor is clipped to a section of track, two thin metal plates rest on top of one of the running rails. These plates are insulated from the rail by a thin paper material on the underside.

Power reaches the Highway Signal through the clip that fastens to the middle rail, and each of the flashing bulbs is then connected to one of the insulated plates to complete the circuit. When the wheels of a train touch first one, then the other of these metal plates, the bulbs flash on and off alternately. The pattern of flashing is not very even, as the wheels on a train are not spaced at regular intervals. Therefore the 154 Highway Signal usually displays a pattern of two quick flashes in a row, followed by a longer pause and then two more quick flashes.

Nevertheless, this method of operation was superior to the previous 79 Highway Warning Signal, which functioned with a bimetallic strip (see Chapters III and IV). Since this signal would not flash alternately for several seconds until the strip warmed up, a passing train could not be used to operate it; by the time the signal began to flash, the train would be gone! Therefore it was connected directly to the transformer and flashed continuously, whether a train was coming or not.

In the years between 1923 and the onset of the Second World War, Lionel developed the concept of simple action accessories to a very high degree, providing young railroaders a wide variety of animated items to accompany their trains. This approach would be further explored in the Postwar years, culminating in the many interesting freight handlers that best represented the company's image during its most successful period, the early and middle 1950s. Perhaps the most significant creation was the inclusion of animated figures, beginning with the universally popular Gateman, the principal subject of the next chapter.

CHAPTER VII

The Busy, Busy Gateman

The most unusual model railroad accessory ever conceived! The gateman is inside his shack and the door is closed until the train approaches. When the locomotive touches a special section of track to which the shack is connected, the door swings open, the gateman rushes out with his lantern raised. When the gateman comes to a stop at the edge of the platform, the lantern is illuminated by a beam of light focused on it from the base. After the last car has passed the special section of track, the gateman returns to his shack and the door swings closed behind him. The action is entirely automatic.

Thus did Lionel's 1935 catalogue introduce the most phenomenal best seller the company would ever produce. The 45 Automatic Grade Crossing Gateman and its successors introduced the exciting concept of figure animation to the toy train world at a very modest cost. It was a time when economic stability was but a dream to most families, and the budget for toys was unlikely to be large in the majority of households. But

This special section of track has a very short insulated portion of one outside rail which causes the Flagman to move his arm rapidly up and down as the train passes. Unlike previously reported versions finished in shades of blue, this Flagman has a black uniform with a very slight dark brown tint, and dark blue swinging arm. At right is an example of the most common figure with an overall dark blue uniform. P. Riddle Collection and photograph.

it has often been said that adversity breeds creativity, and the designers at Lionel spent the Depression years creating the most impressive outpouring of ingenious devices to come from that company until the Postwar years, many of them at prices nearly as attractive as the devices themselves. (This toy was invented by J. L. Bonanno, Pat. No. 2,138,367.)

Introduced at just $3 for either the O Gauge or Standard Gauge version, the 45 Gateman made a most exciting Christmas gift, and was priced within the reach of most parents' budgets in the mid-1930s. It promised the addition of live action to even the simplest train layout, and its appeal was such that millions of these toys have been produced since then, and they are still manufactured today. Although the structure has changed from metal to plastic, and the color scheme has been altered through the years, this toy is perhaps the most universally recognized product of any toy train manufacturer, and helped promote the Lionel trademark to its position of high esteem. (A comprehensive examination of the various Prewar and Postwar versions of this toy is contained in *Greenberg's Guide To Lionel Trains, 1945-1969, Volume II*.)

The mechanism is extremely simple. A pivoting crank is mounted inside the base and connected at one end to a solenoid. The gateman figure, with his swinging right arm and lantern, is attached to the other end, through a curved slot in the base. When the solenoid is activated, the figure pushes out through the door, which is also activated by the crank. At the same time, a bulb beneath the floor lights up, shining on the lantern and giving it a pleasant red glow. All this happens automatically, as the train passes over an insulated track section or Contactor (see Chapter VI).

Partially due to its large size and rugged construction, the Gateman has proven to be a durable toy, and many of the oldest examples still operate well. But its substantial nature creates one drawback: it is realistic in every respect except size, being far too large for O Gauge railroads and even outsized for the Standard Gauge line. At almost 3 inches in height, the figure

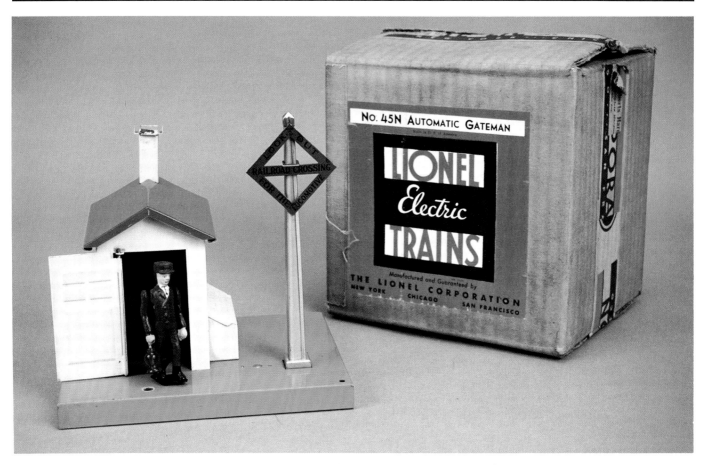

45N Gateman with brass diamond-shaped sign. G. Zippie Collection, B. Schwab photograph.

reaches a scale 12 feet tall in O Gauge! It is unlikely that many children pay much attention to this discrepancy, however, as the large size contributes to the Gateman's attention-getting nature, making it more noticeable and therefore more fun. (American Flyer created a similar toy in the 1950s called Sam the Semaphore Man, with a scale-sized man who emerges from a tiny shack. Although much more realistic, this toy attracts far less attention on the author's layout than Lionel's huge example, especially from the younger set.)

The Gateman figure was made in two versions prior to the War, the first being relatively primitive. Although its painted face and uniform were highly detailed, the composition material from which it was made was somewhat fragile, and could not withstand rough handling. In 1939 a new design was introduced, with a smoother finish, more durable construction and better proportions. This model was continued after the War, and is easily distinguished by its solid left arm, which is part of the main mold. The earlier version has two swinging arms.

The shack itself is rectangular and made of sheet metal, with a peaked roof and a chimney centered toward the rear. A tool shed with a slanted lid is mounted on one wall, and the entire structure is fastened to a rectangular base that holds the mechanism. Toward the front of the base is a post containing a

warning sign. On the earliest models, the post is of open girder construction, and the sign is diamond shaped. According to Ron Morris, Lionel used the 068 Warning Sign as an integral part of the 45 Gateman design, and on the earliest versions, a pea green 068 post was oversprayed aluminum for the 45 application. A solid post (like the 153 Block Signal or 154 Highway Signal) replaced the open girder pole at some point before 1939, and in that year the diamond-shaped sign was replaced by a die-cast crossbuck lettered "RAIL ROAD / CROSSING". The earliest diamond signs are lettered "RAILROAD CROSSING" across the center and "LOOK OUT / FOR LOCOMOTIVE" around the perimeter, but in 1936 a new sign adding the word "THE" ("LOOK OUT / FOR THE LOCOMOTIVE") was substituted.

It is relatively simple to distinguish Prewar examples of the 45 Gateman. All are believed to have chimneys, as well as red celluloid inserts above a clear bulb in the base. Postwar versions have no chimneys, and a red bulb to light up the lantern. There have been a few examples discovered with a mixture of these details, and these were probably made at the close of the War using leftover parts.

Lionel made one other animated figure in the Prewar years: the 1045 Flagman, which stands on a square base beside a warning sign on a pole, and waves a flag in its right hand when a train approaches. This accessory is outrageously over-sized. The 4¼-inch figure is far too large to look right with Standard Gauge, and towers mightily above O Gauge trains. Nevertheless, it was a good seller, and is very attractive in operation.

A small solenoid causes the arm to raise. If connected to a regular section of insulated track or a 41 or 153C Contactor, the Flagman holds his arm up steadily until the train has passed. A more realistic waving action occurs if it is wired to one plate of a 154C Contactor, as the arm moves up and down each time a wheel passes over the plate.

The author's 1045 Flagman was found with an unusual section of insulated Standard Gauge track. In addition to having an entire outside rail insulated, a length of rail 1⅛ inches long has been cut from the end of one outside rail, and isolated by fiber pins. This track section may be factory production, although no mention of it is made in the catalogues, and it does not seem to be listed under its own catalogue number in any existing inventory. Further, the Flagman was not introduced until 1938, by which time Lionel had converted to contactors for accessory activation. It may have been made in a Lionel Service Station, or by a purchaser. Reader information about this special track section is invited.

Lionel's earliest accessory with visible action was the 77 Crossing Gate, introduced on page 39 of the 1923 catalogue with a small drawing tucked in between more colorful semaphores and the 69 Warning Bell. Considering the great success of the Warning Bell two years earlier, a more elaborate presentation of such an innovative item would have been expected. Why Lionel chose to present its first crossing gate in such a low-key manner is a mystery, but sales were brisk from the beginning, and tens of thousands of them were soon in operation on layouts from coast to coast. Later versions have a red bulb mounted toward the narrow end of the gate arm.

The 77 Crossing Gate (and its O Gauge companion 077, identical except for the identification plate) was also an oversized toy. It is speculated that Lionel was more interested in creating rugged and dependable toys than in realism, and opted to make the gates large enough to accommodate a hefty solenoid, as well as to withstand rough handling by children. It was not until 1937 that a scale-sized gate was introduced, and it lasted only until the beginning of the War. The 47

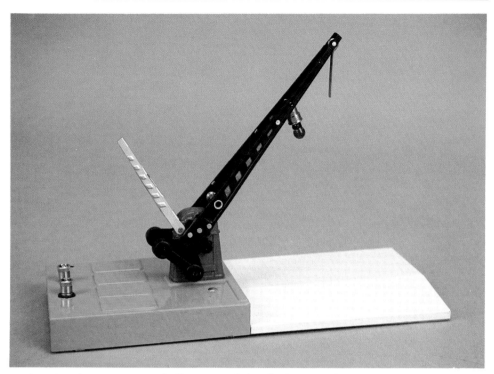

46 Crossing Gate. G. Zippie Collection, B. Schwab photograph.

Double Crossing Gate is a most attractive accessory, containing two tiny gates mounted on pedestals and facing each other over a wide section of roadway. The green sheet metal ends are stamped to suggest paving block sidewalks, and a small pedestrian arm descends to warn tiny inhabitants not to cross the tracks. A miniature red bulb hangs from each gate, enclosed by a fragile metal lantern casing (which is almost always missing when these toys are found today). Two years later a smaller version was produced. The 46 Single Crossing Gate is virtually identical to half of the 47.

Lionel's final Prewar crossing gate design was the 152, a realistic but greatly oversized model with a die-cast base, striped main arm with a red bulb, and a small pedestrian gate. With this model, the company apparently returned to the same philosophy that produced the 77, sacrificing realistic size for durability. The 152 was continued after the War, but the little 46 and 47 were not.

All of these various crossing protectors were quite popular, due to their appealing action and relatively low cost. Following are descriptions of known variations of railroad gates and action figures produced by Lionel between 1923 and 1942.

GD EXC RST

45 AUTOMATIC GATEMAN (1935-36): Standard Gauge.

045 AUTOMATIC GATEMAN (1935-36): O Gauge.

45N AUTOMATIC GATEMAN (1937-42, Postwar): Both Gauges. Steel construction, 45N green base, white or ivory building with matching or light red hinged door and matching attached toolbox with

77 Crossing Gates, four variations. Back to front, lert to right: 77(C), 77(E), 77(D), 77(A), and SS Track in front. G. Zippie and G. Barnett Collections, B. Schwab photograph.

GD EXC RST

"AUTOMATIC GATEMAN / MADE IN U.S. OF AMERICA / THE LIONEL CORPORATION / NEW YORK" embossed on lid or on decal, red peaked roof, chimney (Prewar only) same color as building, steel girder (early, same as 68) or solid pole with brass diamond-shaped warning sign (early, same as 068) or die-cast crossbuck, molded composition figure with elaborate paint scheme and two swinging arms (early) or simpler paint scheme and one swinging (right) arm, translucent red plastic lantern in right hand, hole in base with red acetate insert above clear 12-volt bulb illuminates lantern when figure emerges, packed with and activated by insulated track section (45, 045) or 41 contactor (45N) when train passes, 7″ wide, 5¾″ deep, 4¾″ high to top of chimney. See Chapters IV and VI for discussion of methods of powering track-activated accessories.

(A) 1935, ivory building, aluminum-painted girder pole (painted over pea green), brass or nickel finial, brass diamond-shaped sign with black letters "RAIL-ROAD CROSSING" and "LOOK OUT / FOR LOCOMOTIVE", "45" or "045" rubber-stamped in very small serif black letters on underside within depression

holding post to base, early gateman figure, packed in large box with insulated track section, lockon, wire and instructions; premium for original box and all parts. C. Weber, R. LaVoie and J. Kotil Collections.

25   55   25

(B) 1936, same as (A), but brass sign says "RAILROAD CROSSING" and "LOOK OUT / FOR THE LOCOMO-TIVE", larger rubber-stamped numbers on underside, J. Kotil and R. LaVoie Collections. 25   55   25

(C) 1937, same as (B), but solid 92 gray pole, with 41 Contactor instead of insulated track section, numbered "45N," packed in smaller box. J. Kotil and C. Weber Collections.   25   55   25

(D) 1938, same as (C), but aluminum-painted pole. P. Riddle and G. Zippie Collections.

25   55   25

(E) 1939, ivory building, aluminum-painted pole, nickel finial, die-cast crossbuck at mid-pole position painted white with black lettering, silver decal with blue lettering on toolbox lid with sans-serif "No. 45", late gateman figure. R. LaVoie, C. Weber and J. Kotil Collections.

25   55   25

GD   EXC   RST

(F) 1940, ivory building, 92 gray pole, nickel or black finial, die-cast crossbuck at mid-pole position, silver and blue decal on toolbox lid with serif "No. 45", late gateman figure, box dated 1940. R. LaVoie, C. Weber, and J. Kotil Collections.   **25   55   25**

(G) 1941, white building with light red door, aluminum-painted pole, black finial, die-cast crossbuck in mid-pole position, black rubber-stamped identification rectangle on underside of base, late gateman figure. J. Kotil Collection.   **35   75   25**

(H) 1942, white building, 92 gray pole, black finial, brass warning sign, embossed toolbox lid, white-painted shack and door, later gateman figure. J. Kotil and R. LaVoie Collections.   **25   55   25**

(I) Early 1942 or 1945, white building with light red door, aluminum-painted pole, die-cast crossbuck near top of pole, nickel finial, silver and blue decal with serif "No. 45", light red door, no chimney. Confusion over dating results from a mixture of Prewar and Postwar features: red celluloid over light bulb hole (thought to be Prewar only) and absence of chimney (thought to be Postwar only); possibly assembled from parts on hand during wartime materials shortage. Reader comments are invited. C. Rohlfing Collection.   **NRS**

45 AUTOMATIC GRADE CROSSING (1936): Similar to 45 Gateman, shown in the 1936 Type IV catalogue, with simulated roadway and fence; no known examples.

46 SINGLE CROSSING GATE (1939-42): Steel base with slanting simulated roadway, light red die-cast stanchion supporting solenoid-actuated black and white main gate, small pedestrian gate, socket for miniature bulb, white metal cage lantern clipped to bulb, two terminal posts, decal placed vertically on end lettered "AUTOMATIC / CROSSING GATE / No. 46 / MADE IN THE U.S. OF AMERICA / THE LIONEL CORP., NEW YORK", 8½″ long, 3½″ wide, 6¼″ high to tip of raised gate; must have miniature bulb with attached lantern to bring full excellent price.

(A) 45N green base, ivory roadway, aluminum-painted pedestrian gate, nickel terminal posts. P. Riddle Collection.   **40   75   35**

(B) Same as (A), but 92 gray pedestrian gate, black terminal posts, decal with smaller lettering. J. Flynn Collection.   **40   75   35**

47 DOUBLE CROSSING GATE (1937-42): Same construction and colors as 46, but extended base and second gate, both gates facing inward over wide roadway, 16½″ long, 3½″ wide, 6¼″ high to tip of raised gate; must have two miniature bulbs with attached lanterns to bring full excellent price.

(A) 45N green base, ivory roadway, aluminum pedestrian gates. C. Rohlfing Collection.   **55   100   45**

(B) Same as (A), but 92 gray pedestrian gates. P. Riddle Collection.   **55   100   45**

77 (I) Crossing Gate.   R. Bartelt Collection A. Fiterman photograph.

GD   EXC   RST

77 AUTOMATIC CROSSING GATE (1923-35): Standard Gauge.

077 AUTOMATIC CROSSING GATE (1923-35): O Gauge.

77N AUTOMATIC CROSSING GATE (1936-39): Both Gauges. Steel base and box with cover containing solenoid to actuate 11″-long steel gate with one cutout circle and twelve cutout parallelograms per side, paper insert showing through cutouts, two terminals and brass or nickel plate on base, unlighted or with socket and bulb mounted in circular area near end of gate. See Chapter VI for additional information.

(A) 1923, black base and mechanism box with nickel cover, black gate with white paper inserts, unlighted, brass plate lettered "77 FOR STANDARD GAUGE TRACK" (or "077 FOR O GAUGE TRACK") "PATENTED SEPT. 21, 1915 / THE LIONEL CORPORATION, N.Y." D. Ely Collection.

20   40   20

(B) 1924, same as (A), but with circular cutout showing paper label printed "STOP" in red. D. Ely and C. Weber Collections.   **20   40   20**

(C) 1927-30, pea green base, maroon or terra cotta mechanism box with nickel cover, pea green gate with white paper insert, circular area near end with red warning sign and "STOP" in white letters, unlighted, brass plate same as (A). P. Riddle Collection.

20   40   20

(D) 1931-34, same as (C), but lighted with red bulb in circular cutout. C. Weber Collection.   **20   40   20**

(E) 1935, black base, red mechanism box with black cover, black gate with paper insert and red bulb to illuminate circular cutout, brass plate same as (A).

20   40   20

(F) Same as (E), but pea green mechanism box. D. Ely Collection.   **20   40   20**

(G) Same as (E), but dark green base and maroon mechanism box. D. Ely Collection.   **20   40   20**

(H) 1936-39, same colors as (E), black-painted nickel plate with nickel lettering "77N CROSSING GATE / MADE IN U.S. OF AMERICA / THE LIONEL COR-

GD EXC RST

PORATION, N.Y.", packed with No. 41 Contactor instead of insulated track section. D. Ely Collection.

	20	40	20

(I) 1926-29, made for American Flyer Manufacturing Co. as catalogue No. 2032.　**25　50　25**

(J) 1931-32, made for Ives under catalogue Nos. 1878 (O Gauge) and 1879 (Wide Gauge).　**25　50　25**

(K) Same as (C), but white gate. R. Morris comment.

152 AUTOMATIC CROSSING GATE (1940-42, Postwar): Red die-cast base, 10½"-long solenoid-actuated main gate, 4"-long pedestrian gate (troublesome and often missing), socket and red bulb toward end of gate.

(A) 1940-41, aluminum-painted gates. P. Riddle Collection.　**15　35　15**

(B) 1942, 92 gray gates. D. Ely, J. Flynn and C. Rohlfing Collections.　**15　35　15**

1045 OPERATING FLAGMAN (1938-42, Postwar): Square vermilion base, solid pole with warning sign (same as 45), large Bakelite figure in uniform with flesh-tone hands and face, some with painted details (dark eyes, red lips, brown hair and shoes, white necktie), solenoid-actuated swinging right arm, white flag in right hand, black-painted nickel plate with nickel lettering "No. 1045 FLAGMAN / MADE IN U.S. OF AMERICA / THE LIONEL CORPORATION, N.Y.", 4" wide, 4" deep, 7" high; 4¼"-tall figure. The author's example came with a special section of Standard Gauge track with a 1⅛" portion of one outside rail insulated and wired to one terminal of the Flagman. Wheels passing over this section cause the flag to wave up and down repeatedly as the train passes. If attached to a normal section of insulated track, the flag remains steady up in the air until the train has passed. See Chapters IV and VI for further information.

(A) Aluminum-painted pole, brass warning sign, nickel finial, dark blue uniform, dark flesh tones, painted details. C. Weber Collection.　**20　35　20**

(B) Same as (A), but nickel sign, lighter blue uniform, lighter flesh tones, no painted details. C. Weber Collection.　**20　35　20**

(C) Same as (B), but post painted 92 gray.

	20	35	20

(D) Green base. Confirmation requested.　**NRS**

(E) Same as (A), but black uniform with very slight dark brown tint, and dark blue right arm. Although this combination could indicate a replaced arm, the author obtained this example from the original owner, who believes it was never sent for repair after purchase. Another example was confirmed by J. Flynn.　**NRS**

(F) Same as (E), but brown figure and arm. J. Flynn comment.　**NRS**

1046 MECHANICAL GATEMAN WITH GATE (1936): No known examples, probably not manufactured; catalogued with 1552 Mechanical Railroad Layout.

1575 CROSSING GATE (1933-37): Stamped steel, not lighted, 5½"-long gate, part of 1569 Lionel Junior Accessory Set.

(A) Pea green post, light red base; red, white and black gate.　**5　10　5**

(B) Gray post, black base; red, white and black gate.　**5　10　5**

(E) 1931-32, made for Ives.　**5　10　5**

CHAPTER VIII

Strictly Scenic

The majority of toys that maintain their popularity over a great number of years reflect the people and activities of the world that are observable but generally not manipulated by children. Dolls, and especially baby dolls, existed in the most primitive societies, as children imitated such aspects of family life as child care. Toy soldiers, toy cars and trucks and airplanes, toy telephones and phonographs, have all been popular since the very first real ones appeared. And so it is with trains.

In order to support the play activities associated with such toys, specific accessories accompany them and remain commercially popular items. Clothing, dishes, cribs and strollers are all built to doll-sized proportions, just as houses and gas stations and even miniature airports are manufactured to coordinate with transportation toys.

It is understandable then that children would be attracted to toys that could make their trains seem more a part of the natural world. Among the earliest accessories to appear, after specific railroad items such as stations and tunnels, were lamp posts. Lionel's first one (No. 61) appeared in the 1914 catalogue, a steel pole mounted on a cast-iron base and topped by an ornate gooseneck with shade and bulb. This design was repeated in several different sizes (one of which, No. 58, remained in production after World War II), plus two similar twin-light styles.

Lionel's lamp posts are mostly town or city designs, the types normally seen in residential and business neighborhoods, rather than simpler and more utilitarian designs found in railroad yards. The No. 58 style was patterned after a New York City prototype. The No. 57 lights its own street signs (usually "BROADWAY" and "MAIN STREET"), while others imitate gas lamps and boulevard lights. Largest (at over 20 inches tall) is an industrial floodlight tower topped by two reflector housings.

The next common scenic accessory is railroad related, and appeared in the 1920 catalogue: the 68 Warning Signal. This simple post has a brass diamond-shaped sign that alerts miniature motorists and pedestrians to the potential danger of approaching trains. The same year brought the first of two sizes of telegraph poles, usable either along the right of way or beside the highway. A related but much larger item, the 94 High Tension Tower, came along in 1932.

It is not surprising that Lionel would eventually provide living space for the inhabitants of Lionelville, and this category soon developed into a line of three residential buildings, a diner, and a wide variety of landscaped plots to accompany them. First to appear

53 Lamp Post. P. Riddle Collection and photograph.

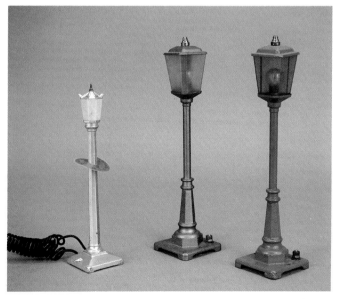

35 and two 56 Lamp Posts; the bronze 56 came mounted on a scenic plot. G. Zippie Collection, B. Schwab photograph.

Two 57 Lamp Posts, showing four different signs. G. Zippie Collection, B. Schwab photograph.

were a Bungalow and two Villas, highly detailed little houses of complex sheet metal design and complete with dormers, porches, chimneys and contrasting windows and doors. The company produced a vast number of lithographed and enameled color combinations. Some of these buildings were modeled upon the actual homes of Lionel executives. According to Ron Hollander in his book *All Aboard*, the 191 model was patterned after the residence of Louis Caruso, the inventor of the latch coupler.

These units were sold for use with either Standard or O Gauge, but were vastly undersized, being closer to HO scale, or half the expected dimensions even for Lionel's smallest trains. Opinions differ on their suitability for layout use, and many operators accept the size discrepancy in favor of authenticity of manufacture on period displays. Their exquisite detailing, especially when combined with Lionel's scenic plots, distracts the eye from the incongruity of size, and viewers usually seem to accept or ignore the fact that the trains tower above them.

Lionel began producing individual landscaped accessories as early as 1927, with the introduction of a small town block called an "Illuminated Terrace," fitted with two lamp posts, three houses and a flag pole. Imitation trees, grass, flowers and shrubbery were

59 and 54 Lamp Posts. G. Zippie Collection, B. Schwab photograph.

placed in artistic designs on a platform measuring 22 by 19 inches. This concept later grew into a whole line of "Scenic Plots" and culminated in 1932 in a magnificent park with nine houses and a wide variety of landscaped details. They were built upon substantial platforms, formed into terraces and hills with a felt composition material, and fitted with lights inside the houses. Wealthier Lionel train owners could provide their imaginary populations with expansive countrysides and substantial residential neighborhoods, and everyone could have Sunday dinner out at the 442 Lionel Diner!

Beginning in 1909 and all throughout the Prewar period, Lionel provided numerous large and small versions of that most fundamental of scenic accessories, the railroad tunnel. The earliest were of pâpier-maché, but the most magnificent were the hand-painted steel creations that debuted in 1920. Built in straight and

curved versions, some with interior lights and detailed with tiny houses and fences, they were made for both Standard and O Gauge trains. In 1932 a line of felt composition tunnels joined the metal ones, and blended in well with the similar style of scenery constructed on the Scenic Plots. These tunnels were also hand painted, and were made until train production ended in 1942 for the duration of the war.

Following are descriptions of known variations of scenic railroad accessories produced by Lionel through 1942. Sets which include several accessories (but not mounted on a single base) must include the original box as noted. Otherwise it is impossible to ascertain whether the components were in fact sold as a set. In all cases, the presence of the original box commands a substantial premium, from 50 to 100 percent depending upon condition.

LAMP POSTS

	GD	EXC	RST

35 BOULEVARD LAMP (1940-42, Postwar): Die-cast combination base and post, eight-sided translucent white lamp enclosure, complex painted plastic cap with central spire and eight pointed projections around the rim (easily broken), embossed "35" and "Lionel Corp." on underside of base, 6⅛" high; premium for intact cap.

		GD	EXC	RST
(A)	1940-41, aluminum.	25	40	20
(B)	1942, 92 gray (casting frequently deteriorated).	25	40	20

52 LAMP POST (1933-41): Die-cast combination base and post painted aluminum, two terminal posts on base, large decorative opalescent (frosted white) bulb, embossed "Made by The Lionel Corporation No. 52" on base, 10¼" or 10½" high.　　**35**　**60**　**30**

63 Lamp Post. G. Zippie Collection, B. Schwab photograph.

58 and 61 Lamp Posts. G. Zippie Collection, B. Schwab photograph.

Four 92 Floodlight Towers. G. Zippie and G. Barnett Collections, B. Schwab photograph.

GD EXC RST

53 LAMP POST (1931-42): Die-cast combination base and post, two terminal posts on base, large decorative opalescent bulb, embossed "53-1" on underside of base, 8½" or 8⅞" high; originated in Ives Bridgeport factory as catalogue No. 308, 1928-30.

	GD	EXC	RST
(A) Light mojave.	25	40	20
(B) Aluminum.	25	40	20
(C) Ivory. C. Rohlfing Collection.	25	40	20
(D) Gray.	25	40	20
(E) White. P. Riddle Collection.	25	40	20
(F) State green. A. Cox Collection.			NRS
(G) Peacock; possibly unique. R. Morris Collection.			NRS
(H) 1931-32, made for Ives under catalogue No. 1882.	45	100	45

54 LAMP POST (1929-35): Cast-iron base with two terminal posts, rolled-steel post, two brass lamp reflector shades suspended from fancy semi-circular ("gooseneck") steel brackets, filigreed (decorative points and curves) within upper curved section of post, two pear-shaped frosted bulbs, usually rubber-stamped

"54" on underside of base, 9½" high; similar to but smaller than late 67.

	GD	EXC	RST
(A) Maroon.	35	60	30
(B) Pea green.	35	60	30
(C) State brown.	35	60	30
(D) 1932, made for Ives under catalogue No. 1905.	35	75	30

56 LAMP POST (1924-42, Postwar): Die-cast base with two terminal posts, usually rubber-stamped "Lionel #56" or "56" on underside of base, rolled-metal post, "gaslight"-style lantern with steel base and cap holding celluloid bulb enclosure (usually found with yellowish discoloration), unfrosted bulb, 7¾" high.

	GD	EXC	RST
(A) Dark green.	30	55	25
(B) Pea green. S. Blotner Collection.	30	55	25
(C) Copper; found on Scenic plots only. D. Ely comment.	40	75	25
(D) Aluminum-painted. D. Ely Collection.	30	55	25
(E) 45N green. D. Ely Collection.	30	55	25
(F) 1939, dark gray.	30	55	25
(G) Aluminum; confirmation requested.			NRS
(H) Mojave. R. Morris Collection.			NRS
(I) Gray.	30	55	25

57 LAMP POST (1922-42): Die-cast base with two terminal posts, rolled-metal post, square sheet metal lantern base and cap holding white celluloid bulb enclosure stamped with various street names in silver or black lettering (either rubber- or heat-stamped, usually found faded or discolored), unfrosted bulb, nickel finial, usually rubber-stamped "Lionel #57" on underside of base, 7½" high; reproductions have been made, and caution should be exercised when purchasing the scarce varieties with street names other than "BROADWAY" and "MAIN STREET". A. G. Thompson comment.

Left to right Warning Signals; 068(A), 68(C), 68(A). R. Bartelt Collection, A. Fiterman photograph.

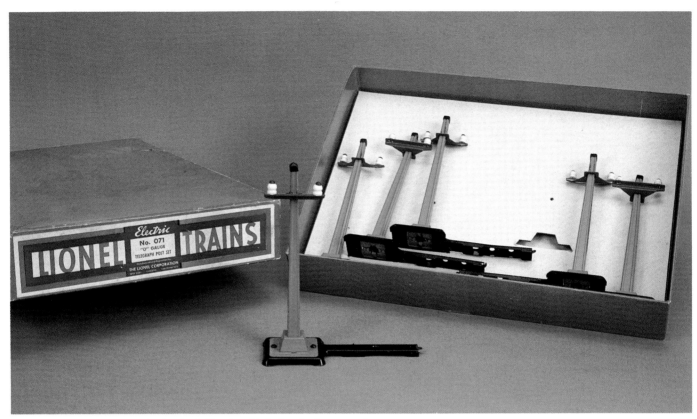

071 Telegraph Post Set. G. Zippie Collection, B. Schwab photograph.

	GD	EXC	RST

(A) 9E orange, "BROADWAY" on two opposing panels and "MAIN" on remaining two sides in serif lettering.
　　　　　　　　　　　　　　　30　　55　　25

(B) Same as (A), but sans-serif lettering.
　　　　　　　　　　　　　　　30　　55　　25

(C) 9E orange, with four different street names: "BROADWAY", "42nd STREET", "FIFTH AVENUE", "21st STREET", in sans-serif lettering; scarce.
　　　　　　　　　　　　　　　50　　90　　45

(D) Yellow, "BROADWAY" on two opposing panels and "MAIN" on remaining two sides in serif lettering; numbered 2013 and made for American Flyer by Lionel and sold in American Flyer box, some with number stamped on base; scarce. R. Morris Collection.
　　　　　　　　　　　　　　　40　　75　　25

(E) 9E orange, "FIFTH AVENUE" on two opposing panels and "42nd STREET" on remaining two sides. D. Ely Collection.　　40　　75　　35

(F) 9E orange, "BROADWAY" on two opposing panels and "21st STREET" on remaining two sides. D. Ely Collection.　　40　　75　　35

(G) 9E orange. "FIFTH AVENUE" on two opposing panels and "21st STREET" on remaining two sides; confirmation requested.　　　　　　**NRS**

(H) Gray, street names unknown; confirmation requested.　　　　　　　　　　　　**NRS**

58 LAMP POST (1922-42, Postwar): Die-cast base with semi-circular back and rectanglar cutout at bottom of three straight sides, two terminal posts, very small diameter metal post, lamp reflector shade suspended from fancy semi-circular ("gooseneck") filigreed steel bracket, five filigree points, pear-shaped frosted bulb, embossed "The Lionel Corporation New York" and rubber-stamped "LIONEL #58" or embossed "58-19" (late) on underside of base, 7⅜" high; smallest version of 59 and 61 style; Postwar examples lack base cutouts, and have four filigree points instead of five, plus slight differences in casting shape.

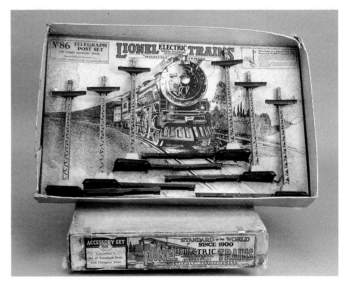

86 Telegraph Post Set. G. Zippie Collection, B. Schwab photograph.

	GD	EXC	RST
(A) 1922-23, dark green. L. Bohn Collection.			
	20	35	15
(B) Maroon; dates uncertain.	20	35	15
(C) 1927, orange. L. Bohn Collection.			
	20	35	15
(D) 1928-34, pea green. L. Bohn Collection.			
	20	35	15
(E) 1935-39, peacock; dates uncertain.			
	20	35	15
(F) 1940-50, cream. P. Riddle Collection.			
	20	35	15
(G) Dark Stephen Girard green. S. Blotner Collection.			
	20	35	15

59 LAMP POST (1920-36): Cast-iron base, some rubber-stamped "LIONEL #59" on underside of base, rolled-metal post, lamp reflector shade suspended from fancy semi-circular ("gooseneck") filigreed steel bracket, pear-shaped frosted or round frosted or unfrosted bulb, 8¹¹⁄₁₆″ or 8¹⁵⁄₁₆″ high; mid-sized version of 58 and 61 style.

	GD	EXC	RST
(A) Dark green, 8¹⁵⁄₁₆″. G. Koff and L. Bohn Collections.	25	45	20
(B) Light green. G. Koff Collection.	25	45	20

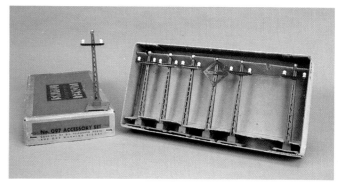

097 Telegraph Post and Signal Set. G. Zippie Collection, B. Schwab photograph.

	GD	EXC	RST
(C) Olive green, 8¹¹⁄₁₆″. G. Koff and L. Bohn Collections.			
	25	45	20
(D) Aluminum; confirmation requested.		NRS	
(E) Peacock; confirmation requested.		NRS	
(F) Cream; confirmation requested.		NRS	
(G) Maroon.	25	45	20
(H) Red.	25	45	20
(I) State brown.	25	45	20

61 LAMP POST (1914-32, 1934-36): Cast-iron base, some rubber-stamped "LIONEL #61" on underside of base, rolled-metal post, lamp reflector shade suspended from fancy semi-circular ("gooseneck") filigreed steel bracket, pear-shaped frosted or round frosted or unfrosted bulb, 12¾″ high; early version with 2⅜″ by 2¼″ base, 1⅝″ reflector shade; late version with 2¼″ square base, 1¼″ reflector shade; Lionel's first lamp post and largest version of 58 and 59 style.

	GD	EXC	RST
(A) Dark green.	30	55	25
(B) Olive green.	30	55	25
(C) Mojave.	30	55	25
(D) Maroon.	30	55	25
(E) State brown.	30	55	25
(F) Black.	30	55	25
(G) Pea green.	30	55	25

63 LAMP POST (1933-42): Die-cast combination base and post painted aluminum, crossarm at top with two fancy torch-style sockets, two large decorative opalescent bulbs, 12¾″ high, embossed or rubber-stamped "#63 / MADE BY / THE LIONEL CORPORATION / NEW YORK" on underside of base. D. Ely Collection. **100 160 100**

64 HIGHWAY LAMP POST (1940-42, Postwar): Die-cast base, very thin steel post, small 64-15 opalescent pear-shaped bulb unique to this lamp with flush fit to socket, 45N green, 6¾″ high (scaled for O Gauge); replacement bulbs available. The original bulbs are flatter on the underside than the reproductions; originals were meant to operate at 12 to 14 volts, and Lou Bohn speculates that most users connected them to higher voltage, accounting for their low survival rate. **20 35 15**

Two 94 High Tension Towers. G. Barnett Collection, B. Schwab photograph.

Three different 184 Bungalows. P. Riddle Collection and photograph.

GD EXC RST

67 LAMP POST (1915-32): Cast-iron base, some rubber-stamped "LIONEL #61" on underside of base, rolled-metal post, two lamp reflector shades suspended from fancy semi-circular ("gooseneck") filigreed steel brackets, two pear-shaped frosted or round frosted or unfrosted bulbs; early version with thick and ornate filigrees, 2 9/16" by 2½" base, 1 9/16" reflector shade, 13" high; late version with thinner and less ornate filigrees (similar to 54), 2¼" square base, 1¼" reflector shade; similar to but larger than 54. The bases on some early dark green versions measure 2¼" by 2⅜". L. Bohn comment.

(A) Dark green. G. Thomson Collection.
50 95 45
(B) Peacock; confirmation requested. NRS
(C) State green. 50 95 45

92 FLOODLIGHT TOWER (1931-42): Steel construction, 5" square base, tapered open-girder tower, rectangular top platform enclosed by fence, two lamp housings in rotating U-shaped brackets, two binding posts and brass or nickel plate at front of base, 20½" high; reproduced by Williams Reproductions and Mike's Train House.

(A) 1931-34, terra cotta base, pea green tower, brass lamp housings, brass plate. G. Barnett and S. Simon Collections. 95 175 90
(B) 1935-41, red base, aluminum-painted tower, nickel lamp housings, nickel plate on base painted black with nickel serif lettering "No 92 FLOODLIGHT / TOWER / THE LIONEL CORPORATION, N.Y." with the "o" raised and underscored. G. Barnett and D. Ely Collections.
95 175 90
(C) 1941-42, same as (B), but light red base, 92 gray tower. P. Riddle and J. Flynn Collections.
95 175 90
(D) Reproduction by Williams Reproductions.
— 50 —
(E) Reproduction by Mike's Train House; issue price 3 / $100. — 50 —
(F) 1932, green, made for Ives under catalogue No. 1902. 95 175 95

POSTS, SIGNS AND TOWERS

60 TELEGRAPH POST (1920-28): Standard Gauge (although sold for use with O Gauge and in O Gauge

GD EXC RST

Scenic Railways prior to 1929), stamped-steel, square base, tapered post of open girder design (alternately described as a "pole" in some catalogues) topped by separate finial, crossarm with two clear glass or white porcelain insulators, with bracket to attach to track beginning in 1929, 8¾" high, 2½" crossarm.

(A) Peacock base and post, maroon crossarm, brass finial, clear insulators. D. Ely Collection.
15 25 15
(B) Peacock base and post, red crossarm, white insulators. C. Weber Collection. 15 25 15
(C) Dark gray base and post, maroon crossarm, white insulators. J. Flynn and D. Ely Collections.
15 25 15
(D) Same as (C), but clear glass insulators. C. Weber Collection. 15 25 15
(E) Apple green base and post, maroon crossarm, white insulators. J. Flynn Collection. 15 25 15
(F) Same as (E), but clear insulators. C. Weber Collection. 15 25 15
(G) Aluminum-painted base and post, light red crossarm, white insulators. C. Weber Collection.
15 25 15
(H) Stephen Girard green base and post, green insulators. D. Ely Collection. 15 25 15

060 TELEGRAPH POST (1929-42): O Gauge, stamped-steel, square base, tapered open girder (early) or solid post topped by separate finial, crossarm with two white porcelain insulators, with bracket to attach to track, 6⅞" high (earlier catalogues state 5½"), 2" crossarm.

(A) 9E orange post, maroon crossarm, brass finial.
15 25 15
(B) Green open girder post, red crossarm, brass finial.
15 25 15
(C) Same as (B), but solid post. 15 25 15

189 Villa.

89 Flag Pole. G. Zippie Collection, B. Schwab photograph.

GD EXC RST

(D) Same as (C), but with black finial.

15   25   15

68 WARNING SIGNAL (1920-39): Standard Gauge, stamped- steel, square base, tapered open girder (early) or solid post topped by separate brass or nickel finial, cutout brass diamond sign 3½" point to point (larger and heavier gauge metal than 068 model), lettered in black or red "RAILROAD CROSSING" across center and "LOOK OUT / FOR LOCOMOTIVE" around border, 8⅞" high, usually rubber-stamped in black "#68"

GD EXC RST

or "#69" on underside of base, as the base was also used for the 69 Warning Bell. The pedestal that supports the post may have an inverted "J" slot. R. Morris comment.

(A) Dark olive, black serif lettering, brass finial. C. Rohlfing and J. Flynn Collections.

8   15   8

(B) Orange, black lettering, brass finial. S. Blotner and J. Flynn Collections. 8   15   8

(C) Maroon, black lettering, brass finial. J. Flynn Collection. 8   15   8

(D) White, red lettering, nickel finial. G. Thomson Collection. 8   15   8

(E) Terra cotta. 8   15   8

068 WARNING SIGNAL (1925-42): O Gauge, stamped-steel, square base punched with two holes, tapered open girder (early) or solid post topped by separate brass or nickel finial, cutout brass diamond sign 2³⁄₁₆" point to point (smaller and lighter gauge metal than 68 model), lettered in black or red "RAILROAD CROSSING" across center and "LOOK OUT / FOR LOCOMOTIVE" around border, 6⁷⁄₁₆" high, usually rubber-stamped in black "LIONEL / #068" on underside of base, packaged with most O Gauge sets from 1927 through 1933.

(A) Pea green, large sans-serif lettering with "LOOK" measuring ⁹⁄₁₆" long. Herzog Collection.

8   15   8

(B) Pea green, large serif lettering with "LOOK" measuring 1¹⁄₁₆" long. C. Weber and Herzog Collections.

8   15   8

(C) Pea green, lettering with very small serifs, "LOOK" measuring 1¹⁄₁₆" long. C. Weber and Herzog Collections. 8   15   8

(D) Same as (C), but dark pea green. C. Rohlfing Collection. 8   15   8

(E) Red base, yellow open girder post with brass finial, white-painted steel diamond with black lettering "RAILROAD" and "CROSSING LOOK OUT / FOR ENGINE" around border and "DANGER" in center, believed made for Lionel by Hafner (shown in mid or late 1930s Hafner catalogue as part of No. 1200 Accessory Set) with diamond made from an Ives die owned by Lionel. The Hafner catalogue announces "SOLE

191 Villa.

442 Diner. R. Bartelt Collection, A. Fiterman photograph.

GD   EXC   RST

EXPORTERS LIONEL CORPORATION". This accessory does not properly belong in either the 68 or the 068 listing. The pole is Standard Gauge size and the diamond is larger than the 068 diamond and smaller than the 68 diamond. It has been rumored that Lionel and Hafner signed an agreement whereby Lionel would end the production of mechanical trains in exchange for handling the overseas distribution of the Hafner line,

90 Flag Pole. G. Zippie Collection, B. Schwab photograph.

and Hafner would not make electrically powered trains. In Volume I of their series, *A Collector's Guide and History to Lionel Trains*, McComas and Tuohy state that the rumor is false, but it persists. Nevertheless, it has been established that Hafner sold products made by Lionel and Lionel distributed Hafner products overseas.   **8   15   8**

(F) 1942, 92 gray with solid post. R. Morris Collection (although he suggests it could have been removed from a 45N Gateman; confirmation requested).

8   15   8

(G) Pea green, base with four holes (one bigger and one smaller than two standard holes), diamond painted orange and rubber-stamped in sans-serif lettering, "LOOK" measures 1³⁄₁₆" long; illustrated on page 13 of the 1926 catalogue. Scarce. J. Flynn comment, C. Weber Collection.   **20   45   8**

(H) 1931-32, made for Ives.   **8   15   8**

70 ACCESSORY OUTFIT (1921-32): Contains 59 Lamp Post, two 62 Semaphores, 68 Warning Signal, in original box.

(A) 1921-26, 1928-32, dark green 59 and white 68.

50   100   50

(B) 1927, pea green 59 and terra cotta 68.

50   100   50

71 TELEGRAPH POST SET (1921-31): Contains six 60 Telegraph Posts, in original box.

60   120   60

071 TELEGRAPH POST SET (1929-42): Contains six 060 Telegraph Posts, in original box.

910 Grove of Trees. G. Zippie Collection, B. Schwab photograph.

	GD	EXC	RST

(A) Orange, open girder posts, maroon crossarms, brass finials, white insulators. D. Ely Collection.

	60	120	60

(B) Green, solid posts, red crossarms, nickel finials, white insulators. D. Ely Collection. 60 120 60

85 TELEGRAPH POST (1929-42): Standard Gauge, stamped-steel, square base, tapered open girder post topped by separate finial, crossarm with two porcelain insulators, with bracket to attach to track, 9″ high, 2½″ crossarm.

(A) 9E orange, maroon crossarm, orange insulators. D. Ely Collection. 20 35 20

(B) Aluminum-painted, red crossarm, white insulators. D. Ely Collection. 20 35 20

86 TELEGRAPH POST SET (1929-42): Contains six 85 Telegraph Posts, in original box.

(A) Orange, maroon crossarms, orange insulators.

	60	120	60

(B) Silver, red crossarms, white insulators.

	60	120	60

94 HIGH TENSION TOWER (1932-42): Stamped-steel, 5″ by 5″ square base, open girder tower, three crossarms each with two hanging porcelain insulators, brass or nickel identification plate on base, packed with spool of 25″ of copper wire, 24″ high; reproduced by Williams Reproductions and Mike's Train House.

	GD	EXC	RST

(A) Terra cotta base, gunmetal or gray tower, brass plate. 100 200 100

(B) Terra cotta base, mojave tower, brass plate. D. Ely Collection. 100 200 100

(C) 1935-41, red base, aluminum-painted tower, nickel plate. D. Ely Collection. 100 200 100

(D) 1942, red base, 92 gray tower. 120 240 100

(E) Reproduction by Williams Reproductions, stamped "WRL". — 50 —

(F) 1986, reproduction by Mike's Train House; issue price 3 / $100. — 50 —

096 TELEGRAPH POST (1934-35): O Gauge, stamped-steel, square pea green base, tapered pea green post topped by separate finial, red crossarm with two white porcelain insulators, without bracket to attach to track, 6⅞″ high, 2″ crossarm. Came only in 097 Telegraph Post and Signal Set. 15 25 15

097 TELEGRAPH POST AND SIGNAL SET (1934-35): Contains six 096 Telegraph Posts, one 068 Warning Signal, in original box. 50 100 50

308 SCALE MODEL SIGNS (1940-42, Postwar): Five signs, white-painted steel with black lettering, 301 "RAILROAD / CROSSING" crossbuck, 302 Y-shaped "YARD LIMIT", 303 "W" (whistle), 304 "RR" and cross in circle, 305 "DANGER / DO NOT / TRESPASS ON / RAILROAD", in light orange box with black lettering.

GD   EXC   RST

(A) Early, rectangular green bases with imitation grass embedded in paint. D. Ely Collection.

12   25   —

(B) Rectangular white bases. D. Ely Collection.

12   25   —

(C) Round white bases. D. Ely Collection.

12   25   —

1569 ACCESSORY SET (1933-37): See Chapter IV.

1571 TELEGRAPH POST (1933-37): Stamped-steel, black square base, U-shaped gray or green pole, two red crossarms, for mechanical trains; part of 1569 Lionel Junior Accessory Set; also made for Ives in 1931-32.   **5   10   5**

HOUSES

184 BUNGALOW (1923-32; uncatalogued and available on Scenic Plots through 1942): Steel construction, enameled or lithographed base, walls, peaked roof and chimney; one dormer usually on left side, chimney at back and usually on the left, separate window inserts, open porch area with shed roof, some with decal or rubber-stamped "MADE BY / THE LIONEL CORPORATION / NEW YORK, U.S.A." and

GD   EXC   RST

either "184 A-1" or "184-1" in black on underside of base, illuminated, early versions varnished, early enameled versions heavier gauge steel (R. Morris comment), 4¾" by 2¾" by 4" high. Over one hundred variations are known. Bases may be lithographed with either grass or flower details, or enameled gray, mojave, Hiawatha gray or yellow-flecked gray. Walls, dormers and porches may be lithographed in white, ivory or gray with a red brick foundation and ivy details plus a brick border around the porch windows, or enameled white, ivory, cream, yellow, mustard or in a textured ivory imitating stucco. Roofs may be lithographed red or green, or enameled maroon, red, light red, rose pink, orange, terra cotta, pea green, apple green or dark green. Window inserts may be ivory, yellow, orange, pea green or apple green, and chimneys may be lithographed brick or enameled white, ivory, cream, yellow, mojave, gray, red or imitation stucco. Reproductions have been made by Frank Bowers in five different enameled color combinations: apple green roof with white walls, wine roof with white walls, red roof with cream walls, dark green roof with white walls, and orange roof with cream walls.

(A) Lithographed base, walls, roof and chimney, enameled window inserts.   **40   75   35**

Compare the trees on this 911 Country Estate, with dark red 191 Villa, with the later version shown on page 91. G. Zippie Collection, B. Schwab photograph.

913 Illuminated Landscaped Bungalow. G. Zippie Collection, B. Schwab photograph.

	GD	EXC	RST
(B) Same as (A), but enameled roof.	40	75	35
(C) Same as (B), but enameled chimney.	40	75	35
(D) Enameled components.	40	75	35

(E) Enameled imitation stucco walls and chimney, gray base, maroon roof, ivory window inserts.

	50	100	35

(T) Enameled, white walls, dark green roof, white chimney, came only with set No. 186.

	40	75	35

(U) Enameled, cream walls, orange roof, white chimney, came only with set No. 186.

	40	75	35

	GD	EXC	RST

(V) 1929-30, made for Ives under catalogue No. 250.

	40	75	35
(W) Reproduction by Frank Bowers.	—	75	—

185 BUNGALOW (1923-24): Same as 184, but not illuminated.

(A) Mixed lithographed or enameled components.

	40	75	35

(B) Enameled, white walls, dark green roof, white chimney, may have come only with set No. 187; confirmation requested.

	40	75	35

(C) Enameled, cream walls, orange roof, white chimney, may have come only with set No. 187; confirmation requested.

	40	75	35

186 ILLUMINATED BUNGALOW SET (1923-32): Five 184 Bungalows in original box.

	250	475	225

187 BUNGALOW SET (1923-24): Five 185 Bungalows in original box.

	225	400	200

189 VILLA (1923-32; uncatalogued and available on Scenic Plots through 1942): Steel construction, two-story 1plus attic design, enameled base, walls, gambrel roof with or without four dormers, chimney at side extending from base through roof, separate window and door inserts, open porch area with shed roof,

911 Country Estate, with yellow 191 Villa. G. Zippie Collection, B. Schwab photograph.

GD EXC RST

some with decal or rubber-stamped "NO. 189 VILLA / MADE BY / THE LIONEL CORPORATION / NEW YORK", in black on underside of base, illuminated, 5⅜" by 4⅞" by 5½" high. Many different variations are known. Bases may be painted mojave, Hiawatha gray, terra cotta or pea green. Walls and porches may be enameled white, ivory, cream, light mustard or sand, and dormers (when present) may be enameled white, ivory, buff, sand or pea green. Roofs may be enameled maroon, peacock, light or medium green, apple green or gray. Window inserts may be white, ivory, cream, buff, sand, peacock, pea green or dark green, and may differ on first and second floors and dormers on the same model. Doors may be ivory, sand, maroon, light red or simulated wood grain. Chimneys may be lithographed brick or enameled red, light red or terra cotta, and are mounted on a foundation enameled mojave or terra cotta, or lithographed in a speckled pattern. Reproductions have been made by Frank Bowers in three different color combinations: peacock roof with white walls, red roof with cream walls, and apple green roof with cream walls.

(A) Enameled components, with dormers.

75 140 75

GD EXC RST

(B) Same as (A), but with lithographed chimney and/or chimney foundation and/or wood-grained doors.

75 140 75

(C) Pea green base, ivory walls, gray or maroon roof, lithographed chimney and chimney foundation, dark green window inserts, wood-grained doors, no dormers.

100 195 75

(D) 1929-30, made for Ives under catalogue No. 251.

NRS

(E) Reproduction by Frank Bowers. **NEW 150**

191 VILLA (1923-32; uncatalogued and available on Scenic Plots through 1942): Steel construction, two-story plus attic design with added wing (variously called "sun porch" or "train room" by collectors), enameled base, walls, hip roof with chimney and with or without two large dormers, separate window and door inserts, open porch area with flat roof surrounded by decorative railing, wing with ten windows and flat roof surrounded by decorative railing, some with decal or rubber-stamped "NO. 191 VILLA / MADE BY / THE LIONEL CORPORATION / NEW YORK", in black on underside of base, illuminated, 7⅛" by 5" by 5¼" high. Many different variations are known. Bases may be painted mojave, tan, Hiawatha gray or pea green.

The landscaping on this 912 Suburban Home, with mustard-colored 189 Villa, differs considerably from the one shown in the next photograph. Lionel scenic plots were hand decorated, and no two are exactly alike. G. Zippie Collection, B. Schwab photograph.

912 Suburban Home with white 189 Villa. G. Zippie Collection, B. Schwab photograph.

GD EXC RST

Walls may be enameled cream, yellow, terra cotta or red crackle, or lithographed to represent dark or light red brick, and porches may be enameled ivory, cream or yellow. Dormers (when present) may be enameled cream, yellow, sand, light red, crackle red or pea green. Roofs may be enameled red, light red, pea green, apple green or gray, and porch roofs may be cream, sand, mustard, mojave or Hiawatha gray. Window inserts may be ivory, pea green, apple green or Stephen Girard green, and doors may be ivory, brown, maroon, red, pea green, apple green, Stephen Girard green or simulated wood grain. Chimneys may be lithographed brick or enameled cream, sand or yellow. Roof railings may be brass, nickel, pea green, dark green or gray. Reproductions have been made by Frank Bowers.

(A) Enameled or lithographed components, with dormers. **100 195 100**

(B) Mojave base, terra cotta walls and dormers, pea green roof, white window inserts, wood-grained doors, green railings, lithographed brick chimney, brass roof. D. Ely Collection. **NRS**

(C) Cream walls, red roof, came only with scenic plots. **120 225 100**

(D) Mojave base, lithographed brick walls, pea green roof, white window inserts, dark green railings, no

GD EXC RST

dormer; uncatalogued, may have come only with scenic plots. **120 225 100**

(E) Dark tan base, terra cotta walls, pea green roof and dormers, cream porch and window inserts, wood-grained doors, lithographed chimney, pea green railings, mustard porch and wing roof; packaged in yellow paper-covered box with white label at one end lettered in red and black "ONE No. 191 / ILLUMINATED / STEEL / VILLA". F. Wasserman Collection. **NRS**

(F) 1929-30, made for Ives under catalogue No. 252. **100 195 100**

(G) Reproduction by Frank Bowers. **NEW 150**

192 ILLUMINATED VILLA SET (1923-32): One 191 Villa, one 189 Villa, and two 184 Bungalows, in original box. **NRS**

SCENIC PLOTS AND RELATED ACCESSORIES

89 FLAG POLE (1923-34): Steel construction, ivory or white pole and base 2½" square, black wooden finial (some possibly gold; confirmation requested), silk American flag, 14" high; also sold under the Ives

914 Park Landscape. G. Zippie Collection, B. Schwab photograph.

	GD	EXC	RST

trademark in 1930 as catalogue No. 87, and in 1931-32 as catalogue No. 1866.   **20**   **35**   **20**

90 FLAG POLE (1927-42): Steel construction, 4½"-diameter base with grass plot and flower border applied, steel ivory pole, black wooden finial, silk American flag, 14¾" high.

(A) Early, brass pedestal, base painted pea green, blue field on flag lighter than variation (B), flag measures 5¾" by 4³⁄₁₆". C. Weber and D. Ely Collections.
    35   **65**   **30**

(B) Later, nickel pedestal, base painted 45N green, flag has navy blue field and measures 5¾" by 3⅞". C. Weber and D. Ely Collections.   **35**   **65**   **30**

(C) Late, similar to (B), but with black oxide pedestal. R. Morris comment.   **35**   **65**   **30**

	GD	EXC	RST

195 ILLUMINATED TERRACE (1927-30): Landscaped plywood platform including 191 Villa, 189 Villa, 184 Bungalow, 90 Flagpole, two 56 Lamp Posts, 22" by 19" Reproduced by Ron Morris, less the buildings.

(A) Original Lionel production.   **400**   **800**   **400**

(B) Base reproduction by Ron Morris.   **NEW 195**

442 LANDSCAPED DINER (1938-42): Steel and wood construction, 610 Pullman roof and body without holes punched for trucks, air tanks, or end doors; mounted on fiberboard foundation and pressed-board base with curved front, fitted with two sets of paperboard and wood steps leading to side doors, shrubbery (curved hedge, two small trees), car insert rubber-stamped in serif letters "EAT" in place of "610" at left

One of these early 913 Landscaped Bungalows has a lithographed building and darker colored foliage (left), while the later version is enameled and has lighter trees and hedges. G. Zippie Collection, B. Schwab photograph.

921 Scenic Park. G. Zippie Collection, B. Schwab photograph.

	GD	EXC	RST

and right and in sans-serif letters "DINER" in place of "PULLMAN" in center, illuminated, 10⅝" by 5½" by 3⅜" high. Base with steps and shrubbery reproduced by Ron Morris; similar building produced by Williams Reproductions.

(A) Ivory walls, light red roof, red doors and windows, red plates, silver lettering, light tan-painted pressed-board base, pink foundation and steps, rectangular paper label on underside with red border printed in red, coded "Form No. 442-16-6.5X — 5-39-TT". C. Rohlfing Collection.   **80   160   75**

(B) Same as (A), but red foundation and steps.

80   160   75

(C) Cream walls, red window and door inserts, roof, and plates, gold lettering, light brown base, pink foun-

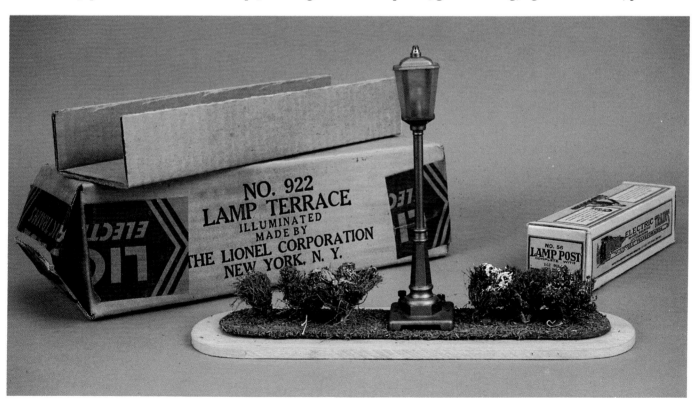

922 Lamp Terrace. G. Zippie Collection, B. Schwab photograph.

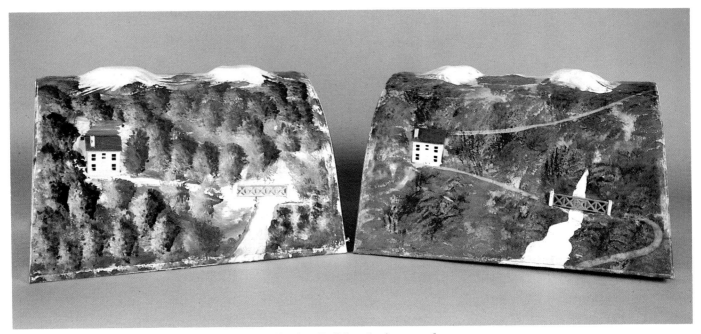

120L Tunnels, early (right) and late. G. Zippie Collection, B. Schwab photograph.

	GD	EXC	RST

dation and steps, same label as (A). Original box dated "8/39". R. Shanfeld Collection.   **80   160   75**

(D) Base reproduction by Ron Morris.   **NEW 25**

910 GROVE OF TREES (1932-42): Rectangular base, paperboard over wood slats or (later) pressed board, covered with imitation grass and trees, some with shrubs, most examples with felt composition rocks, some with brass plate lettered "MADE BY / THE LIONEL CORPORATION / NEW YORK", 16″ by approximately 8″ (latter dimension varies). Reproduced by Ron Morris.

(A) Eleven trees.   **75   150   —**

(B) Six trees, bushes, yellow-orange rock pile, rectangular orange sticker dated "5/39" on underside, base painted green. R. Shanfeld Collection.
   75   150   —

(C) Reproduction by Ron Morris.   **NEW 37.50**

911 COUNTRY ESTATE (1932-42): Rectangular base, paperboard over wood slats or (later) pressed board, covered with imitation grass, trees, hedge and shrubbery, with illuminated 191 Villa, 16″ by 8″; has been found with brass plate. Reproduced by Ron Morris, less building.

(A) Tan base, cream walls and dormers, red roof, cream chimney, white porch, pea green windows and doors, brass railings.   **195   400   175**

(B) Cream walls and dormers, green roof, cream chimney, orange windows. R. Shanfeld Collection.
   195   400   175

(C) Mojave base, red crackle walls, pea green roof, cream trim and chimney. G. Zippie Collection.
   195   400   175

(D) Gray base, yellow walls and chimney, red roof, pea green trim. J. Flynn observation.   **195   400   175**

(E) Base reproduction by Ron Morris.   **NEW 37.50**

912 SUBURBAN HOME (1932-42): Rectangular base, paperboard over wood slats or (later) pressed board, covered with imitation grass, trees, hedge and shrubbery, with illuminated 189 Villa, 16″ by 8″. Reproduced by Ron Morris, less building.

(A) Tan base, cream walls, first-floor windows, and dormers, ivory doors and upper windows, terra cotta chimney.   **175   350   150**

(B) Dark mustard walls, green roof, terra cotta chimney, four dormers, white windows and doors, orange label dated "5/39" on underside. R. Shanfeld Collection.
   175   350   150

(C) Gray base, tan walls, apple green roof, terra cotta chimney, white trim. J. Flynn observation.
   175   350   150

(D) Base reproduction by Ron Morris.   **NEW 37.50**

913 LANDSCAPED BUNGALOW (1932-42): Rectangular base, paperboard over wood slats or (later) pressed board, covered with imitation grass, trees, hedge and shrubbery, with illuminated 184 Bungalow, usually lithographed, 16″ by 8″. Reproduced by Ron Morris, less building.

(A) 1940-42, white lithographed walls, enameled pea green roof, red chimney, orange windows.
   150   300   125

(B) Dark gray base, yellow walls, red roof, yellow chimney, apple green window inserts. R. Shanfeld Collection.   **150   300   125**

(C) Hiawatha gray base, cream walls and chimney, apple green roof, orange windows. J. Flynn observation.
   150   300   125

(D) Hiawatha gray base, white walls and chimney, apple green roof, orange windows.   **150   300   125**

	GD	EXC	RST

(E) Base reproduction by Ron Morris.   **NEW 37.50**

914 PARK LANDSCAPE (1932-36): Elliptical plywood base painted cream with two horseshoe-shaped imitation grass plots, shrubbery and flower garden with cream urn in center, 16″ by 8½″. Reproduced by Ron Morris. D. Ely Collection.

	GD	EXC	RST
(A) Original Lionel production.	100	200	—
(B) Reproduction by Ron Morris.			**NEW 35**

917 SCENIC HILLSIDE (1932-36): Paperboard base over wood slats, with composition felt hill, hand-painted and decorated with trees and shrubbery, with two small red-roofed houses, 34″ by 15″ by 9½″ high. Reproduced by Ron Morris.

	GD	EXC	RST
(A) Original Lionel production.	100	225	—
(B) Reproduction by Ron Morris.			**NEW 145**

918 SCENIC HILLSIDE (1932-36): Paperboard base over wood slats, with composition felt hill, hand-painted and decorated with trees and shrubbery, with one small red-roofed house, 30″ by 10″ by 9½″ high. Reproduced by Ron Morris.

	GD	EXC	RST
(A) Original Lionel production.	100	225	—
(B) Reproduction by Ron Morris.			**NEW 135**

919 PARK GRASS (1932-42, Postwar): Artificial green grass, 8 oz., in cloth bag.   7   15   —

920 SCENIC PARK (1932-33): Rectangular plywood two-section base with rounded corners and raised felt composition terrace, hand-painted and detailed with grass, trees, hedges and shrubbery, two 184 Bungalows, 189 Villa, 191 Villa, either 910 Grove of Trees or 914 Park Landscape (possibly added only outside the factory), 922 Lamp Terrace (possibly added only outside the factory), 57″ by 31½″ by 10″ high. Reproduced by Ron Morris.

	GD	EXC	RST
(A) Original Lionel production.	750	1800	750
(B) Reproduction by Ron Morris.			**NEW 325**

921 SCENIC PARK (1932-33): Rectangular plywood three-section base with rounded corners and raised felt composition terrace, same as 920 with addition of 921C Park Center Section, 85″ by 31½″ by 10″ high. Reproduced by Ron Morris.

	GD	EXC	RST
(A) Original Lionel production.	1200	3000	1200
(B) Reproduction by Ron Morris.			**NEW 450**

921C PARK CENTER SECTION (1932-33): Rectangular plywood base with raised composition terrace, hand-painted and detailed with grass, trees, hedges and shrubbery, 184 Bungalow, 189 Villa, 191 Villa, either 910 Grove of Trees or 914 Park Landscape, 922 Lamp Terrace, illuminated, 28″ by 31½″ by 10″ high; designed to fit between two sections of 920 Scenic Park. Reproduced by Ron Morris.

	GD	EXC	RST
(A) Original Lionel production.	450	1200	450
(B) Reproduction by Ron Morris.			**NEW 185**

922 LAMP TERRACE (1932-36): Elliptical plywood platform painted cream, decorated with imitation grass and flowering shrubbery, 56 Lamp Post in center, 13″ by 3¾″ by 8¼″ high. Reproduced by Ron Morris, less lamp.

	GD	EXC	RST
(A) Copper lamp post (never sold separately). G. Zippie Collection.	100	200	90
(B) Green or pea green lamp post.	90	175	90
(C) Mojave lamp post.	90	175	90.
(B) Base reproduction by Ron Morris.			**NEW 17.50**

927 ORNAMENTAL FLAG PLOT (1937-42): Elliptical plywood platform painted cream, decorated with imitation grass and flowering shrubbery, ivory steel pole with wood finial, silk flag fitted with cord for raising and lowering, 16″ by 8½″ by 14¾″ high. Reproduced by Ron Morris.

	GD	EXC	RST
(A) Original Lionel production.	75	150	75
(B) Reproduction by Ron Morris, less flag.			**NEW 25**
(B) Reproduction by Ron Morris, with reproduction flag.			**NEW 37.50**

TUNNELS

104 TUNNEL (1909-14): Standard Gauge, pâpier-maché hand-painted in shades of brown, gray, green and cream, 13″ by 9″ by 9″ high.   50   100   —

109 TUNNEL (1913): Standard Gauge, hand-painted pâpier-maché, 25″ by 14″ by 12½″ high.

50   100   —

118 TUNNEL (1915-32): O Gauge, hand-painted pâpier-maché or steel, with or without small house on side.

(A) 1915-20, pâpier-maché with steel brace, hotel detail on side, 10″ long.   25   50   —

(B) 1920-32, steel with embossed simulated stone portals, hand-painted to represent wooded mountain with road and snow-capped peak in shades of gray, green, red and yellow, 8″ by 7¼″ by 7″ high. D. Ely Collection.

35   75   35

(C) Same as (B), but brass tunnel. L. Bohn Collection.

35   75   35

(D) Similar to (B), steel interior and portals, brass outer shell, "LIONEL" on keystones at each end, 8″ by 7¼″ by 7½″ high, packed in corrugated box with white label with red and black lettering "LIONEL / ALL / METAL / RAILROAD / TUNNEL", boy wearing engineer's cap on left and "No. / 118" inside red outlines. F. Wasserman Collection.   35   75   35

118L TUNNEL: Same as metal 118, but lighted, plus dormer from 189 on each side and orange-trimmed front porch railing from 191 on each side. R. Morris comment.   40   80   40

119 TUNNEL (1915-42): Standard or O Gauge, hand-painted pâpier-maché or steel.

(A) 1915-19, pâpier-maché with steel brace, house detail on side, 16″ long.   35   75   —

916 Tunnel. G. Zippie Collection, B. Schwab photograph.

GD EXC RST

(B) Circa 1920-23, steel interior and embossed simulated stone portals, brass outer shell, hand-painted to represent wooded mountain with road and snow-capped peak in shades of gray, green, red and yellow, no house detail, "LIONEL" on keystones at each end, 12" by 9" by 9" high. F. Wasserman Collection.

35   75   35

(C) Circa 1924-42, similar to (B), but with house and bridge detail.   35   75   35

119L TUNNEL (1927-33): Same as metal 119, but lighted inside one portal, painted waterfall passing under 3¼" fence, white two-story house with maroon roof and white chimney. D. Ely Collection.

40   80   40

120 TUNNEL (1915-27): Standard or O Gauge, hand-painted pâpier-maché or steel.

(A) 1915-21, pâpier-maché with steel brace, house detail on side, 20" long.   40   80   —

(B) 1922-27, steel construction, painted waterfall passing under 3¼" fence, white two-story house with maroon roof, no chimney, 17" by 12" by 10½" high. D. Ely Collection.   40   80   40

(C) Late version of (B), lighter portal color, house with red roof and chimney. D. Ely Collection.

40   80   40

GD EXC RST

120L TUNNEL (1927-42): Same as metal 120, but lighted with one bulb inside each portal.

(A) Early, subdued colors, two houses with cream walls and chimneys and red roofs, two orange fences with cream posts, rubber-stamped inside "NO. 120-L TUNNEL / MADE BY / THE LIONEL CORPORATION / NEW YORK". G. Zippie Collection.

50   100   50

(B) Late, same as (A), but brighter colors, houses with yellow walls and chimneys and light red roofs, gray fences with yellow posts. G. Zippie Collection.

50   100   50

123 TUNNEL (1933-42): O Gauge, composition corrugated paperboard base, 90-degree curve, hand-painted with trees, shrubs and house detail, 18½" by 16¼" by 10" high. R. Shanfeld Collection.

50   100   50

128 TUNNEL (1920): Same as metal 118, lighted. No known examples; confirmation requested.   **NRS**

129 TUNNEL (1920): Same as metal 119, lighted. No known examples; confirmation requested.   **NRS**

130 TUNNEL (1920): Same as metal 120, lighted. No known examples; confirmation requested.   **NRS**

GD   EXC   RST

130 TUNNEL (1926): O Gauge, steel construction, 90-degree curve, embossed simulated stone portals, hand-painted to represent wooded mountain with five chalet-style houses, waterfall passing under fence, road and snow-capped peak in shades of gray, green, red and yellow, 26″ by 23″ by 14½″ high, portals 4½″ wide by 5½″ high. R. Morris Collection.   **150   300   150**

130L TUNNEL (1927-33): Similar to 130, but lighted.

(A) 1927 only, same size and details as 130; reader confirmation requested.   **160   325   160**

(B) 1928-33, similar to (A), but 24″ by 18½″ by 14½″ high, portals 5″ wide by 6½″ high. R. Morris Collection.   **160   325   160**

140L TUNNEL (1927-32): Standard or O Gauge, steel construction, 90-degree curve, embossed simulated stone portals, hand-painted to represent wooded mountain with seven chalet-style houses, waterfall passing under fence, road and snow-capped peak in shades of gray, green, red and yellow, 37″ by 24½″ by 20″ high, illuminated with one bulb inside each portal.   **200   400   200**

915 TUNNEL (1932-35): Small Standard Gauge, felt composition on wood base, 90-degree curve, hand-painted with trees, shrubs and small houses. Reproduced by Ron Morris.

(A) 1932-33, 65″ by 28½″ by 23½″ high, portals 6¼″ wide by 7¾″ high.   **150   300   150**

(B) 1935, similar to (A), but 60″ by 28¾″ by 20½″ high.   **150   300   150**

(C) Reproduction by Ron Morris.   **NEW 285**

GD   EXC   RST

916 TUNNEL (1932-42): O Gauge, felt composition on wood or corrugated paperboard base, 90-degree curve, hand-painted with trees, shrubs and three chalet-style houses. Reproduced by Ron Morris.

(A) 1932, 37″ by 30½″ by 13½″ high.   **90   180   90**

(B) 1933-42, two white porcelain insulators at forward edge of each portal, 29¼″ by 24″ by 13½″ high. G. Zippie Collection.   **90   180   90**

(C) Reproduction by Ron Morris.   **NEW 145**

923 TUNNEL (1933-42): Standard or O Gauge, felt composition on corrugated paperboard base, 90-degree curve, hand-painted with trees, shrubs and three chalet-style houses, some stamped inside "O G TRACK & STD.", 40¼″ by 23″ by 14¼″ high, portals 7¾″ wide by 8½″ high. Reproduced by Ron Morris.

(A) Original Lionel production.   **100   200   100**

(B) Reproduction by Ron Morris.   **NEW 215**

924 TUNNEL (1935-42): O72 Gauge, similar to 916. Reproduced by Ron Morris.

(A) 1935, 29¼″ by 20½″ by 13½″ high, portals 4¾″ wide by 5⅛″ high.   **90   180   90**

(B) 1936-42, 30⅛″ by 21¼″ by 12¼″ high, portals 4¾″ by 5⅛″ high.   **75   150   75**

(C) Reproduction by Ron Morris.   **NEW 135**

1022 TUNNEL (1935-42): Lionel Jr. and O Gauge, similar to 123, but without house and trees, 18¾″ by 16½″ by 9¼″.   **35   75   35**

1023 TUNNEL (1934-42): Lionel Jr. and O Gauge, felt composition on corrugated paperboard base, 14⅜″ by 10¾″ by 8½″ high, portals 4¼″ wide by 5⅞″ high.   **35   75   35**

CHAPTER IX

Motorization Promises New Excitement

From the introduction of the 77 Crossing Gate in 1923 through 1937, all Lionel action accessories operated by means of a solenoid (see Chapter VI), and their motion was therefore restricted to back-and-forth movement only. The company was already proficient in the production of powerful, reliable electric motors for locomotives, and beginning in 1938 this expertise was applied to creating a series of four sophisticated action toys: the 97 Coal Loader, 164 Log Loader, 165 Magnetic Crane and 313 Bascule Bridge.

A non-reversing motor, smaller than those used in the locomotives but still relatively powerful, was designed for use in these toys. In two of the accessories, the Coal Loader and the Log Loader, it simply applies rotary motion to endless belts, moving the freight from one place to another. The application used in the Crane is much more elaborate, having a complex transmission actuated by a pair of solenoids. The Bascule Bridge mechanism is similarly intricate, employing a worm-drive lifting mechanism and cam-operated leaf switches that maintain power to the motor while shutting off approaching trains to prevent accidents when the bridge is in the up position.

The Coal Loader appeared first, in the 1938 catalogue. It consists of a sheet metal building atop an elevated open structure mounted on a Bakelite (phenolic plastic) base, with an inclined open girder enclosure over a chain-style conveyor belt fitted with tiny buckets. A small motor mounted under the base and fitted with a worm-gear drive turns the conveyor, and the buckets scoop the coal out of a bin and dump them in the storage building at the top. A solenoid opens a gate inside the building to allow the coal to slide down a chute and into a waiting car.

This mechanism is simple and trouble free, requiring only regular lubrication for proper operation. Lionel introduced the Loader at a cost of $5.95, and it was immediately successful. Not only was it the first mass-produced motorized freight mover sold for use with electric trains, it could be purchased with one of the new automatic cars that carried coal and dumped it into the loader's receiving bin by remote control. The play value is immense; young engineers can dump the coal, elevate it into the storage area, then move the train to the opposite side and fill the car with coal again, all by pushing the buttons. (A companion 96 Coal Loader was offered for $2 less and deleted the motorized conveyor belt, substituting a hand crank, but it was much less popular than the automatic version. Least expensive of all was the 98 Coal Bunker introduced a year later, which had no conveyor belt at all. It was the poorest selling of the three coal handlers. By the late 1930s, the Depression had eased enough to allow many purchasers to go first class with the motorized model.)

Motor and transmission from 165 Magnetic Crane. P. Riddle Collection and photograph.

The 164 Log Loader of 1940 is similarly basic, having a pair of endless chains to hoist logs into a holding bin, there to await being rolled into the new automatic log dump cars by solenoid action. Both of these loaders are big and impressive toys, and although the prices were roughly equivalent to the cost of some complete train sets ($7.50 for the Coal Loader and $8.75 for the Log Loader in 1940), the public perceived them as a quality bargain, and many were sold.

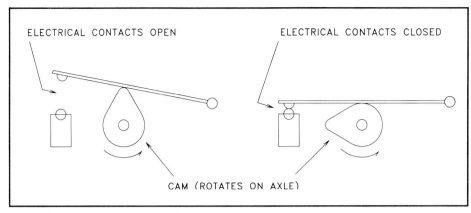

Figure 9-A: Cam and leaf switch mechanism.

Unlike the previous two toys, the 165 Magnetic Crane contains an intricate and extremely versatile mechanism. The motor and transmission are mounted beneath the top plate of an elevated tower, geared to a rotating cab and boom on top. The boom is fitted with a rotating drum and a pulley, over which a miniature rope raises and lowers a hook and electromagnet. The various gears are brought into alignment by the action of two solenoids, allowing the cab to rotate in both directions and the rope to go both up and down, operated by four buttons on the control box. A central control knob turns the magnet on and off, allowing the crane to lift and dump small pieces of scrap metal. Despite this complexity, the Magnetic Crane appeared in 1940 at only $7.95, and the mechanism was adapted after the War for the plastic 182 Magnetic Crane.

Also appearing in the 1940 catalogue was the magnificent 313 Bascule Bridge, a beautiful design that lifts high above model waterways at the touch of a button. Because the bridge span is quite heavy, it requires a strong coil spring to assist the motor in

Motor and transmission from 313 Bascule Bridge. P. Riddle Collection and photograph.

raising it. It employs a worm-gear drive and linkage that pull downward, pivoting the bridge up around a fulcrum. The gearing possesses substantial mechanical advantage, allowing a relatively small motor to exert considerable effort, but the design was faulty in one respect. The constant pressure of the motor and spring cause the Bakelite base to warp, and unless the bridge is mounted on a permanent layout, it can bend or even break. The mechanism was revised slightly after the War to help ease the burden on the base.

The inventor of the Log Loader, Magnetic Crane and Bascule Bridge mechanisms was Henry J. Ferri of Staten Island, New York. Ron Morris reports the patent numbers as follows: Model 164 Log Loader, #2,297,138; Model 165 Magnet Crane, #2,316,680; and Model 313 Bascule Bridge, #2,366,848. Ron also speculates that the mechanism of the bridge would have performed better and lasted longer if the dummy counterweight had actually contained some lead ballast. The author made this modification when restoring one of these toys some years ago, with very positive results.

Even more sophisticated than the mechanism, the electrical connections ensured that once the operator pushed the control button, the bridge would complete its entire up and down cycle without stopping. Furthermore, it could be wired to turn off track power on either side of the bridge to prevent locomotives from trying to cross it when the span was raised. The secret is a set of cam-operated leaf switches.

A cam is simply an oval wheel mounted on an axle, which turns along with the mechanism that lifts the bridge, as shown in the diagram. When the bridge is down, the cam is in the position illustrated at left. Two electrical contacts are kept apart by the lobe of the cam pressing on a flexible leaf switch. When power is applied to start the bridge, the cam begins to rotate as at right, and allows the contacts to close. This completes the circuit to the motor, and causes it to run even if the operator releases the control button. The bridge keeps moving until it has returned to the down position, by which time the cam has turned a full circle and presses on the leaf switch again, cutting off power.

The principle is applied in reverse to stop the trains. When the bridge is down, the train control cam is in the position shown at right, and electrical power travels through the contacts to the track. But when the bridge begins to rise, the cam lifts the switch and shuts off power. (Unlike the design shown in the diagram, this mechanism has a much broader cam lobe that keeps the switch in the "off" position much longer.)

The application of motorization signified a new direction in toymaking, and set the pattern that would characterize many of Lionel's most successful accessories after the War. Further details about the freight handlers may be found in Chapter X, and the Bascule Bridge is described in detail in Chapter XI.

CHAPTER X

Moving the Freight

The introduction of Lionel's first motorized accessory in 1938 represented a fundamental change in philosophy for toy manufacturers, a shift in attitude that would profoundly affect the direction the industry would take in the years that followed the War. Prior to the appearance of the 97 Coal Elevator, the majority of toys depended largely upon the imaginations of their young owners for their success. There were exceptions, most notably construction toys such as Erector and in some respects toy trains themselves, but the things children did with their toys almost always involved fantasy and mental imagery. The Dorfan company produced a motorized crane for railroad use in 1930, but the poor quality of the castings caused them to break easily, and they failed to become popular.

For example, dolls are imperfect representations of human babies, and prior to the battery-operated age, the most sophisticated of them could only drink and wet, close their eyes and cry. It was the mind of the young owner that could visualize their animation and interact with them as if they were alive. Similarly, the things that happened around a real train (passengers boarding and crew members loading and unloading freight) happened only in the imagination of the Lionel operator. Children are adept at creating their own world, in which their toys are manually and mentally assisted in their representation of reality.

A generation or more of children loaded Lionel gondolas and boxcars by hand, and stuffed their stock cars full of toy animals. The miniature people who bought tickets in stations and rode in coaches were placed there by hand, and if a youngster didn't have any little people, imagination sufficed to populate the illusory world. The child of the 1930s could hardly have conceived of a day, less than two decades in the future, when the genius of Lionel and American Flyer designers would turn fantasy into reality with moving milkmen and cattle and passengers and freight of all descriptions.

This revolution in playtime philosophy began on page 39 of Lionel's 1938 catalogue. "At last, Lionel has created an accessory which will actually load model freight cars by remote control!" the text announced. "Imitation coal. . . . is scooped up by a series of buckets traveling on an endless chain. The chain-conveyor lifts the buckets to the top of the building where they are turned upside down, dumping their contents into the loft . . . When the gate is opened, the contents of the loft pour down through a chute into your waiting freight car."

This well-designed toy was the first of many to turn the illusion in a young railroader's mind into reality. All of its functions proceeded without manual intervention. No gargantuan hand was needed to dump the coal into the bin, for Lionel's newly introduced 3659 and 3859 Dump Cars could do it by remote control. The coal (most of it, anyway; a fair amount would spray out on the floor) could be transported by machinery to the storage area, there to await delivery to the next arriving freight car on the opposite side, all at the touch of a button. It was real!

While the illustration in the 1938 catalogue correctly depicts the upper section of this accessory, it is apparent that the design was not final, or that a finished sample was not provided to the artist, in time for delivery to the printer. The base of the Coal Loader is shown as being in one piece, with the receiving bin a part of the main section. Three terminal screws are shown on the side (there are actually five, mounted on top of the base), and the control box resembles that used for the 1121 track switches. The actual 97 Controller has a knob for starting the motor and a push button for opening the delivery gate. The drawing of the 3659 Dump Car, introduced on the same page, is only a rough approximation of the final product, and is shown with a green bin and low mechanism housing instead of the production red bin and high solenoid cover.

The 97 Coal Loader has a separate Bakelite receiving bin hinged to the end of the base. A solenoid is activated when the motor is turned on, and raises the bin to direct the coal toward the buckets. The conveyor

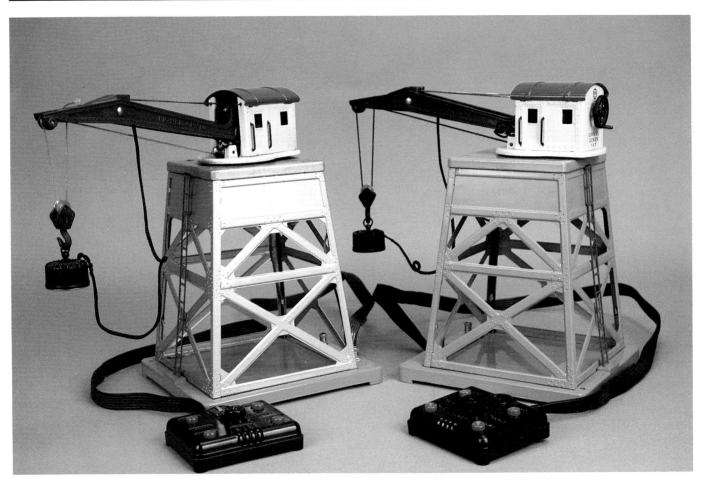

Two 165 Magnetic Cranes, with aluminum-painted (left) and 92 gray structures, showing four-button control boxes. G. Zippie Collection, B. Schwab photograph.

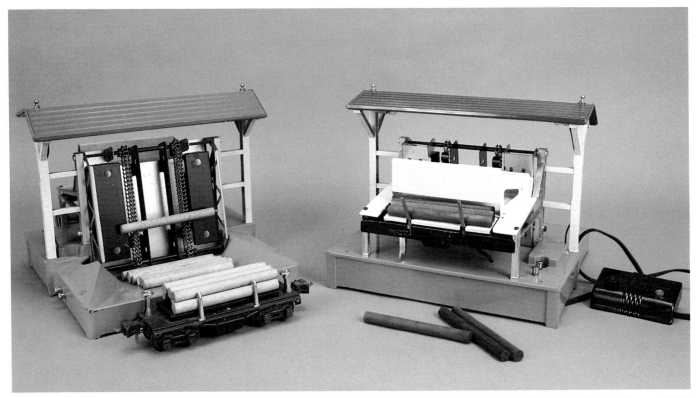

164 Log Loader (right) and orange-roofed 164 Loader from 186 Accessory Set, which included a 3651 Lumber Dump Car and RCS track section. G. Zippie Collection, B. Schwab photograph.

97 Coal Loader. G. Zippie Collection, B. Schwab photograph.

turns inside an open girder column, slanted upward toward the bright yellow loft on top, and the tiny buckets are carried upward and over a pulley arrangement at the top of the column. The coal is held in the loft until another solenoid is activated, opening a gate and dropping the coal down a chute on the side opposite the receiving bin.

Lionel provided this fantastic accessory, complete with a generous sack of imitation coal, for just $5.95, a reasonable sum for such a versatile toy, even before the close of the Great Depression. Even though the price would rise to $7.50 the following year, and increase by yet another dollar in 1941, this captivating plaything

sold in great numbers, encouraging the company to bring out two more motorized freight loaders in 1940.

In order to use all of its features, the Coal Loader must be located between two parallel lengths of straight track, placed approximately 15 inches apart between the center rails. In the instruction sheet, Lionel provided track plans for both O27 and O Gauge to show how the accessory might be placed. These plans require the use of a track switch to create the extra siding. In addition, a remote-control track section is required in front of the receiving bin, in order to make the Dump Car work. Lionel undoubtedly enjoyed extra sales of track products as a result of this arrangement.

The company also packaged the Loader with a Dump Car and remote-control track section at an introductory price of $10.75 (two dollars more the following year) in the 188 Accessory Set.

In 1940 the same technology was applied to create the 164 Log Loader. Its green-painted Bakelite base measures almost a full square foot, and the mechanism rises under a red-painted Bakelite shed roof on top of two columns. A pair of bulbs under the roof illuminate the action. A pair of endless chains propel small semi-circular cradles to lift the logs over a pulley system at the top, where they drop into a sheet metal switch-back receiving bin and come to rest against a pair of hinged upright stakes. A solenoid may be activated to drop the stakes, allowing the logs to fall into a waiting car.

Like the Coal Loader, this accessory must be placed between two tracks 15 inches apart (center to center), and requires a remote-control track section to dump the logs from a 3651 Lumber Car. Lionel offered all three items in an accessory set for $12.25; the Log Loader alone sold for $8.75 in 1940.

Lionel's designers were very busy preparing the 1940 line of accessories. In addition to the huge 313 Bascule Bridge (Chapter XI), the catalogue announced the 165 "Triple-Action Magnetic Crane," the most complex device of its kind ever produced as a toy up to that time. "Totally unlike any other train accessory ever made, this new Lionel model will perform all of the operations of a real crane at the touch of a button. An ingenious remote control motor operates a winch to raise or lower the block and tackle. This same motor by another action revolves the derrick in a complete circle, in either direction. Boom may be raised or lowered by means of a wheel at rear of cab." This 1940 catalogue description was accompanied by a large and accurate drawing of the crane, which was accorded a full page of its own.

Mounted on a tall open-girder platform, the derrick housing and boom are similar to those of the 2660 Work Crane Car. The mechanism (examined in Chapter IX) raises and lowers an electromagnet capable of lifting small pieces of scrap metal. A special control box with four buttons and an on-off knob for the magnet controls all operations. By manipulating the various controls, an operator can pick up a load from trackside, raise and rotate the magnet until it is suspended above a gondola or hopper, and release the load into the car. The action is positive and reasonably trouble free, although frequent lubrication is required to prevent wear of the gear train, a procedure which can only be carried out by detaching the top platform of the elevated structure. It is common for this accessory to be found with dry, worn gears.

Lionel neglected to mention a possible electrical problem inherent in this toy. One of the two wires from the transformer that power the motor is grounded to the metal frame and to the housing of the magnet. This connection must be to the same transformer post as the wire that leads to the outside rails of the track (clip 2 on the Lockon). If not connected in this manner, should the magnet come into contact with any metal parts on a freight car, a short circuit and sparking will result.

The Crane came with a bag of steel scrap and a separate Bakelite receiving bin, but unlike the other two large freight loaders, it was not offered in a set with a car, nor did it require a remote-control track section. Since the crane performed all of the loading and unloading motions alone, no dump car was produced to be used with it, although ingenious children soon learned to place the scrap metal instead of barrels in the 3652 Operating Gondola, introduced the previous year. The 165 Magnetic Crane was priced at an economical $7.95, rising by a dollar in 1941.

Lionel took a giant step forward in promoting the concept of model railroad operation with these three attractive and intriguing accessories. They not only changed the marketing strategy of the company, creating the demand for extra items such as automatic freight cars and track products, they also changed the way in which children conceive of their toys. No longer need a youngster imagine the transfer of products from storage to car and back again; these models actually accomplished the task, in a totally hands-off manner. The remote-control revolution that would dominate the toy market in the years following World War II had begun.

Following are descriptions of known variations of remote-control freight loading accessories produced by Lionel between 1938 and 1942.

GD EXC RST

96 COAL ELEVATOR (1938-40): Rectangular black Bakelite base with hinged coal receiving bin, aluminum-painted tower supporting 1685 cream or yellow loft building, vermilion or light red roof, windows and ladder, black chute at top of tower on side opposite bin, angled girder box enclosing hand-cranked endless chain conveyor with black buckets, solenoid-actuated remote-control dumping mechanism, 11½" long by 6" wide by 12" high, designed to be located between straight tracks located 15" apart (center rail to center rail); operating coal dump car delivers load into bin on one side, receives coal from spout on other side; unmotorized version of 97 Coal Loader.

100 190 90

97 MOTORIZED COAL ELEVATOR (1938-42, Postwar): Similar to 96, but conveyor powered by motor located beneath base, embossed "MADE IN U.S. OF AMERICA / THE LIONEL CORP. N.Y." beside three terminal posts for connecting control box, "COAL ELEVATOR / CONNECT / TO / TRANSFORMER" beside two terminal posts on opposite side.

(A) Black tower, aluminum-painted conveyor enclosure, 1685 cream loft building, light red roof, windows and two-piece ladder. Confirmation requested.

NRS

GD EXC RST

(B) Aluminum-painted tower and conveyor enclosure, yellow loft building, light red roof, windows and two-piece ladder. P. Riddle, G. Zippie and C. Rohlfing Collections. **100 190 90**
(C) 1942, same as (B), but 92 gray tower and conveyor enclosure. D. Ely Collections. **100 190 90**
(D) 92 gray tower and conveyor enclosure, light brown building, orange roof, black windows and two-piece ladder. Confirmation requested. **NRS**

98 COAL BUNKER (1938-40): Similar to 96, but smaller sheet metal base, aluminum plate with black block lettering "No. 98 COAL HOUSE / MADE IN U.S. OF AMERICA" and serif lettering "THE LIONEL CORPORATION, N.Y.", no receiving bin, conveyor or enclosure, 1685 cream house, cream receiving hopper for loading coal manually attached to upper wall of building on side opposite black delivery chute, vermilion or light red roof, windows and ladder, solenoid-actuated remote-control dumping mechanism, requires track on delivery chute side only; identified as "COAL HOUSE" on base, "COAL TIPPLE" on packing box and "ELEVATED COAL STORAGE BUNKER" in 1939 and 1940 catalogues (possibly uncatalogued in 1938). C. Rohlfing and Brueckl Collections.
150 300 135

160 UNLOADING BIN (1938-42, Postwar): Black Bakelite, 8⅜" long, 3¼" wide. **1 2 —**

164 LOG LOADER (1940-42, Postwar): 45N green-painted Bakelite base embossed "No. 164 / LUMBER SHED / MADE IN / U.S. OF AMERICA / THE LIONEL CORP., / NEW YORK", cream die-cast support poles, vermilion or light red roof, nickel finials, girders and posts supporting conveyor mechanism with two endless chains and semi-circular log scoops, cream and black steel delivery bin assembly with two solenoid-actuated stakes to hold or release logs on opposite side, 11¼" long, 10¾" wide, 9" high.

(A) Aluminum-painted mechanism support girders and posts. P. Riddle, D. Ely and C. Weber Collections.
100 190 90
(B) Same as (A), but light red roof. C. Weber Collection.
100 190 90
(C) 1942, same as (B), but 92 gray mechanism support girders and posts. C. Rohlfing Collection.
100 190 90

GD EXC RST

(D) Same as A, but orange roof; came with 186 Accessory Set. G. Zippie Collection. **100 190 90**

165 MAGNETIC CRANE (1940-42, Postwar): 45N green-painted Bakelite base, steel tower, die-cast tower top enclosing motor and gearbox assembly, cream cab (same as 2660) enclosing winding drum, light red roof and ladder, medium green, dark green or olive green Bakelite boom (same as 2660) with string and hook, magnet embossed "CUTLER-HAMMER" hung from hook, manual wheel at back of cab to elevate boom, cab stamped with circular "L" insignia in cream and black above wheel, and in black serif lettering "LIONEL / LINES / 165" below wheel, boom embossed "LIONEL CRANE", base embossed "NO. 165 / REMOTE CONTROL / CRANE", 6½" long, 6" wide, 10" high.

(A) Molded plastic cylinder string support at end of boom, hole for string knot immediately beneath cylinder, another small hole below, nickel inside magnet casing, aluminum-painted tower and top, shiny base. Lemieux Collection. **100 190 90**
(B) Same as (A), but metal pulley at end of boom and single hole for string knot, blued inside magnet casing. P. Riddle, G. Zippie and C. Rohlfing Collections.
100 190 90
(C) 1942, same as (B), but 92 gray tower and top, dull base. G. Zippie and Lemieux Collections.
100 190 90

186 LOG LOADER OUTFIT (1940-41): Set of 164 Log Loader, 3651 Lumber Dump Car, 160 Unloading Bin, RCS Remote Control Track Section, logs, original box required. G. Zippie Collection. **250 450 225**

188 COAL ELEVATOR OUTFIT (1938-41): Set of 97 Coal Loader, 3659X Coal Dump Car, 160 Unloading Bin, RCS Remote Control Track Section, two 206 Sacks of Coal, original box required; "188 Coal Elevator" appears only on the set box. R. Shanfeld Collection.
250 450 225

206 SACK OF COAL (1938-42, postwar): Artificial, approximately ½ lb. **5 10 —**

207 SACK OF COAL (1938-42): Artificial, approximately ¼ lb. **5 10 —**

CHAPTER XI

Bridges

A bridge is more than just a structure of wood or steel spanning a stream or canyon. It is an almost romantic symbol of American life, an image of travel to distant and unexplored places capturing the spirit of adventure inherent in railroading itself. It is probably no accident, therefore, that Lionel's earliest known scenic accessory was a simple overhead truss bridge, designed for use with 2⅞" Gauge trains and offered at least as early as 1902.

313 Bascule Bridge. R. Bartelt Collection, A. Fiterman photograph.

The basic concept of a bridge suggests the need for spanning some sort of gulf, either a waterway or depressed land area. Since the vast majority of Prewar Lionel Trains were played with on a flat floor or table, rather than operated on a scenic layout with submerged details such as rivers, the company helped create the illusion of bridges crossing obstacles by providing some of them with approach ramps to elevate them slightly. A primitive version of this concept was available for even this earliest bridge, a set of twelve cast-iron pillars 8⅜ inches high that could support an entire loop of track. Raising the whole roadbed in this manner might not have been realistic, but it did allow children to place toy boats beneath the bridge, simulating usage in the real world.

Ron Morris suggests that the inspiration for these pillars was the type of structure used to support elevated urban railways (commonly called "Els") in such cities as New York and Chicago. Ron reports that the Hubley company patented and manufactured a clockwork elevated railway in 1896, and that similar toys were made by both Bing and Ives.

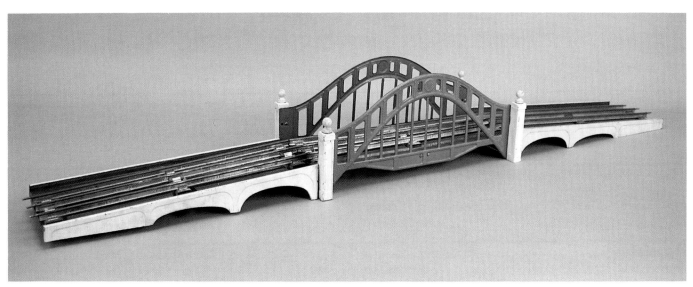

101 Bridge, consisting of 104 Center Span and two 100 Approaches. G. Zippie Collection, B. Schwab photograph.

When the manufacture of 2⅞" Gauge trains was discontinued, to be replaced by the new Standard Gauge models in 1906, Lionel sold only a passenger foot bridge, a design of European origin (probably German) that could span two tracks and had a pair of semaphores and two human figures mounted on top. Two different railroad bridges were listed in the catalogue at different times beginning in 1911, but no examples have been identified, and it is likely they were never made. However, Lionel apparently recognized the appeal of these accessories, since a two-page illustration in the 1915 catalogue promotes Meccano construction toys with an illustration of a Lionel 42 locomotive and three coaches crossing a huge open girder suspension bridge.

The earliest bridges known to be offered for both Standard and O Gauge trains appeared in 1920, and were sufficiently elevated to make the use of approach ramps mandatory. Sets came packaged with one, two or three central spans and two ramps, one for each end, and both the ramps and additional center sections could be purchased separately. The track used on the O Gauge ramps was longer than the standard OS section. These bridges remained available through 1931, and were then replaced by new designs that lie flat on the floor and require no approaches.

The elevated bridges have one undesirable feature: the track tilts upward at a rather severe angle where the approach ramp begins, then returns to horizontal at the center span, only to tilt downward at the opposite end and upward again at the bottom of the far ramp. This causes no problem with trains of the early 1920s, as the locomotives are of box cab design and have high pilots, with plenty of clearance. When steam-outline engines appeared in 1929, however, it was noted that the pilots could and did touch the rails when entering and leaving the ramps. This necessitated the introduction of level bridges, despite the loss in realism for those who operated their trains on a table or the floor.

The early bridges in both gauges were of relatively complex design, featuring four corner posts on the center spans topped by finials and open girder sides painted in contrasting colors. The corner posts were dropped from the 1931 replacements, which now had passenger walkways down each side and nameplates or decals on the sides. Until 1940 only one style was offered in each gauge at any one time, with the exception of the massive 300 Hell Gate design promoted for use with either Standard or O Gauge trains.

The Hell Gate first appeared in 1928, a huge and reasonably faithful representation of the East River landmark in New York City. The stamped-steel sides were cleverly designed to suggest an elevated roadbed, with the heaviest girders forming a raised belt line at the upper level of the tower bases. In fact, the train tracks cross the very bottom of the bridge, allowing the trains to pass through without climbing. Perhaps Lionel designers were already anticipating the production of locomotives incapable of abrupt changes in grade, but it is more likely that approach ramps were considered impractical for a bridge that already measured 28¾ inches in length.

The ends of the Hell Gate are beautifully designed and executed. Tall towers surmount simulated stone bases and contain arched cutouts, complete with imitation iron fencing at the bottoms. A rectangular cornice with ornamental fencing tops each tower. The complex side frames suggest the open girder construction of the prototype, and handrails extend along the outside from end to end.

Toward the latter 1930s, declining sales forecast the end of Standard Gauge production and a concentration upon O Gauge. Lionel brought out new and realistic bridge designs in the smaller size only, which would be continued after the War. The 314 Girder Bridge represents a common type used for short spans across waterways and above roadways in cities. The 315 Trestle (actually an overhead truss bridge, according to Lou Bohn) with its top-mounted and red-capped bulb, and its unlighted companion 316, were similar to open girder structures seen all over North America. Most impressive of all was the first operating lift bridge ever to be produced for model trains, the 313 Bascule Bridge.

"A thousand boys begged us to build it," the 1940 catalogue proclaimed, "a bridge that would open and close by remote control!" The Bascule Bridge featured a Bakelite base and steel girders, pivoting between twin towers and raised and lowered by a motor housed in a peaked roof structure and driving a worm and gear transmission. This building has separate window frame detail, but strangely lacks a door. On the side closest to the lift section, the frame insert is deleted from one window, and the drive rod from the worm gear protrudes through it to the transmission unit inside the base of the tower. This arrangement provides the most obvious clue to identifying Prewar manufacture of this accessory. While the 313 Bascule Bridge was continued through 1950, Postwar units have a revised spring-drive mechanism, which exits the house through a slot in the wall instead of through the window.

This handsome accessory can be used without permanent installation on a layout by means of an alignment frame that extends the full length of the bridge and includes a short section of track at the end of the bridge that rises. A Lockon is attached permanently to this frame to permit connection of track power. Since use of the alignment frame compromises the illusion of open space beneath the bridge, modelers with permanent installations can eliminate its use by securing the receiving track in a fixed location at the end of the bridge. When wired according to the instruction sheet, the Bascule Bridge provides auto-

300 Hell Gate Bridge with original box. G. Zippie Collection, B. Schwab photograph.

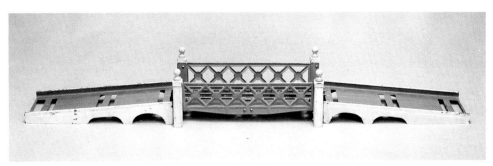

106 Bridge, consisting of 110 Center Span and two 105 Approaches. A. Fiterman photograph.

matic stopping and starting of locomotives, preventing them from trying to enter the span when it is raised. This arrangement and other mechanical details are discussed further in Chapter IX.

While no particular prototype for the 313 Bascule Bridge was specified by Lionel, the design was commonly used in many parts of the United States, and is often referred to simply as a "drawbridge." A drawing of one very similar to Lionel's appears on page 90 of the book *Metropolitan Corridors*, by John R. Stilgoe (New Haven and London, Connecticut: Yale University Press, 1983). Several can also be

viewed just to the east of Interstate Route 93 not far from the center of downtown Boston.

Following are descriptions of known variations of railroad bridges and associated accessories produced by Lionel between 1902 and 1942.

GD EXC RST

26 PASSENGER FOOT BRIDGE (1906-07): Standard Gauge, two sets of steps supporting elevated walkway spanning track, two bases, open grillwork fences, two semaphores at ends of walkway, two miniature figures, 24" long, 17" high, believed to be manufactured in Europe, probably Germany.

NRS

100 BRIDGE APPROACHES (1920-31): Standard Gauge, set of two ramps, steel construction simulating concrete, cream sides, roadbed slotted to receive section of S straight track, used in combination with and gradually elevates track to height of 104 Bridge Center Span, each 14" long, 5½" wide, 2" high at high end of ramp.

(A) Early, lithographed speckled-gray roadbed (simulates gravel).

    10   20   10

(B) Late, light gray roadbed.

    10   20   10

(C) Late, black roadbed.

    10   20   10

(D) 1931-32, made for Ives.

    10   20   10

101 BRIDGE (1920-31): Standard Gauge, set of one 104 Bridge Center Span and one pair of 100 Approaches, 42" combined length.

(A) Early, lithographed speckled-gray roadbed (simulates gravel). P. Riddle Collection.   **30   55   30**

(B) Late, light gray roadbed. G. Zippie Collection.

    30   55   30

(C) Late, black roadbed.   **30   55   30**

(D) 1931-32, made for Ives.   **30   55   30**

102 BRIDGE (1920-31): Standard Gauge, set of two 104 Bridge Center Spans and one pair of 100 Approaches, 56" combined length.

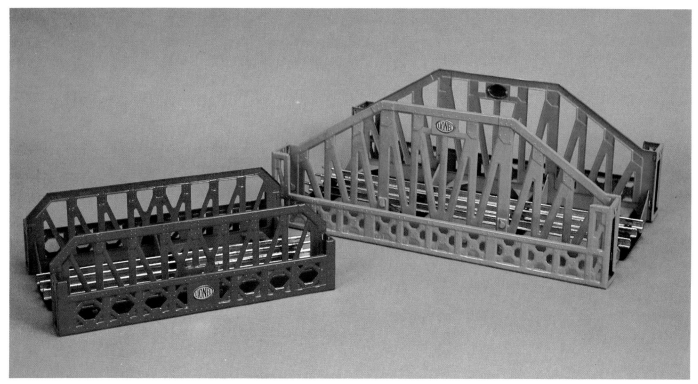

O Gauge 270 (left) and Standard Gauge 280 Bridges. G. Zippie Collection, B. Schwab photograph.

	GD	EXC	RST
(A) Early, lithographed speckled-gray roadbed (simulates gravel).	50	90	50
(B) Late, light gray roadbed.	50	90	50
(C) Late, black roadbed.	50	90	50

103 BRIDGE (1913-15): Standard Gauge, pâpier-maché simulated stone, catalogued but no known examples and believed not manufactured, 28″ long, 6½″ wide. **NRS**

Pea green 280 Bridge with brass plates (left) and 45N green version with nickel plates. G. Zippie Collection, B. Schwab photograph.

314 Girder Bridge. R. Bartelt Collection, A. Fiterman photograph.

	GD	EXC	RST

103 BRIDGE (1920-31): Standard Gauge, set of three 104 Bridge Center Spans and one pair of 100 Approaches, 70″ combined length.

	GD	EXC	RST
(A) Early, lithographed speckled-gray roadbed (simulates roadbed).	70	125	70
(B) Late, light gray roadbed.	70	125	70
(C) Late, black roadbed.	70	125	70

104 BRIDGE CENTER SPAN (1920-31): Standard Gauge, steel, elevated roadbed slotted to receive section of S straight track, pea green suspension-style sides similar to 300 Hellgate Bridge, supported on cream pillars at four corners topped with round wooden finials, assembled with machine screws and bottom brace, used with 100 Approaches, 14″ long, 6½″ wide, 6½″ high.

	GD	EXC	RST
(A) Early, lithographed speckled-gray roadbed (simulates gravel).	20	35	20
(B) Late, light gray roadbed.	20	35	20
(C) Late, black roadbed.	20	35	20
(D) 1931-32, made for Ives.	20	35	20

105 BRIDGE (1911-14): Standard Gauge, wood and pâpier-maché, in five sections each 6″ square, catalogued but no known examples and believed not manufactured. **NRS**

105 BRIDGE APPROACHES (1920-31): O Gauge, set of two ramps, steel simulating concrete, roadbed slotted to receive section of OS straight track, used in combination with and gradually elevates track to height of 110 Bridge Center Span, each 10½″ long, 4½″ wide, 2″ high at high end of ramp.

	GD	EXC	RST
(A) Early, lithographed speckled-gray roadbed (simulates gravel), cream sides.	5	10	5
(B) Late, light gray roadbed, cream sides.	5	10	5
(C) Gray roadbed, light mustard sides.	5	10	5
(D) 1931-32, made for Ives.	10	20	10

106 BRIDGE (1920-31): O Gauge, set of one 110 Bridge Center Span and one pair of 105 Approaches, 31½″ combined length. Lou Bohn reports differences in the lengths of track sections that fit in these bridges and approaches, with at least one example requiring a 10½″ section on the bridge and 10″ sections on the approaches. Reader comments and confirmation are invited.

	GD	EXC	RST
(A) Early, lithographed speckled-gray roadbed (simulates gravel), cream sides and pillars.	20	40	20
(B) Late, light gray roadbed, cream sides and pillars.	20	40	20
(C) Gray roadbed, light mustard sides and pillars.	20	40	20
(D) Gray roadbed, pea green sides, cream pillars. L. Bohn Collection.	20	40	20
(E) 1931-32, made for Ives.	20	50	20

316 Trestle Bridge. R. Bartelt Collection, A. Fiterman photograph.

	GD	EXC	RST

108 BRIDGE (1920-31): O Gauge, set of two 110 Bridge Center Spans and one pair of 105 Approaches, combined length 42".

(A) Early, lithographed speckled-gray roadbed (simulates gravel), cream sides and pillars. **35 70 35**
(B) Late, light gray roadbed, cream sides and pillars. **35 70 35**
(C) Gray roadbed, light mustard sides and pillars. **35 70 35**

109 BRIDGE (1920-31): O Gauge, set of three 110 Bridge Center Spans and one pair of 105 Approaches, combined length 52½" long.

(A) Early, lithographed speckled-gray roadbed (simulates gravel), cream sides and pillars. **50 100 50**
(B) Late, light gray roadbed, cream sides and pillars. **50 100 50**
(C) Gray roadbed, light mustard sides and pillars. **50 100 50**

110 BRIDGE CENTER SPAN (1920-31): O Gauge, steel, elevated roadbed slotted to receive section of OS straight track, pea green latticework sides, supported on pillars at four corners with or without round wooden finials, assembled with machine screws, used with 105 Approaches, 10½" long, 5½" wide, 4" high.

(A) Early, lithographed speckled-gray roadbed (simulates gravel), cream sides and pillars. **15 30 15**
(B) Late, light gray roadbed, cream sides and pillars. **15 30 15**
(C) Gray roadbed, light mustard sides and pillars. **15 30 15**

	GD	EXC	RST

(D) 1931-32, made for Ives. **15 30 15**

270 BRIDGE (1931-42): O Gauge, steel open girder-type construction, pedestrian walkway on each side, elliptical plate or decal lettered "LIONEL" centered near bottom of each side, one section of OS track, 10" long, 6⅜" wide, 3" high.

(A) Maroon, brass plates. **15 30 15**
(B) 1942, vermilion, nickel plates. G. Zippie Collection. **15 30 15**
(C) Probably 1931-34, light red, brass plates with clear lacquer overcoat. L. Bohn Collection. **15 30 15**
(D) Probably 1935-36, same as (C), but nickel plates. Confirmation requested. **NRS**
(E) Probably 1937-40, same as (C), but bright aluminum plates with clear overcoat. C. Rohlfing and L. Bohn Collections. **15 30 15**
(F) Probably 1941-42, same as (E), but aluminum black rubber-stamped plates without clear overcoat. L. Bohn comment. **15 30 15**
(G) Probably late 1941-42 production, cherry red, yellow decals with green "LIONEL" in green ellipse, no slots for plate; difficult to find. Luftkopf Collection. **35 75 15**

271 BRIDGES (1931-33, 1935-40): Set of two 270 Bridges, same colors, combined length 20". **30 60 30**

272 BRIDGES (1931-33, 1935-40): Set of three 270 Bridges, same colors, combined length 30". **45 90 45**

280 BRIDGE (1931-42): Standard Gauge, steel open girder-type construction, pedestrian walkway on each

GD EXC RST

side, elliptical plate lettered "LIONEL" centered near top of each side, one section of S track, 14" long.

(A) 1931-35, gray with pea green portals and walkways, brass plates. **20 35 20**
(B) 1936-42, pea green, brass or nickel plates. G. Zippie Collection. **20 35 20**
(C) Red bridge, brass plates. P. Riddle Collection.
20 35 20
(D) 1939-42, 45N green, nickel plates. G. Zippie Collection.
20 35 20

281 BRIDGES (1931-33, 1935-40): Set of two 280 Bridges, same colors, combined length 28".
40 70 40

282 BRIDGES (1931-33, 1935-40): Set of three 280 Bridges, same colors, combined length 42".
60 105 60

300 HELL GATE BRIDGE (1928-42): Standard Gauge but also promoted for O Gauge, steel construction simulating girder, concrete and stone, suspension-style sides between ornate towers with open archways, flat base to allow table-top use without ramps, railings along pedestrian walkways, elliptical plate centered at top of each side, 28¾" long, 11" wide, 10½" high; reproduced by T-Reproductions and Mike's Train House.

(A) 1928-34, orange base, cream towers, green sides, brass railings and plates. G. Zippie Collection.
400 900 400
(B) 1935-42, red base, ivory towers, aluminum sides, nickel railings and plates. D. Ely Collection.
450 1000 400
(C) 1986-87, reproduction by T-Reproductions, die-stamped on base "T / R", "T / R-NAT", or "T-Reproductions"; 1987 price $295. **— 450 —**
(D) 1987, reproduction by Mike's Train House; issue price $295. **— 450 —**
(E) Same as (A), but terra cotta base. R. Morris comment. **— 450 —**
(F) Same as (B), but black oxide railings and stanchions. R. Morris comment. **— 450 —**

313 OPERATING BASCULE BRIDGE (1940-42, Postwar): 45N green Bakelite base, steel open girder truss bridge and towers, die-cast tower tops, cream building with no door conceals motor and drive mechanism, orange windows, vermilion roof, red R-26 light cap over clear bulb at highest point of bridge, five screw-type terminals on base at forward end of building, cased lifting mechanism beneath tower next to building, heavy coil spring inside opposite tower, black frame with integral power lockon to hold track in alignment in non-permanent installations (often missing but necessary for full value), 23" long bridge, 21½" long base, 10⅛" wide, 9½" high to top of light cap; Postwar mechanism contains revised spring drive, late Postwar (1949-50) light cap is larger.

(A) 1940-41, aluminum-painted bridge. C. Rohlfing Collection. **250 550 250**
(B) 1942, 92 gray bridge. P. Riddle Collection.
250 550 250

314 GIRDER BRIDGE (1940-42, Postwar): Heavy steel base, die-cast sides attached by rivets, rubber-stamped "LIONEL" in black on both sides, small round-cornered rectangle cast in side and lettered "BUILT BY / LIONEL", 10" long, 4½" wide, 1¾" high.

(A) 1940-41, bright aluminum-painted, 9/32" high lettering. C. Rohlfing Collection. **10 20 10**
(B) 1942, 92 gray, 5/16" high lettering (same as 1945-46 version; later postwar versions painted a lighter shade of gray with ⅜" high lettering). P. Riddle Collection. **10 20 10**

315 TRESTLE BRIDGE (1940-42, Postwar): Steel overhead truss-style girder construction, R-26 red light cap over clear bulb centered on top, wire cross braces on top, 24½" long, 4½" wide, 5¾" high.

(A) 1940-41, aluminum-painted. **25 50 25**
(B) 1942, 92 gray. **30 60 25**

316 TRESTLE BRIDGE (1941-42, Postwar): Similar to 315, no light or cross braces, uncatalogued until 1949, 24½" long. Although the 316 was once believed to be of Postwar manufacture only, C. Weber and C. Rohlfing report that the bridge was planned and in fact produced before the War. C. Weber has an aluminum-painted bridge in the original box with a 1941-dated mailing label on it. C. Rohlfing reports a 316 in 92 gray, and believes it was purchased by his parents before the War; nearly all aluminum-painted accessories became 92 gray in 1942. A circular entitled "Lionel Special Promotional Numbers" also implies that a 316 was planned before the War. These facts support the production as an uncatalogued item at least as early as 1941. C. Weber and C. Rohlfing comments.

(A) Aluminum-painted, rubber-stamped on underside "No. 316 BRIDGE / BUILT BY / THE LIONEL CORPORATION / NEW YORK, N.Y. / U.S. OF AMERICA". C. Weber Collection. **25 50 25**
(B) 92 gray, rubber-stamped on bottom "316 TRESTLE BRIDGE". C. Rohlfing Collection.
25 50 25

340 BRIDGE (1902-05): 2⅞" Gauge, black cast-iron construction, very simple overhead truss style with slotted wood ties for strap steel track, 24" long, 6" wide, 10" high. **NRS**

380 TRESTLE PILLARS (1903-05): 2⅞" Gauge, black-enameled cast-iron construction, 6" wide, 8⅜" high, attaches to track with screw and washer; sold in boxes containing one dozen. **NRS**

CHAPTER XII

Technology: Making Everything Work

At the turn of the 20th century, electrification of private homes was still far from universal, being confined primarily to cities and the more heavily populated suburban areas. In addition, various incompatible systems involving direct current, alternating current of differing cycle rates and voltages ranging from 55 to 220 could be found, depending upon locale. In the beginning, electricity was seen primarily as a source of light, and while serviced homes were outfitted with sockets for light bulbs, the concept of plug-in units (such as appliances or table lamps) was still in the future.

This confused situation presented formidable obstacles for manufacturers of electric-powered toys, and varying methods were developed for packaging power sources. Most common was the dry cell, a large and cumbersome unit producing approximately 1½ volts. Such cells were not rechargeable, and were fairly expensive, making their use beyond the means of many purchasers. A set of four cells was sufficient to run a Lionel locomotive, and was listed at $1.20 in the 1902 catalogue, at a time when such a sum represented more than a day's pay for most workers. Alternatively, plunge batteries consisting of glass jars with carbon and zinc terminals embedded in "electric sand" were available at $2.50.

Components to make longer lasting and rechargeable wet cell batteries were sold along with instructions for their use in homes serviced by direct current. These cells could be wired into a lamp socket for charging, as described in the early Lionel catalogues, and consisted of containers fitted with terminal plates into which

Top plate of Lionel A Transformer, showing movable arm and studs for voltage taps. P. Riddle Collection and photograph.

Lionel B Transformer, showing line cord with lamp socket plug. P. Riddle Collection and photograph.

250-watt Model Z TRAINmaster Transformer. P. Riddle Collection and photograph.

water and sulfuric acid were poured. To achieve the proper voltage reduction from the 110-volt line, a light bulb was wired in series with the circuit, and the speed of the train could be adjusted by varying the load rating of the bulb used.

It is difficult today to conceive of employing such an unsafe apparatus in conjunction with a child's toy, but in those years considerable experimentation was required of those who would explore this new technology. It should be remembered that the earliest Lionel trains were promoted primarily as store window displays, and that J. L. Cowen was only just becoming aware of their appeal as toys and the possibility of expanding his market in that direction. The cover of the 1902 catalogue is inscribed "MINIATURE / ELECTRIC / CARS / With full accessories for / WINDOW / DISPLAY / and / HOLIDAY / GIFTS". The word "toy" is not employed. The emphasis suggests that commercial usage rather than the private home market was considered most important.

Batteries, especially the expensive but safer dry cells, remained the primary recommended source of power for Lionel trains through 1905, when the first primitive transformer was introduced, and they stayed in the catalogue (but with ever decreasing emphasis) through 1912. Even after that date, Lionel continued to provide supporting items such as rheostats to provide speed control when used with battery power, although the rapidly expanding network of public power supplies soon made transformers the preferred means of controlling electric toys.

Because their small motors are designed to operate on low voltage as a safety measure, electric trains cannot be connected directly to house power. A transformer is a device that reduces the line voltage available to households by means of a principle called induction. Briefly stated, current is passed through a coil of heavy wire called the "primary" inside the transformer, where it generates both heat and a magnetic field. This field induces a current of lesser voltage in an adjacent and longer coil of wire of lesser thickness (the "secondary"). The relationships between the thickness of the wire and the number of turns in each coil govern the amount of voltage reduction achieved.

A rudimentary type of speed control was realized by providing the secondary coil with a series of connections at various points along its length. According to the point at which the current was tapped from this coil, increasing or decreasing amounts of voltage could be obtained in "steps" of one, two or three volts each. This led to the designation "step-type transformer" that became associated with these devices. A lever on top of the transformer case could be moved over a series of brass studs, each representing a point of connection to the coil, enabling the operator to vary the speed of a locomotive.

Lionel's earliest transformer was shown in the 1906 catalogue, and was adaptable to areas having either 55- or 110-volt alternating current service. The case was made decorative and intended for permanent wall mounting, and the price was a substantial $15. Its promise of eliminating all future battery purchases, however, made the outlay of such a sum

Lionel WX Transformer plate showing 25-cycle designation. These units were produced in the 1930s for such areas as Atlantic Canada where 60-cycle current was not available. P. Riddle Collection and photograph.

Lionel A Transformer showing line cord with wall socket plug, its storage box and cord-mounted storage box cover. P. Riddle *Collection and photograph.*

more practical than extravagant. For areas with direct current, the company replaced the hazardous acid cells with a resistance-type reducer to be used in conjunction with an integrally mounted light bulb. This device sold for $6 in 1907, and improved versions were available as late as 1938 for areas such as parts of New York City where conversion to the more versatile alternating current was delayed.

An improved transformer design was introduced in 1914 at a substantially reduced price: $5 or $7.50, depending upon capacity. These were the first of a series of safe and dependable step-type units (Lionel called them "Multivolt" beginning in 1915) that would be sold until the Second World War. (Ron Morris reports that the output of some early Lionel transformers was as high as 30 and even 45 volts, hardly a safe level for toys meant for children to play with. By the 1920s, the maximum voltage was restricted to 25 volts in even the largst models.)

Standardization in the electric industry was slow to develop, and companies such as Lionel were forced to offer their products with adaptations for a variety of local conditions. In addition to units for direct current, transformers suited to uncommon rates of alternating current were produced for some areas. While 60-cycles-per-second was the most common, 50-cycle and 25-cycle generating plants persisted throughout North America for decades. (While transformers could be built that would operate on all three systems, they produced the least voltage when used in the prevalent 60-cycle systems, and it was more efficient to manufacture these accessories in separate versions tailored to individual markets. The 25-cycle transformers can be connected safely to 60-cycle lines, but the reverse is not true; 60-cycle units will overheat on a 25-cycle line.) Furthermore, only newer homes were being equipped with the recently developed wall plugs for portable lamps and other electrical appliances, and for many

168 Magic Electrol Controller, back plate and inside view, showing rectifier disk. P. Riddle Collection and photograph.

years Lionel transformers were equipped with screw-in plugs for attachment to lamp sockets, as shown in the photograph.

The advent of the wall plug was a significant advance, forecasting the widespread use of portable appliances throughout a household. Lionel took special care in packaging them, to prevent damage to the breakable plug housing and to reduce the possibility of bending the prongs. A special wooden box was provided with some models, with the line cord inserted through a hole in the box lid, supposedly to encourage storage of the plug in its box when the transformer was not in use.

Although much safer than the exposed wet cells of the early years, Lionel Multivolt transformers had no built-in protection against short circuits. If children left the units operating while faulty connections or derailed trains shorted out their terminals, excessive heat was generated and fires could result. Beginning in 1932 an external circuit breaker was offered, intended to be wired between the transformer and the track. This unit would interrupt the current in the presence of a short circuit, preventing the possibility of overheating, but since their use was not mandatory, and the circuit breaker was an unexciting accessory unlikely to be requested by young engineers, many layouts went unprotected until the introduction of

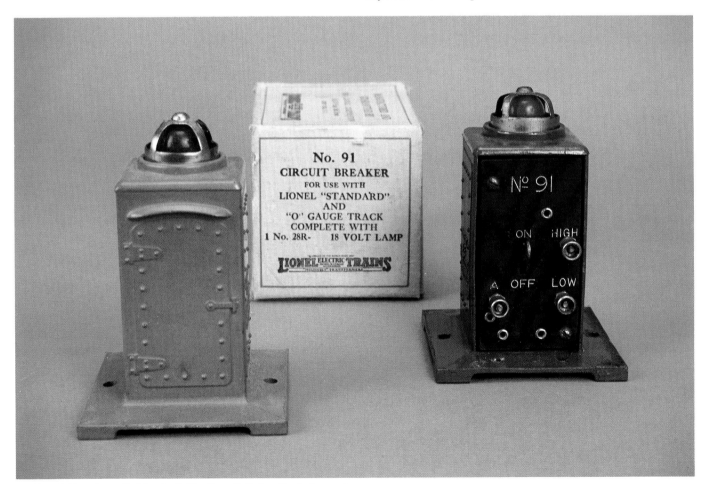

91 Circuit Breaker. G. Zippie Collection, B. Schwab photograph.

Lionel Bild-a-Motor No. 1 for O Gauge (left) and No. 2 for Standard Gauge. G. Barnet Collection, B. Schwab photograph.

such transformers as the "TRAINmaster" series (see below) in the late 1930s.

Multivolt transformers delivered manageable amounts of voltage for running trains, accessories and lights, and had but one major drawback. When the control arm was moved from stud to stud to increase voltage, there was a momentary loss of contact and a slight interruption of power to the track. This produced no ill effects until the introduction of automatic reverse units in the mid-1920s.

The Ives Corporation developed the first remote-control reverse unit in 1925, an ingenious device that allowed a locomotive to move forward or backward, and even stand in neutral with its lights still burning. This sequence was achieved by use of a revolving drum, against which tiny brass fingers made and broke electrical contact to reverse direction of current through the motor field to the brushes and commutator. A solenoid rotated the

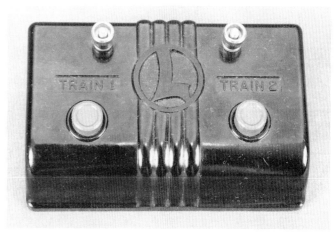

168 Magic Electrol Controller, front view. P. Riddle Collection and photograph.

drum, advancing it to the next position each time power to the track was interrupted and reestablished.

Since the Ives device was patented, Lionel quickly developed a competing but inferior design that allowed forward and reverse travel but lacked the neutral position. Because it was also actuated by interruptions in power flow, the step transformers caused it to trip every time an operator attempted to increase or decrease speed. To counteract this problem, Lionel produced rheostat control devices (like the earlier battery rheostats) which could be wired between the transformer and the track. These units consist of a coil of resistance wire similar to the secondary coil of the transformer, against which a metal contact slides. Depending upon the position of this contact, these devices tap into the coil to deliver varying amounts of voltage without interruption, preventing the solenoid in the reverse unit from moving.

Lionel continued to offer step-type transformers with external rheostats long after other manufacturers (notably American Flyer and the Jefferson Manufacturing Company) had combined the two in a single case. Instead of employing a separate coil, the speed control arm in these transformers simply wiped across the secondary coil. They were both cheaper to build and more efficient, as less heat was generated by the single coil and more current was available for operating the trains. According to Ron Morris, the term "rheostat" is not technically correct when applied to transformers with secondary coil wipers, but Lionel used that term in catalogue descriptions.

Lionel finally offered low-powered transformers with integral rheostats in the latter 1930s, but it was not until 1939 that the company produced the first of a modern series of powerful and versatile units, some capable of handling as many as four trains with ease. Housed in steel cases and fitted with up to four separate rheostats, these TRAINmaster transformers provide pinpoint control of large layouts with a minimum of wiring and a high degree of safety and convenience. Built-in circuit breakers afford protection against inadvertent short circuits, and high wattage ratings, as much as 250 for the Z model, allow multi-train operation from a single control device. TRAINmasters were continued briefly after the War, and then developed into a similar but superior line (RW, KW, ZW) incorporating both whistle and directional controls.

In 1940 a few locomotive models were offered with a special remote-control reversing mechanism called Magic Electrol. Unlike the standard E-unit, which reversed the motor at any interruption of the current, Magic Electrol was a relay-operated device that responded to a small amount of DC current super-imposed upon the AC track power. The company used this device to allow the independent reversing of two locomotives on one track, as exemplified by their set No. 1061, first offered in 1940. This set contains two complete trains, a 1666 Locomotive with three passenger cars and a 1663 Magic Electrol Switcher with three freight cars. The 1666 has a conventional E-unit.

With this set came the interesting 168 Controller. The author's example, obtained with a complete two-train set from Gordon Bosworth at the York TCA meet in October of 1992, looks very much like the control box of a 1019 Remote Control Track section. However, it has two screw-type terminals, and the buttons are labeled "Train 1" and "Train 2" instead of "Uncouple" and "Unload" as on the 1019 box. This controller is wired into the circuit between the transformer and the track, and contains a rectifier disk, similar to the ones in whistle controllers. One button interrupts the track current and operates the E-unit in the 1666, while the other imposes the DC current to operate the relay in the 1663. In this manner, the reverse units in the two locomotives operate independently of each other.

Early Lionel catalogues displayed a line of "New Departure" motors and accompanying accessories, including pulley systems (referred to as "countershafting") for powering various types of toys, as well as one of the earliest electric fans every marketed. These were joined by the improved "Peerless" motors in 1915, and in 1928 by Bild-a-Motor units which were designed for easy screwdriver assembly, and were included in a few locomotives.

Throughout the Prewar years, Lionel offered train-related hardware such as car lighting kits, remote-control whistle and reverse actuators, wiring aids (Lockons and Contactors), tubes of lubricant and replacement light bulbs. As the trains became more sophisticated, some were supplanted by built-in units. Passenger cars were provided with internal lighting at the factory, and as early as 1938, a transformer with a built-in whistle controller came with some low-priced sets. While less glamorous than the signals and buildings that were featured prominently in the catalogue, these items were essential to efficient operations in Lionelville, and the company paid proper attention to producing quality items to fill every need.

Following are descriptions of the technology-oriented accessories produced by Lionel between 1901 and 1942. Transformers are listed in a separate section following miscellaneous devices.

GD EXC RST

NO NUMBER WHISTLE DEMONSTRATOR (1935): Plywood box painted light yellow, red art deco lettering "A REAL WHISTLE BY LIONEL" on side, rectangular opening to right of lettering, large sideways T-shaped opening on rear, O Gauge track and rubber roadbed mounted on top, wooden bumper at

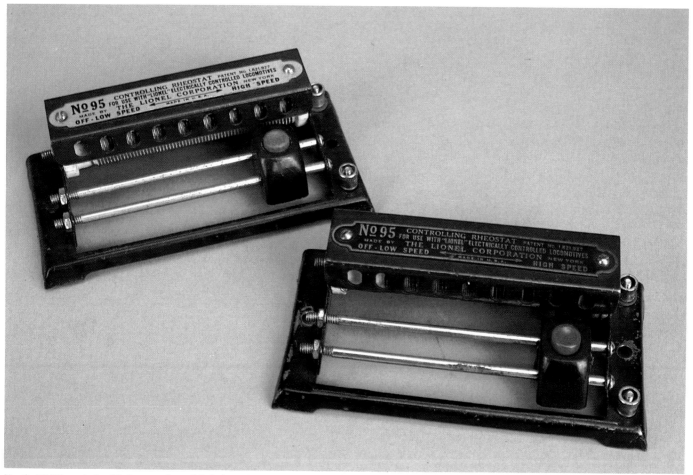

Early 95 Rheostat with brass plate (right) and later version with nickel plate. G. Zippie Collection, B. Schwab photograph.

GD   EXC   RST

right end, two wires soldered to track, 18" long, 4" wide, 4¼" high; special dealer promotional device. Reader information requested. Anderson Collection.   **NRS**

A MINIATURE MOTOR (1904): 2⅞" long, 2⅞" wide, 2¼" high.   **50   100   50**

B NEW DEPARTURE MOTOR (1906-16): 3¼" long, 3" wide, 2" high.   **50   100   50**

C NEW DEPARTURE MOTOR (1906-16): Similar to B, wound to operate on single or double cell battery power.   **50   100   50**

D NEW DEPARTURE MOTOR (1906-16): Similar to B, on-off switch, reversing device, maroon base and winding cover, chrome ends, eyelet on top, decal lettered "NEW DEPARTURE / TYPE D", 3⁵⁄₁₆" high. D. Ely Collection.   **50   100   50**

E NEW DEPARTURE MOTOR (1906-16): Similar to B, two speeds.   **50   100   50**

F NEW DEPARTURE MOTOR (1906-16): Similar to B, two speeds, reversing device.   **50   100   50**

G FAN MOTOR (1909-14): Battery-powered, similar to (B) with fan blades, mounted on elevated stand.
    50   100   50

GD   EXC   RST

K SEWING MACHINE MOTOR (1904-06): Reader information requested.   **50   100   50**

L SEWING MACHINE MOTOR (1905): Reader information requested.   **50   100   50**

M PEERLESS MOTOR (1915-20): Battery-powered, single speed, non-reversing.
    50   100   50

OTC LOCKON (1923-36): O Gauge, fiber clip-on device with two wiring terminals, supplies power to middle rail and ground connection to outer rail of track.
    —   1   —

R PEERLESS MOTOR (1915-20): Battery-powered with reversing device, black base 4⅝" long and 2⁵⁄₁₆" wide, red fiberboard reverse switch, drives 2" brass gear on axle with wide belt-drive spool on opposite end, additional ⁷⁄₁₆" slotted drive wheel permits two-speed operation, 1⅜"-long and ⅜"-wide brass plate with sans-serif lettering "PEERLESS BATTERY MOTOR / TYPE "R" / THE LIONEL MANUFACTURING COMPANY / NEW YORK", packaged in dark gray box with silver rubber-stamped lettering on one end "PEERLESS / BATTERY MOTOR / TYPE R / MADE BY / THE LIONEL MANUFACTURING CO. / NEW YORK", with original sales slip from "Central Electric

GD EXC RST

& Lock Co. / 13 N. Thirteenth St. / Philadelphia, PA" dated "1 / 22 / 1916" suggesting 1915 year of manufacture; similar to motor in four-wheel U-frame 33 Locomotive. D. Ely Collection. **35 75 35**

STC LOCKON (1923-36): Standard Gauge, fiber clip-on device with two wiring terminals, supplies power to middle rail and ground connection to outer rail of track. **— 1 —**

UTC LOCKON (1936-42): Universal, fiber clip-on device with two wiring terminals, two-way locking lever clamps to either Standard Gauge or O Gauge track (also O27, O72), supplies power to middle rail and ground connection to outer rail of track.

1 2 —

Y PEERLESS MOTOR (1915-20): Battery-powered, three-speed, reversing device. **40 80 40**

1 BILD-A-MOTOR (1928-29): O Gauge, reported as single speed, non-reversing. The 1928 and 1929 catalogues claim reverse capability, and show a reverse lever in the illustration. Confirmation requested.

60 125 60

1 BILD-A-MOTOR (1930-31): O Gauge, similar to above, three-speed gear mechanism and reversing device, nickel-plated sides, red or black base and trim on main pulley wheel, 5½" long, 3" wide, 3" high, one example packaged in two-piece box with 2¼"-wide and 3"-high white label lettered "No. 1 / 'BILD-A-MOTOR' / TRADE-MARK PATENTS PENDING" with illustration and additional description, rubber-stamped "11-83T" on cover. D. Ely comment. G. Barnett Collection.

60 125 60

2 BILD-A-MOTOR (1928-29): Standard Gauge, similar to 1, red or black base, 7" long, 3⅝" wide, 4" high, reported as single speed, non-reversing. The 1928 and 1929 catalogues claim reverse capability, and show a reverse lever in the illustration. Confirmation requested. **60 125 60**

2 BILD-A-MOTOR (1930-31): Standard Gauge, similar to above, three-speed gear mechanism and reversing device. G. Barnett Collection.

60 125 60

2 COUNTERSHAFT (1904-11): Shaft and three-pulley mechanism, 11½" long, 4" wide, 7½" high. **NRS**

20 DIRECT CURRENT REDUCER (1906): Speed regulator with on-off switch. **NRS**

27 LIGHTING SET (1911-23): Three sockets, 3½-volt bulbs and contacts, 5' flexible wire, for battery or DC operation; used to light car interiors.

10 20 10

41 CONTACTOR (1936-42): Pressure-operated single-pole, single-throw (SPST) switch; fits below track ties to activate accessories. **5 10 —**

43/043 BILD-A-MOTOR GEAR SET (1929): Converts Standard Gauge (43) or O Gauge (043) Bild-A-

GD EXC RST

Loco into a Bild-A- Motor; packaged in 58 Lamp Post box with overpasted labels on ends. D. Ely Collection.

30 60 —

65 WHISTLE CONTROLLER (1935): Black steel box, four terminal posts, three red buttons, black-bordered nickel plate with black block lettering "TRANSFORMER" and "TRACK" above serif lettering "No. 65 WHISTLE CONTROLLER / MADE IN U.S. OF AMERICA PAT PEND. / THE LIONEL CORPORATION, N.Y." followed by operating instructions in block lettering, two slanted L-shaped internal brackets (66 and 67 are straight), brown-painted Mallory rectifier disk with thin bolt and stamped "Pat. 164974 ET AL", small rectangular transformer casing with round coil covered with black wire, 3⅜" long, 2¾" wide, 2½" high; came in train sets with whistle tenders and with whistle tenders packaged for separate sale. C. Rohlfing Collection.

5 10 5

66 WHISTLE CONTROLLER (1936-38): Black steel box, four terminal posts, three red buttons, black-bordered nickel plate with black block lettering "CONNECT THESE 2 / POSTS TO TRANSFORMER" and "CONNECT THESE 2 / POSTS TO TRACK" above serif lettering "WHISTLE CONTROLLER No. 66" with the "o" in "No." spaced up and underscored, and block lettering "FOR ALTERNATING CURRENT ONLY / MADE IN U.S. OF AMERICA BY THE LIONEL CORPORATION, N.Y. / PATENTS PENDING", followed by operating instructions (more detailed than 65), two galvanized L-shaped mounting brackets wrapped with asbestos-insulated fine wire inside, two black-painted squares stamped "MALLORY / TYPE 65 / MADE IN U.S.A / PAT. 1649741 ET AL" around edges and small "R" in upper right corner, enclosing two rectifier disks and secured with large central bolt, small square transformer coil wound with maroon wire, 3⅜" long, 2¾" wide, 2⅞" high; differs considerably from 167 components. P. Riddle and R. LaVoie Collections.

5 10 5

67 WHISTLE CONTROLLER (1936-38): Same as 66 except for number; internal components appear identical. The 67 may possibly produce greater voltage than 66, as the 1936 and 1937 catalogues list the former with Standard Gauge sets and the latter with O Gauge sets. Reader confirmation requested. P. Riddle Collection. **5 10 5**

81 RHEOSTAT (1927-33): Black steel frame with two terminal posts, green steel cover with brass plate enclosing ceramic core wrapped with resistance wire grounded to frame, circuit completed through spring steel slide contacting wire coil at any point along its length, on-off switch on slide; designed to accommodate up to 18 volts AC; also made for Ives under catalogue No. 1894. L. Bohn comment. P. Riddle and Weisblum Collections. **5 10 5**

GD EXC RST

88 BATTERY RHEOSTAT (1915-27): Similar to 81, designed to accommodate up to 12 volts DC. P. Riddle Collection.   **5   10   5**

88 DIRECTION CONTROLLER (1933-42): Black steel case, red normally-on push button, used for momentary current interruption to actuate remote-control reverse units in locomotives.   **1   2   —**

91 CIRCUIT BREAKER (1930-42): Die-cast base, brass or nickel cap over red bulb; to be wired between transformer and track to provide protection against short circuits.

(A) Early, mojave base, brass light cover, two terminals. G. Zippie Collection.   **10   20   10**
(B) Late, State brown base, nickel light cover, three terminals. L. Bohn and D. Ely Collections.
                              10   20   10
(C) Same as (A), but State brown base.
                              10   20   10
(D) 1931-32, made for Ives under catalogue No. 1877.
                              20   45   10

95 RHEOSTAT (1934-42): Similar to 81, but with red push button instead of on-off toggle switch on slide,

GD EXC RST

used for momentary current interruption to actuate three-position remote-control reverse (E-unit).

(A) Black frame, dark green cover, brass plate. P. Riddle and G. Zippie Collections.
                              —   5   105
(B) Same as (A), but nickel plate. G. Zippie Collection.
                              5   10   5

106 AC REDUCER (1909-14): 110-volt AC, click-step speed control.   **5   10   5**

106 RHEOSTAT (1911-14): Step-type, 110- or 220-volt.   **5   10   5**

107 DC REDUCER (1911-38): 220 (1911-13 only) or 110 volts, four porcelain tubes wound with resistance wire enclosed and ventilated by perforated and asbestos-lined steel cover, steel base, sliding lever to tap current from coils, supplied with four porcelain supports and screws for mounting on wall or table, used instead of transformer in areas (such as parts of New York City) that supplied Direct Current household electricity; generated considerable heat. L. Bohn comment.

(A) 110-volt. Weisblum Collection.   **NRS**

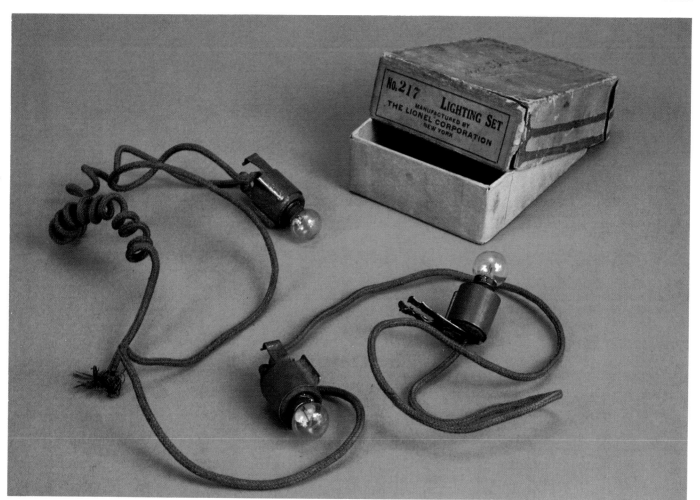

217 Car Lighting Kit. G. Zippie Collection, B. Schwab photograph.

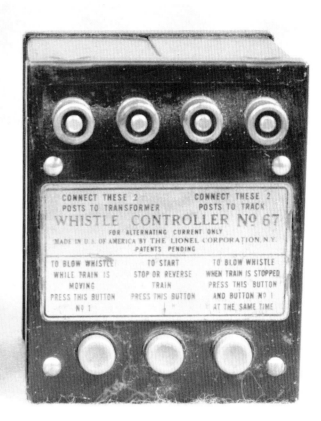

Left to right: No. 66 and 67 Whistle controllers.

GD EXC RST

(B) 220-volt. **NRS**

(E) 1931-32, made for Ives under catalogue No. 1893.

5 10 —

108 BATTERY RHEOSTAT (1912-14): Rotary design. **NRS**

111 BULB ASSORTMENT (1920-31): Boxed set of fifty or (later) seventy assorted 12- and 18-volt replacement bulbs.

(A) Early, wooden box, wooden bulb containers. R. Morris Collection. **50 100 —**
(B) Later, light yellow cardboard box, cardboard bulb containers. R. Morris Collection. **50 100 —**

153C BLOCK CONTROL CONTACTOR (1941-42, Postwar): Pressure-operated single-pole, double-throw (SPDT) switch; fits below track ties to control lights on 153 Block Signal and to activate insulated blocks of track for two-train operation.

10 25 10

159C BLOCK CONTROL CONTACTOR SET (1940-42): Pressure-operated single-pole, double-throw (SPDT) switch, lockon, two fiber pins; fits below track ties to control lights on Block Signal and to activate insulated blocks of track for two-train operation; similar to 153C. **10 25 10**

GD EXC RST

160 AC REDUCER (1909-14): 220-volt AC. **NRS**

166 WHISTLE CONTROLLER (1938-39): Externally similar to 66, but nickel plate with more condensed sans-serif lettering, copper-oxide selenium rectifier disk mounted with speed clip to rivet and insulating Bakelite washer on wide metal bar instead of L-shaped bracket, asbestos-insulated wire coil mounted on lower bar surface, L-shaped bracket holding small square transformer winding as in 66; represents evolutionary development and improvement of whistle control devices culminating in superior two-button design (167) and finally transformer-mounted controls. P. Riddle, R. LaVoie and C. Rohlfing Collections. **5 10 5**

167 WHISTLE AND DIRECTION CONTROLLER (1939-42, Postwar): Black Bakelite case, two maroon buttons separated by protrusion on case, "WHISTLE" on left and "REVERSE" on right, copper-oxide rectifier disk mounted on flanged steel bottom plate by speed clip, asbestos insulation with four turns of wire on plate, square transformer housing wrapped with green wire, 3⅞" wide, 3¼" deep, 1¼" high. Postwar version has flangeless bottom plate, no protrusion between buttons, rectifier disk mounted on Bakelite washer concealed beneath metal plate, five turns of wire around asbestos

	GD	**EXC**	**RST**

insulation, black transformer windings, rubber-stamped "J. B." on metal plate. P. Riddle and R. LaVoie Collections. **5 10 5**

167X WHISTLE AND DIRECTION CONTROLLER (1940-42): Similar to 167, but for OO Gauge.
5 10 5

168 MAGIC ELECTROL CONTROLLER (1940-42): Bakelite box with two push buttons, to actuate reverse mechanisms in two-train Magic Electrol set.
(A) Case similar to 167 Whistle Controller.
15 30 15
(B) Case similar to control box of 1019 remote-control track section. P. Riddle Collection. **15 30 15**

169 DIRECTION CONTROLLER (1940-42): Steel case, two buttons for reversing Magic Electrol and uncoupling Teledyne train sets. **15 30 15**

170 DC REDUCER (1914-38): Similar to 107, 220 volts, resistance coil with slide tap, used instead of transformer in areas (such as parts of New York City) that supplied Direct Current household electricity; generated considerable heat. L. Bohn comment.
NRS

171 DC TO AC INVERTER (1936-42): Variable voltage switch, on-off switch, four fixed voltage binding posts, 115-volt DC input, 2- to 30-volt AC output. L. Bohn comment. **3 5 3**

172 DC TO AC INVERTER (1939-42): Same as 171, but 220- volt DC input. L. Bohn comment.
3 5 3

217 LIGHTING SET (1914-23): Three wooden sockets, 14-volt bulbs and nickel clamps, green cloth-covered wire, for AC operation; used to light car interiors. G. Zippie Collection. **10 20 10**

270 LIGHTING SET (1915-23): Two sockets and 8-volt bulbs, 3' flexible wire, for battery or DC operation; used to light car interiors. **10 20 10**

271 LIGHTING SET (1915-23): Similar to 270, but with two 14-volt bulbs, for AC operation.
10 20 10

301 DRY CELLS (1901-05): Set of four, with wire.
NRS

302 PLUNGE BATTERY (1902): Reader information requested. **NRS**

303 CARBON CYLINDER (1902): Reader information requested. **NRS**

304 COMPOSITE ZINC (1902): Reader information requested. **NRS**

305 ELECTRIC SAND (1902): Reader information requested. **NRS**

306 GLASS JAR (1902): Reader information requested. **NRS**

370 WET CELL BATTERIES (1902-03): Set of two.
NRS

439 PANEL BOARD (1928-42): Rectangular frame with curved shoulders at base (similar to 440C Panel Board described in Chapter IV), stamped-steel construction, black simulated marble composition panel board fitted with six knife switches with black Bakelite handles embossed "L" on each side, two simulated meters with nickel rims, space for two switch controllers with or without pre-drilled holes on frame below simulated marble panel, arched sheet steel extension at top of frame with hooded central socket and bulb, flanked by identification plates, plate near bottom of base lettered "MADE BY / THE LIONEL CORPORATION / NEW YORK", 7$\frac{3}{16}$" wide, 8$\frac{3}{16}$" high; designed by Joseph Bonanno to include working voltmeter and ammeter, but deleted for economy.

(A) 1928-42, crackle red frame, white marble composition panel board, brass switches, meter rims, lamp hood, and identification plates. **50 100 50**
(B) 1935, same as (A), but black panel board.
50 100 50
(C) Same as (A), but aluminum-painted panel board. J. Flynn comment. D. Ely Collection. **50 100 50**
(D) Similar to (A), but bright red frame, black panel board, nickel switches, meter rims, lamp hood and plates. D. Ely Collection. **50 100 50**
(E) Similar to (A), but maroon frame.
50 100 50
(F) Similar to (A), but crackle maroon frame.
50 100 50
(G) 1932, made for Ives under catalogue No. 1901.
50 100 50

925 LUBRICANT (1935-42, Postwar): Petroleum-based lubricant, two ounces. **1 3 —**

926 LUBRICANT (1942): Much smaller tube than 925. **1 2 —**

TRANSFORMERS

Cases were constructed of cast iron through 1921 and steel thereafter, except for TRAINmaster models, which are housed in Bakelite cases.

A (1916, 1921-37): Multivolt, 60-cycle, stepped voltage output.

	GD	**EXC**	**RST**
(A) 1921-31, 40-watt.	5	10	5
(B) 1931-37, 60-watt.	5	10	5

B (1916-38): Multivolt, 60-cycle, stepped voltage output.

	GD	**EXC**	**RST**
(A) 1916-17, 50-watt.	5	10	5
(B) 1917-21, 75-watt.	5	10	5
(C) 1921-31, 50-watt.	5	10	5
(D) 1932-38, 75-watt.	5	10	5

	GD	EXC	RST

C (1922-31): Multivolt, 75-watt, 25- to 40-cycle, stepped voltage output. **5 10 5**

F (1931-37): Multivolt, 40-watt, 25- to 40-cycle, stepped voltage output. **5 10 5**

H (1938-39): Multivolt, 75-watt, 25- to 40-cycle, stepped voltage output. **5 10 5**

J: Multivolt, stepped voltage output, universal 90- to 250-volt, 40- to 133-cycle, intended to be adapted to varying locales prior to delivery; announced but not manufactured. Instruction sheets were printed; L. Bohn reports them in English, French and Spanish. **NRS**

K (1913-38): Multivolt, 60-cycle, stepped voltage output.
(A) 1913-17, 150-watt, 29-volt output, slate top. **10 20 10**
(B) 1917-21, 200-watt. **10 20 10**
(C) 1921-38, 150-watt, brass plate. C. Rohlfing Collection. **15 25 15**
(D) Same as (C), but nickel plate. **15 25 15**

L (1913-16): Six fixed voltage taps, 75-watt, 60-cycle. **2 5 2**

L (1933-38): Multivolt, 50-watt, 60-cycle, stepped voltage output. **5 10 5**

N (1941-42): Multivolt, 50-watt, 60-cycle, stepped voltage output. **2 5 2**

Q (1914-15): Three fixed voltage taps, 50-watt, 60-cycle. **2 5 2**

Q (1938-42, Postwar): TRAINmaster, continuous dial rheostat (secondary winding wiper), 75-watt, 60-cycle. **10 20 10**

R (1938-42, Postwar): TRAINmaster, two continuous dial rheostats (secondary winding wipers), 100-watt, 60-cycle. **20 35 20**

S (1914-17): Multivolt, 50-watt, 60-cycle, stepped voltage output. **5 10 5**

S (1938-42, Postwar): TRAINmaster, continuous dial rheostat (secondary winding wiper), whistle and direction controls, 80-watt, 60-cycle. **10 20 10**

T (1919-28): Multivolt, 60-cycle, stepped voltage output.
(A) 1914-17, 75-watt. **5 10 5**
(B) 1917-21, 150-watt. **10 15 10**
(C) 1921-22, 110-watt. **5 10 5**
(D) 1922-28, 100-watt, brass plate, control arm, binding posts and nuts, cloth-covered line cord. **5 10 5**

(E) Same as (D), but nickel plate, control arm, binding posts and nuts, rubber-covered line cord. **5 10 5**

U (1932-33): "ALLADIN", 50-watt, 60-cycle, stepped voltage output; also made for Ives under catalogue No. Y. **5 10 5**

V (1938-42, Postwar): TRAINmaster, four continuous dial rheostats (secondary winding wipers), 150-watt, 60- cycle. **30 60 30**

W (1933-42): Multivolt, 75-watt, 60-cycle, stepped voltage output; also made for Ives. **5 10 5**

WX (1933-42): Multivolt, 75-watt, 25-cycle, stepped voltage output. **5 10 5**

Y (1932-33?): 50-watt, 60-cycle, stepped voltage output; also made for Ives, same as U. **5 10 5**

Z (1938-42): TRAINmaster, four continuous dial rheostats (secondary winding wipers), 250-watt, 60-cycle. **55 100 55**

1012 (1931-33): "WINNER" transformer in lithographed station (see Chapter V). **20 35 15**

1017 (1932-33): "WINNER" transformer in lithographed station (see Chapter V). **15 30 15**

1027 (1933-34): Lionel Junior transformer in lithographed station (see Chapter V). **15 30 15**

1028 (1935): Lionel Junior transformer in lithographed station (see Chapter V). **15 30 15**

1029 (1935-39): Continuous lever rheostat (secondary winding wiper), 25-watt, 60-cycle. **3 5 3**

1030 (1935-38): Continuous lever rheostat (secondary winding wiper), whistle control, 40-watt, 60-cycle. **5 10 5**

1037 (1940-42): Continuous lever rheostat (secondary winding wiper), 40-watt, 60-cycle. **3 5 3**

1038 (c. 1940, uncatalogued): Continuous lever rheostat (secondary winding wiper), 30-watt, 60-cycle. **3 5 3**

1039 (1937-40): Continuous lever rheostat (secondary winding wiper), 35-watt, 60-cycle. **5 10 5**

1040 (1937-39): Continuous lever rheostat (secondary winding wiper), whistle control, 60-watt, 60-cycle. **5 10 5**

1041 (1939-42, Postwar): Continuous lever rheostat (secondary winding wiper), whistle control, 60-watt, 60-cycle. **5 10 5**

CHAPTER XIII

Trackwork

An intelligently planned and convenient system of trackwork, while neither glamorous nor exciting, is basic to the success of any line of toy trains. It must provide the flexibility to create interesting layouts, the durability to withstand repeated assembly, and accurate and consistent alignment to keep the trains from derailing.

Lionel's earliest track, a two-rail design in 2⅞" Gauge, can best be described as primitive. It consists of rails made from thin metal straps that fit into slotted wooden ties, which were originally connected by brass plates mounted on some of the ties. The design was improved in 1902, when the strap rails were bent to be

joined by means of right-angle tab and slot extensions at the ends. Two lengths of rail were made, 15 inches and 13 inches; for a curved track section, the longer length forms the outside rail while the shorter one is used inside, and two equal length straps can be paired for a straight section. Beginning in 1902, switches and a 90-degree crossing were also offered, along with a short section containing a bumper and a trestle bridge with integrally mounted track (see Chapter XI).

At the same time, European manufacturers and the Ives Corporation in the United States had already adopted sectional track, not unlike the familiar toy train product still in use today. The Lionel product was

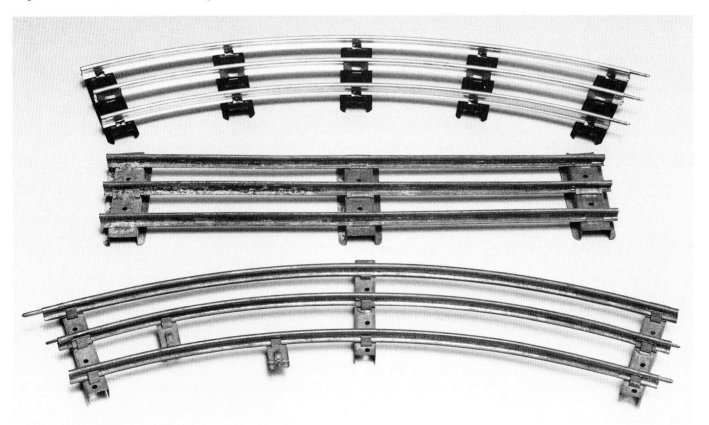

Top to bottom: Reproduction Standard Gauge, later Standard Gauge and early Standard Gauge. B. Greenberg Collection, A. Fiterman photograph.

far less convenient, requiring much more assembly and providing an inferior running surface for the train wheels (a thin steel edge as compared with Ives' rounded rail tops). Throughout his career, however, J. L. Cowen frequently employed bluster and hyperbole to turn a disadvantage into a virtue in the text of his advertisements. He was seldom given to understatement. The 1904 catalogue proclaims "our track is perfect in construction, can be laid and taken up without any trouble and made into any shape desired." Such exaggeration was no doubt meant to overshadow the advantages of standardized sectional track produced by Lionel's major competitors, but it is significant that when the new line of Standard Gauge trains appeared in 1906, sectional track following the Ives concept was introduced without fanfare.

The earliest Lionel Standard Gauge designs formed very tight curves (36 inches in diameter), and were replaced the following year with somewhat broader radius sections making circles 42 inches in diameter. A three-rail system replaced the earlier two-rail concept used for 2⅞" Gauge trains, allowing Lionel to forego insulating the car and locomotive wheels from the frames and from each other. (On all Lionel trains built after 1905 except two-rail OO Gauge, all wheels provide a ground for the electric circuit through the running rails, and power is picked up by a shoe that contacts the middle rail.) Inverted U-shaped metal ties were clamped onto the now common tubular rails, the center one being insulated from the ties by fiber strips, and pointed track pins were placed in one end of each rail to fit into the end of an adjacent section.

Once this pattern was established, it continued in use and is still employed today; the first O Gauge track introduced in 1915 is compatible with Lionel products now being produced. Various refinements were implemented over the years, such as shaped track pins with indentations to provide better contact, and track accessories such as switches and crossings were designed with closer tolerances to make for smoother running, but the basic concept has remained unchanged. The only exceptions during the Prewar period are the short-lived OO Gauge line, made in both two- and three-rail versions on composition bases rather than metal ties, and the more realistic wide-radius system of T-shaped solid rails produced beginning in 1935 and required for the scale Hudson in 1937.

When Lionel took over control of the Ives Corporation at the end of the 1920s, the parent company inherited the tooling for that Bridgeport, Connecticut, firm's line of lightweight trackage, which was built to O Gauge (1¼ inches) between the running rails) but formed a circle only 27 inches in diameter, compared with Lionel's 31-inch O Gauge line. This trackage was somewhat less durable but was less expensive to produce, and Lionel offered it in the economical Winner and Ives sets and later with Lionel Jr. trains. In 1937 these low-priced offerings were renamed "O27 Gauge" to reflect the space between the rails (O Gauge) and the diameter of a circle (27 inches). A two-rail version of this Ives track design was offered with clockwork trains of the 1930s.

In 1934 Lionel moved toward more realistic trains with the production of the first Union Pacific streamliner, designed after the early diesel locomotives that had just been placed in service on America's railroads. The long and graceful coaches of this set could not negotiate 31-inch O Gauge curves, and Lionel began manufacturing O72 trackage, measuring a full 6 feet across a circle. The gauge was compatible with the regular line of track, and all O Gauge trains could run on O72 as well, but the Union Pacific set and similar

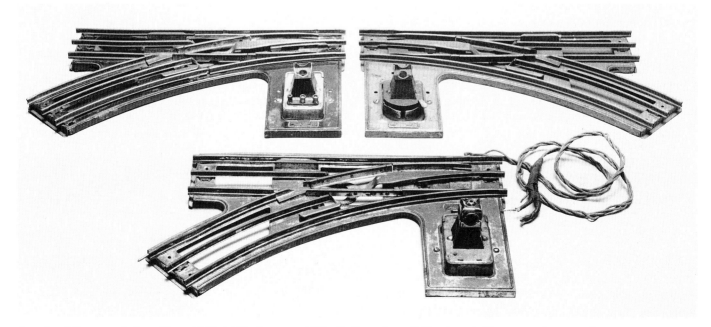

Standard Gauge switches. Top: 223L, 210R. Bottom: 222L. B. Greenberg Collection, A. Fiterman photograph.

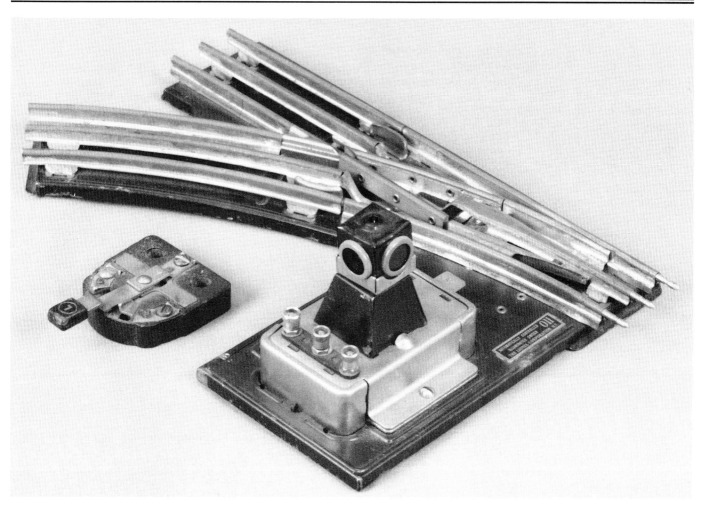

011 Remote Control Switch. P. Riddle Collection and photograph.

large trains produced later (for example, the Hiawatha and semi-scale Hudson) were confined to broad-radius operation.

Lionel's most realistic O Gauge trackage consists of solid rails shaped like the prototype, with flat tops and flanged bases. These rails were mounted on ties at the factory, but joining them together requires attaching separate fishplates with miniature nuts and bolts, a time-consuming process. Achieving the extra degree of realism exacts a heavy toll in loss of convenience, but the 700E scale Hudson can not be run satisfactorily on tubular track, due to its small wheel flanges (although an "X" version of the 700E was built for tubular rail use). The semi-scale Hudson has larger flanges and operates successfully on regular O72 sections.

The earliest switches and crossings were somewhat crude, with large spaces between the rails where the routes crossed each other. Pickup shoes and rollers were subject to particular abuse when passing over these accessories, and sometimes bent or broke off after repeated jolts from dropping into the joints. Machining and design techniques gradually improved, and highly refined O and O72 switches were developed with the introduction of molded Bakelite for bases and guardrails in the mid-1930s. These improved the per-

formance of the trains substantially, but Standard Gauge never benefited from the same technology. Sales of the large toys had declined dramatically in those days of economic hardship, and most of the company's innovations (scale rolling stock, automatic uncoupling and operating freight cars) were confined to the O Gauge line. (Standard Gauge fans did receive one of Lionel's most attractive features of the 1930s, however: the remote-control whistle!)

Until 1926 all Lionel switches were manually operated by means of a lever on the base, but when the remote-control reverse unit appeared, the company began to promote the concept of "Distant Control," by which an operator could run the trains without moving away from the transformer. It was therefore logical that an electric switch should be created, and the 1926 catalogue trumpeted the new solenoid-powered Standard Gauge switches with considerable enthusiasm but in a silly illustration (page 39 of the catalogue) showing a tiny siding made up of two curved sections incapable of accommodating even the shortest train. An O Gauge "Distant Control" switch appeared in 1927.

Non-derailing automatic switches first appeared in Standard Gauge in 1931, and two years later in O Gauge. The 1933 catalogue describes their operation as follows: "Suppose that your Lionel Limited were tearing along the track, around a curve close to a switch and then suppose that, through an oversight, the switch were set against the train. Would the train jump the track and tumble over? Not if you had the new Lionel Non-Derailing Distant Control Switches, for when the train approaches an open switch of this type, instantly and just like magic, a patented automatic mechanism sets the track in a clear position and the train rolls along its way." This feature operates by means of an insulated rail on each approach track, which is grounded to the control solenoid. Whenever a train's wheels touch this rail, they complete the ground and cause the points to move in the proper direction.

Special sections of track with one insulated running rail were produced to activate automatic accessories (see Chapters IV and VI), and bumpers were built in both O and Standard Gauge sizes. A special rubber roadbed was also produced in both sizes, and helped deaden the rumble of the trains while affording a more realistic ballasted appearance. Overall, track products received a generous amount of attention in the catalogues, as part of the company's effort to promote the concept of large layouts and the accompanying potential for greater sales of all kinds of accessories.

With the exception of the solid rail "Model Builders" trackage first advertised in 1935 and the OO Gauge products, all Lionel sectional trackage is constructed of

20 Crossing. P. Riddle Collection and photograph.

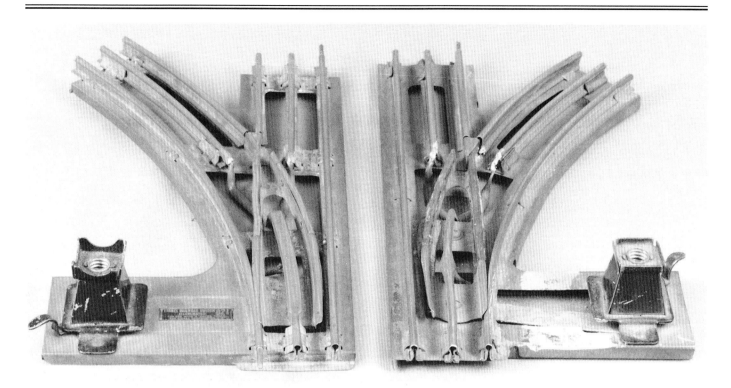

Comparison of early O Gauge Switch (right) with later version, top view. Note closed base with brass plate, fiber rail inserts, wider middle rail, and curved-sided lantern bases on later model. P. Riddle Collection and photograph.

GD EXC RST

rolled-steel rail of tubular design, clamped to inverted U-shaped metal ties. Switches and crossovers have similar rail mounted on metal or Bakelite bases. Following are descriptions of track products and accessories produced by Lionel between 1923 and 1942.

C CURVED TRACK (1906-42): Standard Gauge, three, four or five ties, eight sections to a 36"- (1906 only) or 42"-diameter circle, 14", 16" or 16½" long.
.10 .50 —

½C CURVED TRACK (1906, 1934-42): Standard Gauge, two (1906 only) or three ties, half section, 7" (1906 only) or 8" long. .10 .50 —

CC CURVED TRACK (1915-22): Similar to C with electrical connectors, 16" or 16½" long.
.10 .50 —

MS STRAIGHT TRACK (1933-38): Two-rail for clockwork (windup) trains, three ties, 9" long.
.05 .25 —

MWC CURVED TRACK (1933-38): Two-rail for clockwork (windup) trains, three ties, eight sections to a 27"-diameter circle, 9½" long. .05 .25 —

OC CURVED TRACK (1915-42, Postwar): O Gauge, three ties, eight sections to a 28½"- (through 1919) or 31"-diameter circle, 11½" (through 1919) or 11" long. .10 .50 —

½OC CURVED TRACK (1934-42, Postwar): O Gauge, two ties, half section, 6½" long.
.10 .50 —

OCC CURVED TRACK (1915-22): Similar to OC with electrical connectors, 11½" or 11" long.
.10 .50 —

OCS CURVED TRACK (1933-42): Similar to OC, one outside rail insulated for operating accessories, 11" long. .10 .50 —

OS STRAIGHT TRACK (1915-42, Postwar): O Gauge, three ties, 10¼" long. .10 .50 —

½OS STRAIGHT TRACK (1932-42): O Gauge, two ties, half section, 5" long. .10 .50 —

OSC STRAIGHT TRACK (1915-22): Similar to OS with electrical connectors, 10¼" long.
.10 .50 —

OSS STRAIGHT TRACK (1922-42): Similar to OS, one outside rail insulated for operating accessories, 10¼" long. .10 .50 —

RCS REMOTE CONTROL TRACK SECTION (1938-42, Postwar): O Gauge, molded Bakelite base, two extra narrow rails between running rails, four screw-type terminals, with two-button Bakelite control box and four-wire cable, for uncoupling and operating remote-control freight cars, 10" long. 3 10 5

S STRAIGHT TRACK (1906-42): Standard Gauge, three or four ties, 12" (1906 only) or 14" long.
.10 .50 —

½S STRAIGHT TRACK (1906-42): Standard Gauge, two ties, half section, 6" (1906 only) or 7½" long. .10 .50 —

Comparison of early O Gauge Switch (right) with later version, bottom view. Note differences in shape of middle rail connector plate and frame cutouts. The bottom plate of the later version has been removed to show the linkage between the control lever and the swivel rails. The wire brings current from the middle rail to the lantern bulb socket. P. Riddle Collection and photograph.

	GD	EXC	RST

SC STRAIGHT TRACK (1915-22): Similar to S with electrical connectors, 14″ long.   .10   .50   —

SCS CURVED TRACK (1933-42): Similar to C, one outside rail insulated for operating accessories, 16″ long.   .10   .50   —

SMC CURVED TRACK (1935-36): Two-rail, three ties with trips for Mickey Mouse clockwork trains with operating stoker tender, eight sections to a 27″-diameter circle, 9½″ long.   .05   .25   —

SS STRAIGHT TRACK (1922-42): Similar to S, one outside rail insulated for operating accessories, 14″ long.   .10   .50   —

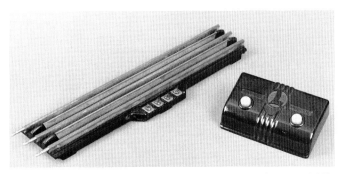

RCS Remote Control Track Section with controller. P. Riddle Collection and photograph.

	GD	EXC	RST

Various changes in O Gauge switch and crossing designs cannot be dated accurately from the illustrations or descriptions in the catalogues, as Lionel frequently initiated changes but retained earlier artwork. For example, the introduction of fiber insulation strips on the pivoting rails of the open frame switch design preceded the change to an open frog design in 1923, but is never mentioned in the catalogue. The following descriptions are based upon examination of available switches and assumptions drawn from catalogue illustrations and text.

011 PAIR OF REMOTE CONTROL SWITCHES (1933-37): O Gauge, one 011L and one 011R, lighted, with two controllers.   20   40   20

011L LEFT HAND REMOTE CONTROL SWITCH (1933-37): O Gauge, lighted, left-hand, non-derailing, similar to 012 but with solenoid mechanism in housing beneath lantern stand, raised to provide clearance for lever mechanism, three screw-type terminals for wire connections, with controller and three-wire cable; non-derailing feature activated by grounding switch machine solenoid to insulated rails on straight and curved approach tracks.

(A) 1933, green-enameled base with nickel control housing and maroon lantern support, brass plate.   10   20   10

Comparison of switch stand sockets of lighted 021 (right) and unlighted 022 Switches, the latter having no threaded receptacle for a bulb. P. Riddle Collection and photograph.

GD   EXC   RST

(B) 1934-37, catalogue illustration indicates color change to black base with nickel control housing and red lantern support; exact date of color change is undetermined, reader confirmation requested.

10	20	10

(C) Same as (B), but black lantern support, black-enameled nickel plate lettered "011 / AUTOMATICALLY CONTROLLED / ILLUMINATED SWITCH / THE LIONEL CORPORATION, N.Y."

10	20	10

(D) 1931-32, made for Ives under catalogue No. 1897.

10	20	10

011R RIGHT HAND REMOTE CONTROL SWITCH (1933-37): Same as 011L, but right-hand only.

012 PAIR OF REMOTE CONTROL SWITCHES (1927-33): O Gauge, one 012L and one 012R, lighted, with two controllers. **20   40   20**

012L LEFT HAND REMOTE CONTROL SWITCH (1927-33): O Gauge, steel construction, lighted, closed base with no open areas on bottom, center rails interconnected by Y-shaped metal plate, swivel points and fixed open frog with guardrails, wide base supporting solenoid-actuated control mechanism in housing

GD   EXC   RST

beneath trapezoidal lantern stand with socket and bulb, surmounted by removable square signal lantern with rounded corners and cut out for two red and two green celluloid disks held in place by circular frames, three screw-type terminals for wire connections, with controller and three-wire cable. **10   20   10**

012R RIGHT HAND REMOTE CONTROL SWITCH (1927-33): Same as 012L, but right-hand only.

013 REMOTE CONTROL SWITCH SET (1929-31): O Gauge, pair of 012 Switches and 439 Control Panel, in original box. **85   175   85**

20 90-DEGREE CROSSING (1909-42): Standard Gauge, steel construction, permanent electrical connections between middle rails.

(A) 1909-25?, small square base, rails extending beyond base with separate ties at ends, with or without pickup shoe support in center, 12" square. The design of this crossing probably changed to that described under (B) below at some point earlier than 1925, and possibly as early as 1917, when the O Gauge 020X

GD   EXC   RST   GD   EXC   RST

45-degree Crossing was introduced. The latter has a base similar to 20(B). Reader confirmation requested.

       2   **5**   **3**

(B) 1926?-42, steel construction, large pea green or black base extending to ends of rails and curved in concave fashion between them, brass or nickel plate usually labeled "No 20 / CROSSING / THE / LIONEL CORP. / NEW YORK", composition pickup shoe support in center, 12″ square.   **2**   **5**   **3**

(C) Same as (B), but black with black composition pickup shoe support.   **2**   **5**   **3**

(D) 1931-32, made for Ives under catalogue No. 1899.

       2   **5**   **3**

As is the case with O Gauge track accessories, the various changes in Standard Gauge switch and crossing designs cannot be dated accurately from the illustrations or descriptions in the catalogues, as old artwork was often retained after changes were initiated. For example, the introduction of fiber insulation strips on the pivoting rails of the open frame switch design preceded the change to an open frog design in 1923, but is never mentioned in the catalogue. The change from wire connections between center rails to steel connections is neither mentioned nor illustrated. The following descriptions are based upon examination of available switches and assumptions drawn from catalogue illustrations and text.

20X 45-DEGREE CROSSING (1928-32): Standard Gauge, construction similar to 20(B), but with metal pickup shoe support in center, 16⅞″ long.

       5   **10**   **5**

020 90-DEGREE CROSSING (1915-42, Postwar): O Gauge, steel construction, permanent electrical connections between middle rails.

(A) 1915-25, catalogue states "Similar in construction to No. 20" (the Standard Gauge version), which is illustrated as having a small square base, rails extending beyond base with separate ties at ends, with or without pickup shoe support in center, 10¼″ square. The design of all early 020 Crossings was probably the same as the O Gauge 020X 45-Degree Crossing introduced in the 1917 catalogue and 020(B) described below. Reader confirmation requested.   **NRS**

(B) 1926-42, steel construction, green or black base extending to ends of rails and curved in concave fashion between them, brass or nickel plate usually labeled "No 020 / CROSSING / THE / LIONEL CORP. / NEW YORK", composition pickup shoe support in center, 10¼″ square.   **2**   **5**   **3**

(C) Same as (B), but black with black composition pickup shoe support.   **2**   **5**   **3**

(D) Same as (C), but no identification plate, model information molded into central black molded crossing insulator. L. Bohn Collection.   **2**   **5**   **3**

020X Crossing. B. Greenberg Collection, A. Fiterman photograph.

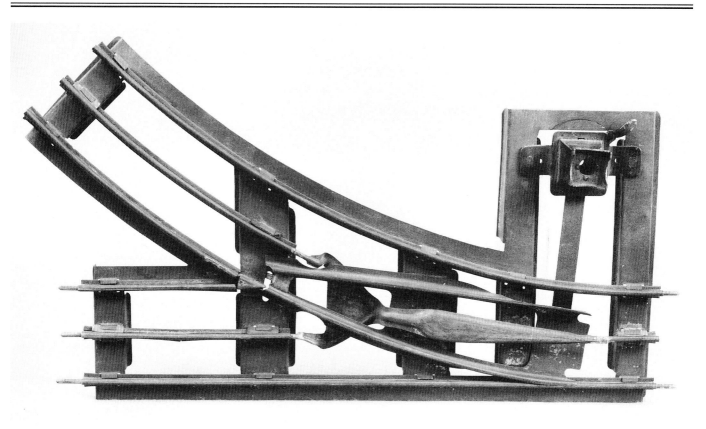

22 Manual Switch. B. Greenberg Collection and photograph.

	GD	EXC	RST

020X 45-DEGREE CROSSING (1917-42, Postwar):
O Gauge, construction similar to 20(B), 10¼" long.
R. Morris reports one example in an original Lionel
box with speckled base and no nameplate or stamping.   5   10   5

21 90-DEGREE CROSSING (1906): Standard
Gauge, similar to 20(A), 8" square base; reader confirmation requested.   **NRS**

21 MANUAL SWITCH (1915-25): Standard Gauge,
steel construction, frame with cutouts supporting rails,
swivel rails with continuous frog, wide base with two
cutout areas supporting control lever mechanism
beneath steel trapezoidal tower with socket and bulb,
surmounted by removable square signal lantern with
rounded corners and punched out for two red and two
green celluloid disks held in place by circular frames.

(A) 1915-16, catalogue states "equipped with electric
signal, having a 3½-volt bulb which can be easily
removed". If the voltage specification is correct, this
bulb would have had a short life when powered by track
current, but if separately lighted by dry or wet cells, it
would have required more wiring; reader confirmation
requested.   3   10   5

(B) 1917, same catalogue illustration as 1915-16,
text describes an electric bulb but does not specify its
voltage.   3   10   5

(C) 1918-22, same catalogue illustration as 1915-16,
text specifies 14-volt bulb.   3   10   5

	GD	EXC	RST

(D) 1923-25, closed control mechanism base (formerly
open area inside rectangle eliminated), wire no longer
connects center rails, two heavy fiber strips inserted
where the rails cross, catalogue illustration depicts O
Gauge version only, p. 35, 1923, brass plate.
                                                   3   10   5

021 PAIR OF MANUAL SWITCHES (1915-37): O
Gauge, one 021L and one 021R, lighted.
                                                   5   10   5

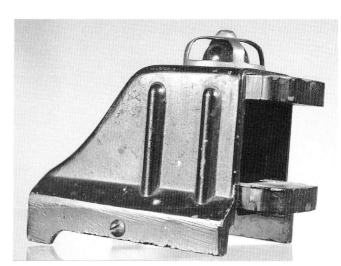

*025 Illuminated Bumper. B. Greenberg Collection, A. Fiterman
photograph.*

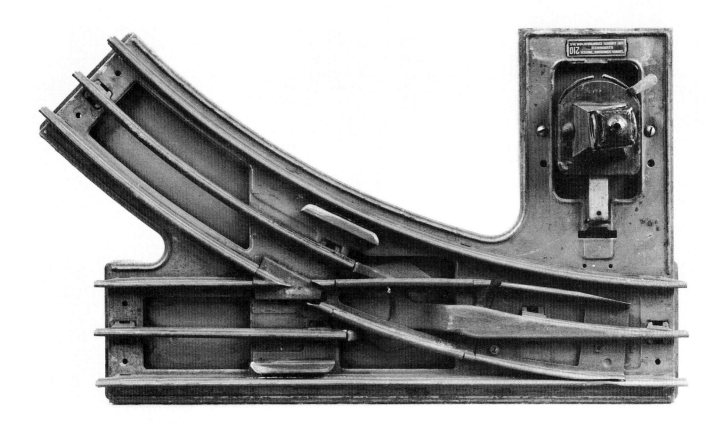

210 Switch. B. Greenberg Collection and photograph.

GD   EXC   RST

021L LEFT HAND MANUAL SWITCH (1915-37):
O Gauge, lighted, steel construction, frame with cutouts supporting rails, no bottom plate, swivel rails with continuous frog, wide base with central cutout area supporting control lever mechanism beneath steel trapezoidal tower with socket and bulb, surmounted by removable square signal lantern with rounded corners and punched out for two red and two green celluloid disks held in place by circular frames.

(A) 1915-22, catalogue states "similar to No. 21 switch" (the Standard Gauge version).   **2   5   3**

(B) 1923-25, closed control mechanism base (formerly open area eliminated), two heavy fiber strips inserted where the rails cross, catalogue illustration depicts O Gauge version only, p. 35, 1923, brass plate lettered "021 / LIONEL RAILROAD SWITCH / ILLUMINATED / FOR USE WITH 'O' GAUGE TRACK / THE LIONEL CORPORATION, N.Y." located between rails and control lever housing   **2   5   3**

(C) 1931-32, made for Ives under catalogue No. 1895.
5   10   5

021R RIGHT HAND MANUAL SWITCH (1915-37):
Same as 021L, but right-hand only.

22 MANUAL SWITCH (1906-25): Standard Gauge, cast-iron (through 1915) or steel switch stand, unlighted; replaced by 220 in 1926.

GD   EXC   RST

(A) 1906-07, rails clamped to ties, no frame supporting structure, swivel rails with continuous frog, switch stand control mechanism mounted on single tie, red-and white-enameled signal disc, center rail ends in diamond-shaped pickup shoe support, 14″ long, 8″ wide, 4½″ wide, catalogue text states "all parts work on spring bearing"; reader confirmation requested.   **NRS**

(B) 1908-12, catalogue illustration same as (A), but text referring to "spring bearing" deleted; reader confirmation requested.   **NRS**

(C) 1913, catalogue illustration same as (A), length specified as 16½″. It is speculated that the switch did not change size, but that Lionel changed the method of measuring the item. The description claims "perfectly insulated" for the first time, but it is not known if this means that part of the pivoting rails are now insulated; reader confirmation requested.   **NRS**

(D) 1914, new catalogue illustration (probably based on a photograph), supporting frame, center rail widens but without earlier distinctive diamond pattern, control lever supported by rectangular extension of the frame with a hollow area inside the rectangle, two wires connecting center rail closest to mechanism with the straight section center rail and curved section center rail, text states "Signals are red and white enameled".   **3   10   5**

(E) 1915-16, same catalogue illustration and text as 1914, but text states "Signal discs are red and green

GD EXC RST

GD EXC RST

enameled" instead of "red and white". It is speculated that the new design pictured on the same page for the 21 lighted switch was actually used for the 22 in 1915 and 1916, rather than the earlier style; reader confirmation requested. **3 10 5**

(F) 1917, new catalogue illustration identical to 21, wide base with two cutout areas supporting control lever mechanism beneath steel trapezoidal tower, hole for but not including socket and bulb, surmounted by removable square signal lantern with rounded corners and punched out for two red and two green disks held in place by circular frames, text states "signal lanterns have red and green disks" but does not indicate whether they are translucent, illustration lacks lines radiating from signal to indicate illumination as shown on 21 drawing. **3 10 5**

(G) 1918-19, not illustrated in catalogue, but assumed to be identical to 21 without bulb. **3 10 5**

(H) 1920-22, same catalogue illustration as 1917. **3 10 5**

(I) 1923-25, closed control mechanism base (formerly open area inside rectangle eliminated), center rails interconnected without wires by Y-shaped metal plate, two heavy fiber strips inserted where the rails cross, catalogue illustration depicts O Gauge version only, p. 35, 1923, brass plate. **3 10 5**

022 PAIR OF MANUAL SWITCHES (1915-26): O Gauge, one 022L and one 022R, unlighted.

5 10 5

022L LEFT HAND MANUAL SWITCH (1915-26): O Gauge, unlighted, steel construction, frame with cutouts supporting rails, no bottom plate, swivel rails with continuous frog, wide base with central cutout area supporting control lever mechanism beneath steel trapezoidal tower with hole for but lacking socket and bulb, surmounted by removable square signal lantern with rounded corners and punched out for two red and two green disks held in place by circular frames, text states "signal lanterns have red and green disks" but does not indicate whether they are translucent, illustration lacks lines radiating from signal to indicate illumination as shown on 021 drawing.

(A) 1915-22, same as 021 but unlighted; 1915-16 catalogue states "similar to No. 22 switch" (the Standard Gauge version) which was shown as an older and different design; believed manufactured in 021 style only. **2 5 3**

(B) 1923-25, closed control mechanism base (formerly open area eliminated), two heavy fiber strips inserted where the rails cross, catalogue illustration depicts O Gauge version only, p. 35, 1923, brass plate lettered "022 / LIONEL RAILROAD SWITCH / NOT ILLUMINATED / FOR USE WITH 'O' GAUGE

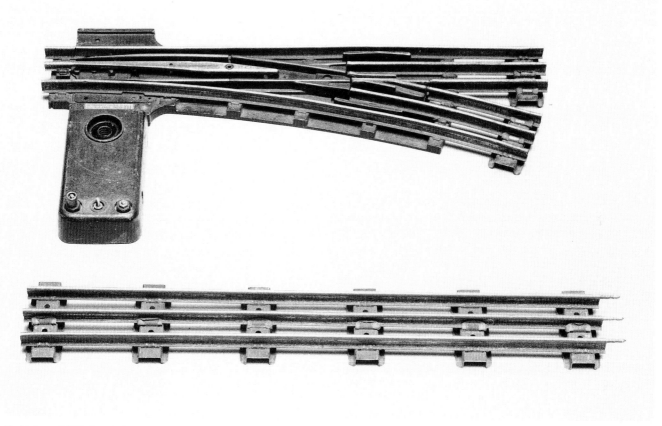

711R Switch and 762 Straight Track. B. Greenberg Collection, A. Fiterman photograph.

GD   EXC   RST   GD   EXC   RST

TRACK / THE LIONEL CORPORATION, N.Y." located between rails and control lever housing.

| | 2 | 5 | 3 |

022R RIGHT HAND MANUAL SWITCH (1915-26): Same as 022L, but right-hand only.

022 PAIR OF REMOTE CONTROL SWITCHES (1938-42, Postwar): O Gauge, one 022L and one 022R, with controllers.   **35   75   50**

022L LEFT HAND REMOTE CONTROL SWITCH (1938-42, Postwar): O Gauge, lighted, Bakelite base and motor housing (detachable to mount on either side), plastic lantern with two red and two green translucent inserts, non-derailing, Bakelite control box with vertical lever and red and green bulbs indicating position of rails (matching lantern on switch), 10½" long.   **20   40   25**

022R RIGHT HAND REMOTE CONTROL SWITCH (1938-42, Postwar): Same as 022L, but right-hand only.

23 BUMPER (1906-33): Standard Gauge, steel construction, two spring-loaded plunger assemblies.

(A) 1906-07, catalogue illustration depicts two U-shaped steel straps mounted on ties between two T-shaped rails, two spring-loaded rods with dome-shaped buffers, black; reader confirmation requested.   **NRS**

(B) 1908-13, solid triangular vertical side frames painted red or black and mounted on section of S track, two black rectangular spring-loaded buffers mounted one above the other.   **5   10   5**

(C) Same as (B), but cutout frames.   **5   10   5**

23 90-DEGREE CROSSING (1912): Same as 20 Crossing, appears only in 1912 catalogue with illustration identical to 20; reader confirmation requested.

| | 2 | 5 | 3 |

023 BUMPER (1915-33): O Gauge, similar to but smaller than 23(C), painted red or black; also made for Ives under catalogue No. 340-0.   **5   10   5**

25 ILLUMINATED BUMPER (1927-42): Standard Gauge, die-cast with two solid projecting buffers, two rounded vertical ribs on each side, light socket and bulb in top covered by brass or nickel cutout light guard, attaches to track with two screws.

(A) 1927-33, cream with red ribs, brass light guard.   **10   25   10**

(B) 1934-42, black with nickel light guard.   **10   20   10**

772 Straight T-Rail Track with plates, screws and nuts. B. Greenberg Collection, A. Fiterman photograph.

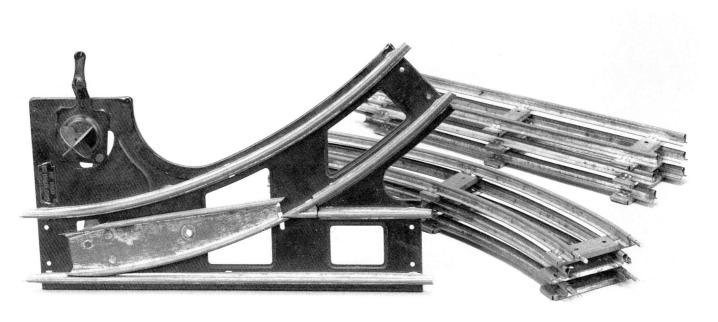

1550 Switches with MS and MWC Track. R. Bartelt Collection, A. Fiterman photograph.

	GD	EXC	RST

(C) 1928-30, made for Ives under catalogue No. 339.

	10	20	10

025 ILLUMINATED BUMPER (1928-42): O Gauge, similar to but smaller than 25.

(A) 1928-33, cream with brass light guard.

	10	25	10

(B) 1928-33, black with nickel light guard.

	10	20	10

(C) 1934-42, semi-gloss black, brass light guard.

	5	10	5

(D) Same as (C), but vertical red stripe painted on side.

(E) Same as (C), but nickel light guard.

	5	10	5

(F) 1928-30, made for Ives under catalogue No. 339-0.

	5	15	5

30 CURVED RUBBER ROADBED (1931-37): Standard Gauge, sponge rubber, molded edges simulating ballast, fits one track section. **NRS**

030 CURVED RUBBER ROADBED (1931-39): O Gauge, sponge rubber, molded edges simulating ballast, fits one track section. **NRS**

31 STRAIGHT RUBBER ROADBED (1931-37): Standard Gauge, similar to 30. **NRS**

031 STRAIGHT RUBBER ROADBED (1931-39): O Gauge, similar to 030. **NRS**

0031 CURVED TRACK (1939-42): OO Gauge, molded Bakelite base with closely spaced ties, two-rail, twelve sections to a 48"-diameter circle, 13" long.

	1	2	—

32 90-DEGREE CROSSING RUBBER ROADBED (1931-37): Standard Gauge, similar to 30. **NRS**

032 90-DEGREE CROSSING RUBBER ROADBED (1931-39): O Gauge, similar to 030. **NRS**

0032 STRAIGHT TRACK (1939-42): OO Gauge, molded Bakelite base with closely spaced ties, two-rail, 12" long.

	1	2	—

33 45-DEGREE CROSSING RUBBER ROADBED (1931-37): Standard Gauge, similar to 30. **NRS**

033 45-DEGREE CROSSING RUBBER ROADBED (1931-39): O Gauge, similar to 030. **NRS**

34 PAIR OF SWITCH RUBBER ROADBED (1931-37): Standard Gauge, similar to 30. **NRS**

034 PAIR OF SWITCH RUBBER ROADBED SECTIONS (1931-39): O Gauge, similar to 030. **NRS**

0034 CURVED TRACK (1939-42): OO Gauge, similar to 0032 with electrical connectors, 13" long.

	1	2	—

042 PAIR OF MANUAL SWITCHES (1938-42, Postwar): O Gauge, one 042L and one 042R.

	20	40	20

042L LEFT HAND MANUAL SWITCH (1938-42, Postwar): O Gauge, lighted, same as 1938 022, but with manual-control lever.

	10	20	10

042R RIGHT HAND MANUAL SWITCH (1938-42, Postwar): Same as 042L, but right-hand only.

0051 CURVED TRACK (1939-42): OO Gauge, molded Bakelite base with closely spaced ties, three-rail, twelve sections to a 27"-diameter circle, 7" long.

	1	2	—

0052 STRAIGHT TRACK (1939-42): OO Gauge, molded Bakelite base with closely spaced ties, three-rail, 7" long.

	1	2	—

GD EXC RST

0054 CURVED TRACK (1939-42): OO Gauge, similar to 0051, with electrical connectors, 7" long.

1 2 —

60 PAIR OF AUTOMATIC TRACK TRIPS (1906-12): Standard Gauge, flat metal strips mounted on ties outside of running rail, leaf spring or spring plunger, actuates reverse mechanisms. **NRS**

0061 CURVED TRACK (1938): OO Gauge, molded Bakelite base with closely spaced ties, three-rail, twelve sections to a 27"-diameter circle, 7" long.

1 2 —

62 AUTOMATIC TRACK TRIP (1914-16): Standard Gauge, boomerang-shaped revolving cam for mounting on tie outside of running rail, actuates reverse mechanisms. **NRS**

0062 STRAIGHT TRACK (1938): OO Gauge, molded Bakelite base with closely spaced ties, three-rail, 6¾" long.

1 2 —

0063 CURVED TRACK (1938-42): OO Gauge, molded Bakelite base with closely spaced ties, three-rail, half section, 3½" long.

1 2 —

0064 CURVED TRACK (1938): OO Gauge, similar to 0061, with electrical connectors, 7" long.

1 2 —

0065 STRAIGHT TRACK (1938-42): OO Gauge, molded Bakelite base with closely spaced ties, three-rail, half section, 3⅜" long.

1 2 —

0066 STRAIGHT TRACK (1938-42): OO Gauge, molded Bakelite base with closely spaced ties, three-rail, partial section, 5⅝" long.

1 2

0070 90-DEGREE CROSSING (1938-42): OO Gauge, molded Bakelite base with closely spaced ties, three-rail, 6¾" square.

5 10 —

0072 PAIR OF REMOTE CONTROL SWITCHES (1938-42): OO Gauge, molded Bakelite base with closely spaced ties, three-rail, lighted, with lighted Bakelite control boxes.

35 75 —

0072L REMOTE CONTROL SWITCH (1938-42): OO Gauge, same as 0072, left-hand only.

20 40 —

0072R REMOTE CONTROL SWITCH (1938-42): OO Gauge, same as 0072, right-hand only.

125 TRACK TEMPLATE (1938): Cutout drawing aid for tracing O72, O, and O27 track, switches, and crossovers, described on page 36 of 1938 catalogue.

2 5 —

210 PAIR OF MANUAL SWITCHES (1926-42): Standard Gauge, one 210L and one 210R, lighted.

15 30 15

210L LEFT HAND MANUAL SWITCH (1926-42): Standard Gauge, successor to 21, steel construction, lighted, closed base with no open areas on bottom, center rails interconnected without wires by Y-shaped

metal plate, swivel points and fixed open frog with guardrails, wide base supporting control lever mechanism encased in steel trapezoidal tower with socket and bulb, surmounted by removable square signal lantern with rounded corners and cut out for two red and two green celluloid disks held in place by circular frames.

(A) 1926-27, unpainted metal base with black lantern support or pea green-enameled base with red lantern support, brass number plate.

8 15 8

(B) 1928-33, catalogue illustration on page 40 suggests revised smaller control lever housing (not confirmed), pea green base, dark green control housing, red lantern support.

8 15 8

(C) 1934, catalogue illustration indicates color change to black base with nickel control housing and red lantern support; exact date of color change is undetermined, reader confirmation requested.

8 15 8

(D) 1935-42, no catalogue illustration, but expected color change to black base with black lantern housing as per 222 model; reader confirmation requested.

8 15 8

(E) 1931-32, made for Ives under catalogue No. 1896.

8 15 8

210R RIGHT HAND MANUAL SWITCH (1926-42): Same as 210L, but right-hand only.

220 PAIR OF MANUAL SWITCHES (1926): Standard Gauge, one 210L and one 210R, unlighted.

15 30 15

220L LEFT HAND MANUAL SWITCH (1926-42): Standard Gauge, successor to 22, steel construction, unlighted and similar to 210, but with empty hole where socket and bulb are installed in 210.

(A) 1926-27, unpainted metal base with black lantern support or pea green-enameled base with red lantern support, brass number plate.

8 15 8

(B) 1928-33, catalogue illustration on page 40 suggests revised smaller control lever housing (not confirmed), pea green base, dark green control housing, red lantern support.

8 15 8

(C) 1934, catalogue illustration indicates color change to black base with nickel control housing and red lantern support; exact date of color change is undetermined, reader confirmation requested.

8 15 8

(D) 1935-42, no catalogue illustration, but expected color change to black base with black lantern housing as per 222 model; reader confirmation requested.

8 15 8

220R RIGHT HAND MANUAL SWITCH (1926-42): Same as 220L, but right-hand only.

222 PAIR OF REMOTE CONTROL SWITCHES (1926-31): Standard Gauge, one 222L and one 222R, lighted, with two controllers.

30 60 30

GD EXC RST

222L LEFT HAND REMOTE CONTROL SWITCH (1926-31): Standard Gauge, lighted, similar to 210 but with solenoid mechanism in housing beneath lantern stand, raised to provide clearance for lever mechanism, wires permanently connected on underside or three screw-type terminals for wire connections, with controller and three-wire cable.

(A) 1926-27, unpainted metal or pea green-enameled base with nickel control housing and red lantern support, permanent wire connections, brass plate.

15   30   15

(B) 1928-30, closed base with no open area from bottom, revised control housing with three screw-type terminals for connection of wires from controller (shown on track side of lantern in catalogue but actually on side opposite track).   15   30   15

(C) 1931, non-derailing, catalogue states "Should a train approach an open switch, which would ordinarily derail it, the new automatic device instantly sets the track in a clear position so that train can go on its way without derailing"; non-derailing feature activated by grounding switch machine solenoid to insulated rails on straight and curved approach tracks.

15   30   15

222R RIGHT HAND REMOTE CONTROL SWITCH (1926-31): Same as 222L, but right-hand only.

223 PAIR OF REMOTE CONTROL SWITCHES (1932-42): Standard Gauge, one 222L and one 222R, lighted, with two controllers.   30   60   30

223L LEFT HAND REMOTE CONTROL SWITCH (1932-42): Standard Gauge, lighted, non-derailing, same as 222(C).

(A) 1932-33, green-enameled base with nickel control housing and red lantern support, brass plate.

15   30   15

(B) Catalogue illustration indicates color change to black base with nickel control housing and red lantern support; exact date of color change is undetermined, reader confirmation requested.   15   30   15

(C) 1931-32, made for Ives under catalogue No. 1897.

15   30   15

223R RIGHT HAND REMOTE CONTROL SWITCH (1932-42): Same as 223L, but right-hand only.

225 REMOTE CONTROL SWITCH SET (1929-32): Standard Gauge, pair of 222 Switches with 439 control panel, in original box.   100   200   100

310 STRAP STEEL TRACK (1901-05): 2⅞" Gauge, 12"-long tinned-steel straps with angled ends forming hooks and slots, wood ties, forms one dozen sections.   NRS

320 MANUAL SWITCH (1902-05): 2⅞" Gauge, matches 310, 4½"-high stand with control lever and

GD EXC RST

red- and white-enameled disks mounted on two extended ties, 17½" long, 8" wide.   NRS

330 90-DEGREE CROSSING (1902-05): 2⅞" Gauge, matches 310, 6" square base instead of ties, with strap rails attached.   NRS

350 BUMPER (1902-05): 2⅞" Gauge, black cast-iron construction, triangular posts, spring-loaded buffer, mounted on 4"-long section of strap steel track with wood ties.   NRS

711 PAIR OF REMOTE CONTROL SWITCHES (1935-42): O72 Gauge, one 711L and one 711R, with two controllers.   75   150   75

711L LEFT HAND REMOTE CONTROL SWITCH (1935-42): O72 Gauge, Bakelite base and motor housing (detachable to mount on either side), plastic lantern with two red and two green translucent inserts, non-derailing, die-cast control box with vertical lever and red and green bulbs indicating position of rails (matching lantern on switch), both straight and curved rails extend beyond base and are mounted to tie at end opposite control box, 14⅜" long.   40   75   45

711R RIGHT HAND REMOTE CONTROL SWITCH (1935-42): Same as 711L, but right-hand only.

720 90-DEGREE CROSSING (1935-42): O72 Gauge, steel construction, metal base similar to 020, curved in concave fashion between rails and not extending to their ends, one tie at end of each track lead, central Bakelite pickup shoe support, 14½" square.

15   25   15

721 PAIR OF MANUAL SWITCHES (1935-42): O72 Gauge, one 721L and one 721R.   50   100   60

721L LEFT HAND MANUAL SWITCH (1935-42): O72 Gauge, similar to 711, lighted, Bakelite base and control housing (detachable to mount on either side), plastic lantern with two red and two green translucent inserts, manual control lever, 14⅜" long.

25   50   30

721R RIGHT HAND MANUAL SWITCH (1935-42): Same as 721L, but right-hand only.

730 90-DEGREE CROSSING (1935-42): O72 Gauge, similar to 720, but solid T-shaped rails.

20   35   20

731 PAIR OF REMOTE CONTROL SWITCHES (1935-42): O72 Gauge, one 731L and one 731R with two controllers.   75   150   75

731L LEFT HAND REMOTE CONTROL SWITCH (1935-42): O72 Gauge, similar to 711, but solid T-shaped rails.   40   75   45

731R RIGHT HAND REMOTE CONTROL SWITCH (1935-42): Same as 731L, but right-hand only.

760 TRACK PACK (1938-42, Postwar): O72 Gauge, contains sixteen sections 761 curved track, with original box.   20   40   16

GD EXC RST   GD EXC RST

761 CURVED TRACK (1934-42, Postwar): O72 Gauge, six ties, sixteen sections to a 72"-diameter circle, 14" long.   **1   2   1**

762 STRAIGHT TRACK (1934-42): O72 Gauge, six ties, 15" long.   **1   2   1**

762S STRAIGHT TRACK (1934-42): O72 Gauge, similar to 762, one outside rail insulated for operating accessories, 15" long.   **1   2   1**

771 CURVED TRACK (1935-42): O72 Gauge, solid T-shaped rails, ten ties, sixteen sections to a 72"-diameter circle, 14" long.   **2   5   3**

772 STRAIGHT TRACK (1935-42): O72 Gauge, solid T-shaped rails, ten ties, 15" long. **2   5   3**

772S STRAIGHT TRACK (1935-42): O72 Gauge, similar to 772, one outside rail insulated for operating accessories, 15" long.   **2   5   3**

773 FISH PLATE SET (1935-42): O72 Gauge, rectangular steel plates with two holes each, used for connecting solid T-shaped rail track sections together; contains fifty fishplates, one hundred bolts, one hundred nuts, socket wrench.   **NRS**

1013 CURVED TRACK (1933-42, Postwar): O27 Gauge, three ties, eight sections to a 27"-diameter circle, 9½" long.   **.25   .50   —**

1018 STRAIGHT TRACK (1933-42, Postwar): O27 Gauge, three ties, 9" long.   **.25   .50   —**

1019 REMOTE CONTROL TRACK SECTION (1938-42, Postwar): O27 Gauge, similar to RCS, for uncoupling and operating remote-control freight cars, 8⅞" long.   **3   10   5**

1021 90-DEGREE CROSSING (1933-42, Postwar): O27 Gauge, similar to 020, black, 7⅜" square.   **2   5   3**

1024 PAIR OF MANUAL SWITCHES (1935-42, Postwar): O27 Gauge, one 1024L and one 1024R.   **4   10   6**

1024L LEFT HAND MANUAL SWITCH (1935-42, Postwar): O27 Gauge, steel base with cutouts, manual-control lever, one-piece Bakelite swivel rail unit with continuous frog design, unlighted, 9⅛" long.   **2   5   3**

1024R RIGHT HAND MANUAL SWITCH (1935-42, Postwar): Same as 1024L, but right-hand only.

1025 BUMPER (1940-42): O27 Gauge, same as 025 with one section 1018 track.   **5   10   5**

1121 PAIR OF REMOTE CONTROL SWITCHES (1937-42, Postwar): O27 Gauge, lighted, steel base, Bakelite solenoid housing with one red and one green lens per side, three screw-type terminals, one-piece Bakelite swivel rail unit with continuous frog design, 9⅛" long, sold in pairs only, with one lighted Bakelite control box containing two levers and two pairs of red and green lenses.   **25   50   30**

1550 PAIR OF MANUAL SWITCHES (1933-37): Two-rail for clockwork (windup) trains, lightweight steel construction, manual control lever, red and green signal disks, swivel rail unit with continuous frog design, 9½", sold in pairs only.   **5   10   5**

1555 90-DEGREE CROSSING (1933-37): Two-rail for clockwork (windup) trains, lightweight steel construction, 7" square.   **2   5   3**

CHAPTER XIV

Scenic Railways, Layouts and Dealer Displays

The Lionel catalogue for 1922 announced a revolutionary new concept in toy marketing: the Scenic Railway. For a period of two years, customers could purchase complete train layouts mounted permanently on sturdy tables with detachable legs and complete with scenery, buildings, signals, bridges and trains. Trackage and accessories were fully wired and required only the addition of a power source (batteries, transformer or direct current reducer) for operation.

The Scenic Railways were handsomely finished and featured novel and creative details, such as a waterproof lake area beneath the bridges that could be stocked with goldfish. It is believed that they came completely finished, requiring no assembly by the purchaser. The cost of these displays was very high for an era in which a $5 weekly salary would be considered adequate by many families. The smallest retailed at $50 east of the Mississippi, while the largest sold for $335. It is believed that few were sold for home use,

173 Layout (Scenic Railway). G. Zippie Collection, B. Schwab photograph.

and that dealers using them as promotional displays were the primary market. Not many are known to have survived intact, and it is supposed that dealers often dismantled them and sold the components separately.

In order to reduce costs and to promote the Scenic Railways for greater consumer use, the company revised the concept in 1924 by changing to a less expensive wood and composition board design for the table and eliminating the trains. Owners could place their existing train sets on the layout, or purchase a new set of their choice. The accessories were packaged separately from the platform, and were to be assembled by the buyer and connected to the wiring, which was already in place. The cost of the two-section O Gauge and three-section Standard Gauge layouts were thereby kept to $50 and $80 respectively, making their acquisition a possibility for many more families, although it seems likely that relatively few took advantage of it, as only a small number can be found today. These prices were maintained until the layouts were dropped from the catalogue after 1928, but it is believed they were also available in 1928.

The concept was revived in 1932 with the 173 Complete Railroad Layout, although the term Scenic Railway would have been more appropriate for this unit. From 1923 through 1941, Lionel also marketed special outfits which are distinguished from simple train sets by the inclusion of accessories, and called them "Complete Railroads" or simply "Outfits," but these came without tables or fixed scenery. By contrast, the 173 was a "Scenic Railway" in every respect except catalogue description. A similar and very economical model built on a platform without legs, the 1053E Lionel-Ives Complete Electric Railroad, was produced in 1933. This evolved into the 1057E Lionel Junior "Distant Control" Railroad in 1934, followed by a similar model 1066E in 1935 and 1936.

While production of the 1923-1924 Scenic Railways involved a considerable amount of hand work by Lionel employees, the revised 1924 and later models utilized standardized components, each of which had its own catalogue number. These included tunnels and plot sections fashioned from steel and painted and detailed with a wide variety of scenic touches. They were described in the catalogue with such labels as "Corner Elevation," "Corner Grass Plot" and "Heart-Shape Grass Plot." Similar units made from painted composition board represented mountains and sky. The company also produced tree and shrub modules for inclusion on the displays. This standardization reduced manufacturing time and therefore lowered the overall cost of the Scenic Railways.

As with the earlier versions, very few complete layouts made from these standardized components may be found today, although the constituent parts are still encountered. Despite Lionel's efforts to advertise them to the general public, most of these

layouts were probably purchased by dealers for display, rather than by individual consumers, and it is believed the dealers often dismantled them and sold off the parts when the promotional purpose had been served.

The outfits that included accessories but no platform were more successful in the marketplace. The author believes this was due to the manner in which toy trains are played with by most children. Much of the fun lies in putting together, taking apart and reassembling the track and accessories, and while the Scenic Railways were undoubtedly beautiful, the only play value they offered was in the running of the equipment. Most children like to rearrange, at least as much as simply play with, their toys. Lionel capitalized on this concept in the years immediately preceding World War II, with a number of train sets featuring the new operating cars and packaged with one of the big motorized freight loaders. Sets were advertised with the 97 Coal Loader or 164 Lumber Loader, plus one or more of the appropriate operating dump cars, as well as with the 165 Magnetic Crane. The cost of these outfits was less than the sum of their prices if purchased separately, and represented true value in the marketplace.

In the listings that follow, the presence of original boxes is assumed in the case of any complete outfit, as there is no other way to verify that the components were sold as a unit. Without boxes, the values are limited to the sum of their component parts.

                GD   EXC   RST

131 CORNER ELEVATION (1924-28): Steel construction, section of 198 and 199 Scenic Railways.
                150   300   150

132 CORNER GRASS PLOT (1924-28): Steel construction, section of 198 and 199 Scenic Railways.
                150   300   150

133 HEARTSHAPE GRASS PLOT (1924-28): Steel construction, section of 198 and 199 Scenic Railways.
                150   300   150

134 OVAL GRASS PLOT (1924-28): Steel construction, section of 198 and 199 Scenic Railways.
                150   300   150

135 SMALL CIRCULAR GRASS PLOT (1924-28): Steel construction, section of 198 and 199 Scenic Railways.
                150   300   150

136 LARGE ELEVATION (1924-28): Steel construction, section of 198 and 199 Scenic Railways. **NRS**

172 COMPLETE RAILROAD LAYOUT (1923): Packaged set of trains and accessories: 150 Locomotive, three 600 Pullmans, 118 Tunnel, 62 Semaphore, 68 Warning Sign, 88 Rheostat, O Gauge Track.
                350   700   350

173 COMPLETE RAILROAD LAYOUT (1923): Packaged set of trains and accessories: 150 Locomotive, two 603 Pullmans, 604 Observation, 118 Tunnel,

GD EXC RST

106 Bridge, six 60 Telegraph Poles, 88 Rheostat, O Gauge Track.   **400   800   400**

173 AND 173E COMPLETE RAILROAD LAYOUT (1932-34): Scenic Railway mounted on table with folding legs, 48″ by 42″, with trains and accessories, landscaped.

(A) 1932, O Gauge, contains 248 Locomotive, two 629 Pullmans, 630 Observation, felt composition Tunnel, 1012X Station, two 184 Bungalows, 435 Power Station, four 060 Telegraph Poles, pair 021 Switches, O Gauge Track, Y Transformer.   **NRS**
(B) 1933, same as (A), but substitutes 259E Locomotive with 259T Tender, 603 Pullman, 604 Observation, 1560 Station, plus 88 Rheostat.   **NRS**
(C) 1934, same as (B), but L Transformer.   **NRS**

173S COMPLETE RAILROAD LAYOUT (1932): Scenic Railway mounted on table with folding legs, 48″ by 42″, with trains and accessories, landscaped; O Gauge, contains 259 Locomotive, 259T Tender, 529 Pullman, 530 Observation, felt composition Tunnel, 1012X Station, two 184 Bungalows, 435 Power Station, four 060 Telegraph Poles, pair 021 Switches, O Gauge Track, Y Transformer.   **NRS**

174 COMPLETE RAILROAD LAYOUT (1923-31): Packaged set of trains and accessories.

(A) 1923, contains 154 Locomotive, 602 Baggage Car, two 603 Pullmans, 119 Tunnel, 106 three-section Bridge, 121 Station, six 60 Telegraph Poles, 62 Semaphore, 68 Warning Sign, pair 022 Switches, O Gauge Track, 88 Rheostat.   **700   1400   700**
(B) 1924-25, same as (A), but substitutes 153 Locomotive, two 603 Pullmans, 604 Observation.   **700   1400   700**
(C) 1926-27, contains 252 Locomotive, two 607 Pullmans, 608 Observation, 119 Tunnel, 106 three-section Bridge, 121 Station, six 60 Telegraph Poles, two 62 Semaphores, 068 Warning Sign, pair 022 Switches, O Gauge Track, 88 Rheostat.   **600   1200   600**
(D) 1928, same as (C), but substitutes 122 Station, pair 021 Switches; 252 Locomotive listed, but 253 Locomotive shown in catalogue illustration. R. Morris comment.   **600   1200   600**
(E) 1929-31, same as (D), but substitutes 253 Locomotive, has one 62 Semaphore, 89 Flag Pole.   **600   1200   600**

175 COMPLETE RAILROAD LAYOUT (1928-29): Packaged set of trains and accessories: 254E Locomotive, two 610 Pullmans, 612 Observation, 119L Tunnel, 106 three-span Bridge, 437 Signal Tower, eight 60 Telegraph Poles, 069 Warning Signal, 080 Semaphore, 90 Flag Pole, pair 012 Switches, O Gauge Track, 81 Rheostat.   **900   1800   900**

176 COMPLETE RAILROAD LAYOUT (1923-25, 1930-31): Packaged set of trains and accessories.

(A) 1923, contains 156 Locomotive, two 610 Pullmans, 612 Observation, 119 Tunnel, 121 Station, 109 five-sec-

GD EXC RST

tion Bridge, eight 60 Telegraph Poles, 62 Semaphore, pair 022 Switches, O Gauge Track, 88 Rheostat.   **800   1600   800**
(B) 1924-25, same as (A), but substitutes 254 Locomotive.   **650   1300   650**
(C) 1930-31, contains 260E Locomotive and Tender, two 710 Pullmans, 712 Observation, 119L Tunnel, 437 Signal Tower, 106 three-section Bridge, eight 060 Telegraph Poles, 069 Warning Signal, 080 Semaphore, 90 Flag Pole, two 56 Lamp Posts, pair 012 Switches, O Gauge Track, 81 Rheostat.   **800   1600   800**

177 SCENIC RAILWAY (1922-23): Wooden table with detachable legs, fitted with trains, accessories and scenery.

(A) 1922, O Gauge, contains 150 Locomotive, two 603 Pullmans, 604 Observation, 119 Tunnel, six Illuminated Metal Houses (see note at end of listing), 124 Station, two-span Bridge (three 110 spans are illustrated in the catalogue), five 60 Telegraph Poles, 069 Warning Signal, 62 Semaphore, two 022 Switches, nine OC Track, seven OS Track, OCC Track, 72″ by 48″, with landscaping and packaged in wooden case; original price $150. The catalogue illustrations of the Illuminated Metal Houses do not closely resemble any of the bungalows or villas introduced the following year; descriptions of these buildings are requested.   **NRS**
(B) 1923, O and Standard Gauges, contains 150 Locomotive, 603 Pullman, 604 Observation, 33 Locomotive, 35 Pullman, 36 Observation, five 184 Bungalows, 189 Villa, 191 Villa, 124 Station, 110 Bridge, two 104 Bridges, three 60 Telegraph Poles, 69 Warning Signal, 62 Semaphore, five 58 Lamp Posts, 57 Lamp Post, 89 Flag Pole, O and Standard Gauge Track, 78″ by 57″, with landscaping; original price $200.   **NRS**

178 SCENIC RAILWAY (1922-23): Wooden table with detachable legs, fitted with trains, accessories and scenery.

(A) 1922, O Gauge, contains 150 Locomotive, two 603 Pullmans, 604 Observation, four Illuminated Metal Houses (see note at end of listing), 124 Station, two-span Bridge (three 110 spans are illustrated in the catalogue), five 60 Telegraph Poles, 069 Warning Signal, seven OC Track, two OS Track, OCC Track, 60″ by 36″, with landscaping and packaged in wooden case; original price $100. The catalogue illustrations of the Illuminated Metal Houses do not closely resemble any of the bungalows or villas introduced the following year; descriptions of these buildings are requested.   **NRS**
(B) 1923, O Gauge, contains 150 Locomotive, 603 Pullman, 604 Observation, 118 Tunnel, five 184 Bungalows, 124 Station, two 110 Bridges, five 60 Telegraph Poles, 069 Warning Signal, 62 Semaphore, four 58 Lamp Posts, 57 Lamp Post, 89 Flag Pole, O Gauge Track, 60″ by 36″, with landscaping; original price $150.   **NRS**

GD   EXC   RST

180 SCENIC RAILWAY (1923): Wooden platform fitted with trains, accessories and scenery; O Gauge, contains 150 Locomotive, two 600 Pullmans, three 184 Bungalows, 127 Station, two 60 Telegraph Poles, 62 Semaphore, two 58 Lamp Posts, 89 Flag Pole, eight OC Track, 36" by 36", with landscaping; original price $50. **NRS**

183 SCENIC RAILWAY (1922): Two-piece wooden table connected by steel bolts and with detachable legs, fitted with trains, accessories and scenery; Standard Gauge, contains 38 Locomotive, two 35 Pullmans, 36 Observation, 120 Tunnel, nine Illuminated Metal Houses (see note at end of listing), 124 Station, two-span Bridge, Foot Bridge (see note at end of listing), eleven 60 Telegraph Poles, 69 Warning Signal, 62 Semaphore, two 67 Lamp Posts, seven C Track, nine S Track, CC Track, 72" by 48", with landscaping and packaged in wooden case; original price $335. The catalogue illustrations of the illuminated metal houses do not closely resemble any of the bungalows or villas introduced the following year, nor are catalogue numbers given for the bridges. Descriptions of these items are requested. **NRS**

198 SCENIC RAILWAY (1924-28): Two-section wood and composition board table fitted with accessories and scenery but no trains; O Gauge, contains 130L Tunnel, 131 Corner Elevation, 132 Corner Grass Plot, two 133 Heartshape Grass Plots, 134 Oval Grass Plot, two 504 Rose Bushes, three 505 Oak Trees, 184 Bungalow, 189 Villa, 191 Villa, 092 Signal Tower, 069 Warning Signal, 076 Block Signal, 077 Crossing Gate, 56 Lamp Post, 58 Lamp Post, 89 Flag Pole, O Gauge Track, 72" by 28"; original price $50. Components of these railways differed throughout the years. For example, the 1927 catalogue lists the following additional planting items: four 500 Pine Bushes, two 501 Small Pine Trees, three 502 Medium Pine Trees, three 503 Large Pine Trees, and four 510 Canna Bushes. **NRS**

199 SCENIC RAILWAY (1924-28): Three-section wood and composition board table fitted with accessories and scenery but no trains; Standard Gauge, contains 120 Tunnel, 131 Corner Elevation, 132 Corner Grass Plot, two 133 Heartshape Grass Plots, two 134 Oval Grass Plots, 135 Circular Grass Plot, 136 Large Elevation, eight 504 Rose Bushes, sixteen 505 Oak Trees, 124 Station, three 184 Bungalows, 189 Villa, 191 Villa, 092 Signal Tower, 66 Semaphore, 69 Warning Signal, 77 Crossing Gate, 78 Train Control Signal, 57 Lamp Post, three 58 Lamp Posts, two 61 Lamp Posts, 89 Flag Pole, Standard Gauge Track, 90" by 60"; original price $80. Components of these railways differed throughout the years. For example, the 1927 catalogue lists the following additional planting items: four 500 Pine Bushes, four 501 Small Pine Trees, four 502 Medium Pine Trees, four 503 Large Pine Trees, and four 510 Canna Bushes. **NRS**

GD   EXC   RST

269W LAYOUT (1940): Packaged set of trains and accessories: 225 Locomotive, 2235 Tender, 3651 Lumber Car, two 2652 Gondolas, 2657 Caboose, 165 Magnetic Crane, O Gauge Track.   **600   1200   600**

273W LAYOUT (1940): Packaged set of trains and accessories: 226 Locomotive, 2226 Tender, three 3811 Lumber Cars, 2817 Caboose, 164 Lumber Loader, O Gauge Track.   **850   1700   850**

405 COMPLETE RAILROAD LAYOUT (1924-26, 1932-33): Packaged set of trains and accessories.

(A) 1924-26, contains 402 Locomotive, 5 Locomotive, 11 Flatcar, 12 Gondola, 13 Cattle Car, 14 Boxcar, 15 Tank Car, 16 Ballast Car, 17 Caboose, 418 Pullman, 419 Combine, 490 Observation, 120 Tunnel, 121 Station, 101 Bridge, four 184 Bungalows, 189 Villa, 191 Villa, eight 60 Telegraph Poles, 65 Semaphore, 66 Semaphore, 69 Warning Signal, two 77 Crossing Gates, 89 Flag Pole, four 57 Lamp Posts, two 59 Lamp Posts, three pair 22 Switches, two 23 Bumpers, Standard Gauge Track, K Transformer.   **NRS**

(B) 1932, contains 9E Locomotive, 424 Pullman, 425 Pullman, 426 Observation, 915 Tunnel, 917 Mountain, 921 Park, 114 Station, 155 Station, 436 Power Station, 438 Signal Tower, 440 Signal Bridge, 80 Semaphore, 90 Flag Pole, 550 Figure Set, pair 223 Switches, Standard Gauge Track, 81 Rheostat, T Transformer.   **NRS**

(C) 1933, same as (B), but substitutes K Transformer.   **NRS**

407 COMPLETE RAILROAD LAYOUT (1927-31): Packaged set of trains and accessories.

(A) 1927-29, contains 408E Locomotive, 418 Pullman, 419 Combine, 431 Dining Car, 490 Observation, 380E Locomotive, 211 Lumber Car, 212 Gondola, 213 Cattle Car, 214 Boxcar, 215 Tank Car, 216 Coal Hopper, 217 Caboose, 218 Dump Car, 219 Crane, 140L Tunnel, 124 Station, 101 Bridge, 436 Power Station, 437 Switch Signal Tower, 438 Signal Tower, three 184 Bungalows, 189 Villa, 191 Villa, twelve 60 Telegraph Poles, 69 Warning Signal, two 76 Block Signals, two 77 Crossing Gates, 78 Train Control Signal, 80 Semaphore, 84 Semaphore, 89 Flag Pole, four 56 Lamp Posts, two 57 Lamp Posts, two 59 Lamp Posts, two 67 Lamp Posts, three pair 222 Switches, Standard Gauge Track, two 23 Bumpers, K Transformer, two 81 Rheostats.   **NRS**

(B) 1930-31, contains 408E Locomotive, 412 Pullman, 413 Pullman, 414 Pullman, 416 Observation, 390E Locomotive and Tender, 212 Gondola, 217 Caboose, 218 Dump Car, 219 Crane, 140L Tunnel, 128 Station with Terrace, 300 Hellgate Bridge, 840 Power House, 195 Terrace, twelve 85 Telegraph Poles, 69 Warning Signal, two 77 Crossing Gates, 78 Train Control Signal, 79 Flashing Signal, 80 Semaphore, 87 Railroad Crossing Signal, four 56 Lamp Posts, two 67 Lamp Posts, 208 Tool Set, 209 Barrel Set, four pair 222 Switches, Stand-

GD EXC RST

ard Gauge Track, two 23 Bumpers, K Transformer, two 81 Rheostats. **NRS**

424 COMPLETE RAILROAD LAYOUT (1923): Packaged set of trains and accessories: 42 Locomotive, 12 Gondola, 13 Cattle Car, 14 Boxcar, 15 Tank Car, 16 Ballast Car, 17 Caboose, 18 Pullman, 19 Combine, 190 Observation, 120 Tunnel, 121 Station, two 65 Semaphores, 66 Semaphore, two 67 Lamp Posts, 217 Car Lighting Set, pair 21 Switches, Standard Gauge Track, K Transformer. **NRS**

500 PINE BUSHES (1927-28): Dealer display and part of some Scenic Railways. 35 75 —

501 SMALL PINE TREES (1927-28): Dealer display and part of some Scenic Railways. 35 75 —

502 MEDIUM PINE TREES (1927-28): Dealer display and part of some Scenic Railways.

35 75 —

503 LARGE PINE TREES (1927-28): Dealer display and part of some Scenic Railways. 35 75 —

504 ROSE BUSHES (1924-28): Dealer display and part of some Scenic Railways. 35 75 —

505 OAK TREES (1924-28): Dealer display and part of some Scenic Railways. 35 75 —

506 COMPOSITION BOARD PLATFORM (1924-28): Two-section decorated table; dealer display and part of 198 Scenic Railway. 75 150 —

507 COMPOSITION BOARD PLATFORM (1924-28): Three-section decorated table; dealer display and part of 199 Scenic Railway. 100 200 —

508 COMPOSITION BOARD SKY (1924-28): Two-section painted background, dealer display and part of 198 and 199 Scenic Railways. 75 150 —

509 COMPOSITION BOARD MOUNTAINS (1924-28): Painted background, dealer display and part of 198 and 199 Scenic Railways. 75 150 —

510 CANNA BUSHES (1927-28): Dealer display and part of some Scenic Railways. 35 75 —

831W LAYOUT (1941): Packaged set of trains and accessories: 225 Locomotive, 2235 Tender, 3651 Lumber Dump Car, 3652 Operating Gondola, 3659 Coal Dump Car, 2757 Caboose, 97 Coal Elevator, O Gauge Track. 650 1300 650

869W LAYOUT (1941): Packaged set of trains and accessories: 225 Locomotive, 2235 Tender, two 2652 Gondolas, 3651 Lumber Dump Car, 2757 Caboose, 165 Magnetic Crane, O Gauge Track. 650 1300 650

878W LAYOUT (1941): Packaged set of trains and accessories: 226 Locomotive, 2226 Tender, 2812 Gondola, 3811 Lumber Dump Car, 3814 Operating Merchandise Car, 2957 Caboose, 164 Lumber Loader, O Gauge Track. 950 1900 950

1007 LAYOUT (1932): Scenic Railway mounted on platform, 43¼" by 29½", with trains and accessories, landscaped; contains 1035 Winner Locomotive, 1016 Tender, 1020 Baggage Car, 1011 Pullman, 1019 Observation, felt composition tunnel, 1017 Transformer Station, 913 Illuminated Landscaped Bungalow, O27 Track. **NRS**

1053E LIONEL-IVES COMPLETE ELECTRIC RAILROAD (1933): Scenic Railway mounted on platform, 43¼" by 29½", with trains and accessories, landscaped; contains 1651E Locomotive and Tender, two 1690 Pullmans, 1691 Observation, felt composition Tunnel, 1017 Transformer Station, 913 Illuminated Landscaped Bungalow, O Gauge Track. **NRS**

1057E LIONEL JUNIOR RAILROAD (1934): Scenic Railway mounted on platform, 43¼" by 29½", with trains and accessories, landscaped; contains 1681E Locomotive and Tender, two 1690 Pullmans, 1691 Observation, felt composition Tunnel, 1027 Transformer Station, 913 Illuminated Landscaped Bungalow, O Gauge Track. **NRS**

1066E DISTANT CONTROL RAILROAD (1935-36): Scenic Railway mounted on platform, 43¼" by 29½", with streamlined train and accessories, landscaped; contains 1700E Power Car, 1701 Coach, 1702 Observation, felt composition Tunnel, 1560 Station, 1028 (1935) or 1029 (1936) Transformer, 913 Illuminated Landscaped Bungalow, O Gauge Track. **NRS**

1095W LAYOUT (1938-40): Packaged set of trains and accessories: 1666E Locomotive, 2689W Tender, 2620 Floodlight Car, 2680 Tank Car, 3659 Coal Dump Car, 2657 Caboose, 96 Coal Elevator, pair 1121 Switches, O27 Gauge Track, 1040 Transformer.

500 1000 500

1099 LAYOUT (1940): Packaged set of trains and accessories: 1666 Locomotive, 2689 Tender, three 3651 Lumber Dump Cars, 2657 Caboose, 164 Lumber Loader, pair 1121 Switches, O27 Gauge Track, 1041 Transformer. 500 1000 500

1195W LAYOUT (1941): Packaged set of trains and accessories: 1666 Locomotive, 2666 Tender, 2620 Floodlight Car, 2680 Tank Car, 3659 Coal Dump Car, 2672 Caboose, 97 Coal Elevator, pair 1121 Switches, O27 Track, 1041 Transformer. 500 1000 500

1199W LAYOUT (1941): Packaged set of trains and accessories: 1666 Locomotive, 2666 Tender, three 3651 Lumber Dump Cars, 2672 Caboose, 164 Lumber Loader, pair 1121 Switches, O27 Track, 1041 Transformer. 500 1000 500

1526 LIONEL-IVES MECHANICAL FREIGHT LAYOUT (1933): Scenic Railway mounted on platform, with trains and accessories, lithographed landscaping with tunnel, bridge and animal cutout; contains 1506L Locomotive, 1502 Tender, 1512 Gondola, 1514 Boxcar, 1517 Caboose, eight MWC Track. **NRS**

GD EXC RST

1527 LIONEL-IVES MECHANICAL PASSENGER LAYOUT (1933): Same as 1526, but with three 1811 Pullmans instead of freight cars. **NRS**

1528 LIONEL-IVES MECHANICAL PASSENGER LAYOUT (1933-34): Packaged set of trains and accessories: 1506L Locomotive, 1502 Tender, 1813 Baggage Car, 1811 Pullman, 1812 Observation, 1560 Station, six 1571 Telegraph Poles, 1572 Semaphore, 1573 Warning Sign, 1574 Clock, pair 1550 Switches, ten MWC Track, six MS Track. **NRS**

1536 MICKEY MOUSE CIRCUS TRAIN LAYOUT (1935): Packaged set of trains and accessories: 1508 Locomotive, 1509 Stoker Tender with Mickey Mouse figure, Circus Diner Car, Circus Animal Car, Circus Band Car, cardboard accessories (tent, gas station, automobile, sign and circus tickets), Mickey Mouse

GD EXC RST

Barker figure; values given for complete set with all cardboard items in original box. **1000 2000 —**

1537 MICKEY MOUSE PASSENGER LAYOUT (1935): Packaged set of trains and accessories: 1508 Locomotive, 1509 Stoker Tender with Mickey Mouse figure, 1813 Baggage Car, 1811 Pullman, 1812 Observation, 1560 Station, six 1571 Telegraph Poles, 1572 Semaphore, 1573 Warning Sign, 1574 Clock, pair 1550 Switches, ten MWC Track, six MS Track. **NRS**

1552 MECHANICAL RAILROAD LAYOUT (1936): Packaged set of trains and accessories: 1511 Locomotive, 1516 Tender, two 1811 Pullman, 1812 Observation, six 1571 Telegraph Poles, 1572 Semaphore, 1574 Clock, eight MWC Track, four MS Track; catalogued with 1046 Mechanical Gateman and Crossing but probably not manufactured. **NRS**

CHAPTER XV

Not Strictly Railroad

A study of the fortunes of the Lionel Corporation, from its founding at the turn of the century until its near collapse and reorganization in 1969, indicates that despite various attempts at diversification, its greatest successes were invariably train related. This is especially true of the late 1950s and early 1960s, after the retirement of the founder, Joshua Lionel Cowen, when a number of misguided decisions led the firm into the production of a number of unprofitable sidelines. During the Prewar period, a few attempts were made to branch out into non-train toys, and although the products were of high quality, they never successfully competed with such broad-based toy manufacturers as Louis Marx, and did not enjoy long life spans.

Cowen was more than a superb designer and electrical engineer; he was at heart an enthusiast and devotee of railroads and railroading, loving especially the powerful steamers that even today, long after their disappearance from the landscape, evoke the most powerful images of industrial America. His trains are magnificent! His single-minded promotion of these products, and his sometimes ruthless competitive tactics toward Ives and American Flyer, resulted in one of the most pervasive corporate images ever established. To millions of consumers, the name "Lionel" was inseparable from electric trains.

Despite clever ideas and well-executed designs, Lionel's other toys never received the promotional attention accorded to the trains. They were generally back-of-the-book items in the catalogue, and the company never succeeded in establishing in the mind of the buyer a link between the brand name and anything other than toy trains.

With one exception, the 455 Electric Range, all of Lionel's toys were transportation-related items. This reflected in part a definite marketing bias toward male children, in an era when gender stereotyping was almost universally accepted and unchallenged. Electric train catalogues from every manufacturer tended to depict boys playing with the products while their sisters were shown as admiring observers, rather than as participants in the fun. It is speculated that Cowen understood well the techniques of promoting his wares to the young male, but was woefully ignorant of (and probably uncaring about) the likes and dislikes of female children.

In fact, many Lionels were purchased for young girls, the author's wife and sister among them, despite the advertising bias. The company's belated but famous attempt at winning the distaff market, the pink and pastel Girl's Train of 1957, was a spectacular failure, however. The company simply did not realize that girls who liked trains would want them to *look* like trains, not like confections from a fashion magazine. The author's wife, Gay, who owned both Ives and Lionel passenger sets while growing up, further suggests that girls did not want their trains to look different from those owned by boys.

The Electric Range was a substantial and attractive product, standing tall enough for use by young apprentice homemakers and constructed of porcelain-coated steel. Unlike simpler ovens produced by other companies after the Second World War, which bake miniature cakes with the heat from a light bulb, Lionel's stove contained heating elements that operated on a full 110 volts. Despite claims of cool operation due to heavy asbestos insulation, the two exposed surface elements were rated at 625 watts each, and the oven contained both broiling and baking units. The entire appliance, if turned on full, consumed 2500 watts of power, and produced a considerable amount of heat.

For very young children, this was an unsafe toy. For older girls who could be expected to understand the dangers involved and take proper precautions, the oven did in fact duplicate the functions of the full-sized kitchen range. It is speculated, however, that youngsters capable of using this toy could be trusted by their mothers to use the real thing. Given the choice, they would do so, making the Lionel product redundant.

455 Electric Range. A. Cox Collection, **Classic Toy Trains** *photograph.*

The range was introduced on the back of the 1930 catalogue at a price of $29.50, and was advertised again in 1932, although it is believed production was halted earlier and sales continued only until existing stock was disposed of. The high cost in those Depression years contributed to the lack of public acceptance of this toy, but the Electric Range probably failed for the more fundamental reason that it was not really a toy, but a miniature appliance, and an unsafe one. It was not perceived by the consumer as a plaything, and one cooking device in the household was usually considered sufficient. While mostly affluent families acquired them, they never achieved the broad acceptance that would have made them profitable.

An automobile from the 80 / 81 / 84 / 85 Racing Automobile Set.

The catalogues stated that five utensils were included with the stove, but did not list them. An illustration in the 1930 catalogue showed a frying pan and a sauce pan, while the pocket catalogue shows a frying pan, bread pan, muffin pan, square cake pan and coffee pot. The 1932 and 1933 illustrations show a sauce pan, spoon and coffee pot. Whereas this list includes seven different items, reader information is requested concerning which utensils were actually included in any given year.

The 80 and 81 Racing Automobile sets of 1912 were, like the trains, directed toward boys. That they never achieved the wide popularity of miniature railroads may have been due to the limitations in their play value. The cars were offered in basic sets with a single vehicle and a circle of track, or in the two-car set No. 84 with two concentric circles of track. The most elaborate version (No. 85) included straight sections, allowing the cars to compete on an oval.

As a competitive racing toy, these cars were less than satis-

factory, as the inner car had far less distance to travel in order to make a complete circuit, and thus an advantage over the outer one. Although extra track for expanding the system was available, it was not heavily promoted, and no switches were developed to allow the

43 Pleasure Boat. G. Zippie Collection, B. Schwab photograph.

cars to take different routes. While trains could be expanded with track and accessories to make ever more interesting layouts, the Racing Automobiles never received a similar support system, and this limitation kept them from developing into a self-sustaining product. Not until the slot car phenomenon of the 1960s would miniature racers achieve anything like the following among children enjoyed for decades by the electric train. Lionel's Racing Automobiles were sold through 1916, and have been reproduced recently by Lionel Trains, Inc. for the collector market.

Two handsome spring-powered motor boats were introduced during the 1930s, the 43 Lionel Craft Pleasure Boat in 1933 and the 44 Racing Boat two years later. Both were substantial steel models 17 inches long, and came with supporting display stands, but since they were designed to operate, most found their way to nearby streams in the hands of their young owners. Finding pristine examples of these toys is a rare occurrence today, as they were subject to rust if not thoroughly dried after use. They operated well and were fitted with adjustable rudders that could be set to keep them turning in circles, but it is likely that far more Lionel boats sailed away and eventually came to rest at the bottoms of lakes than ever ended up in toy collectors' display shelves.

One other transportation toy, the 50 or 55 Airplane and associated Airport accessory of 1936-1939, suffered the same type of limitation as the Racing Automobiles. The plane was tethered to the top of a tall trapezoidal pylon by a rigid supporting arm, and "flew" in circles above a colorful cardboard platform printed to suggest runways, terminals and destination cities. The catalogue illustration and text promoted the remote-control features of the airplane, suggesting the fun to be had in "Loops, side-slips, tail-spins, power dives," but lasting play value was lacking in this toy. After a number of revolutions, the plane ceased to have the appeal of trains, whose routes and buildings could be endlessly rearranged and whose cars could be shuffled and loaded with toys and imagined cargo and passengers.

Had the Airplane been more versatile, it might have enjoyed considerable popularity, as the public was becoming increasingly aware of and fascinated by air travel in the 1930s. Pan American had already established scheduled and dependable passenger service, and air mail routes were expanding almost daily. It is interesting to note the use of the term "joy stick" in the catalogue description of the control unit. This phrase enjoys wide use currently as a result of computer game applications, but was apparently also a term familiar to the aviation-minded public in the years preceding World War II.

Power for the airplane is obtained directly from house current, without the use of a transformer. The text claimed the toy was "practically indestructible," while in fact it proved to be somewhat fragile and is

50 Remote Control Airplane. A. Cox Collection, **Classic Toy Trains** *photograph.*

rarely found undamaged today. It first appeared at $10.95 in 1936, rising to $15 in the 1937 catalogue, but a drastic reduction to $9.95 the following year suggests that sales were disappointing. It was dropped after 1939.

The boats and racing cars of the Prewar period were marginally more successful than Lionel's other ventures outside the train sphere, but overall the company achieved the best sales with products its management understood best. Following are descriptions of known miscellaneous accessories produced by Lionel between 1912 and 1942.

GD EXC RST

43 LIONEL CRAFT PLEASURE BOAT (1933-36, 1939-41): 2Steel construction, white hull, beige deck, vermilion bottom, brass or nickel fittings, two molded and painted figures in forward cockpit beginning in 1935, flag, clockwork motor, display stand, 17″ long; reproduced by Lionel Trains, Inc. G. Zippie Collection.

(A) Original Lionel.   **250   450   225**
(B) 1990, reproduction by Lionel Trains, Inc., catalogue No. 13802, embossed "LTI" or "Lionel Trains, Inc."   **—   475   —**

44 LIONEL CRAFT RACING BOAT (1935-36): Steel construction, white hull, dark brown deck, green bottom, nickel fittings, simulated engine and two molded figures in rear cockpit, large numerals "44" centered on sides, clockwork motor, display stand, 17″ long; reproduced by Lionel Trains, Inc.

(A) Original Lionel.   **300   550   275**
(B) 1991, reproduction by Lionel Trains, Inc., catalogue No. 13805, embossed "LTI" or "Lionel Trains, Inc."   **—   475   —**

GD EXC RST

49 AIRPORT (1937-39): Lithographed two-piece circular cardboard, 58″ in diameter, sold separately to be used as base for 50 or 55 Airplane. **50 100 —**

50 REMOTE CONTROL AIRPLANE (1936): Steel construction, red body and 12″-wide wings, soft rubber propeller (which became brittle with age) on nose, 30″-high trapezoidal pylon enclosing motor and power supply, rotating support arm from top of pylon to body of plane, die-cast control box with joy stick.

100 200 90

51 AIRPORT (1936, 1938): Lithographed two-piece square heavy paper stock, sold separately to be used as base for 50 or 55 Airplane. **50 100 —**

55 REMOTE CONTROL AIRPLANE (1937-39): Similar to 50, but with aluminum-painted wing and stabilizer trim, some mechanical variations in mechanism. **150 325 125**

80 RACING AUTOMOBILE SET (1912-16): Metal construction, racing-style body with fenders, fuel tanks and suspension details, simulated brake and throttle handles, ten-spoked wheels, replaceable solid rubber tires, spare tire mounted on rear deck, driver figure holding the steering wheel with mechanic figure sitting beside him, powered by electric motor, shoe at rear for third-rail current pickup, 8½″ long; eight sections steel L or O curved track forming circle 36″ in diameter, with central channel for insulated third rail (one section with wiring connections), starting post.

750 1200 700

81 RACING AUTOMOBILE SET (1912-16): Same as 80, but with 30″-diameter I curved track.

750 1200 700

84 DOUBLE RACING AUTOMOBILE SET (1912-16): Two-car set (80 and 81) allowing concentric placement of track circles; reproduced by Lionel Trains, Inc.

(A) Original Lionel. **1500 2400 1400**
(B) 1991, reproduction by Lionel Trains, Inc., catalogue No. 13803, embossed "LTI" or "Lionel Trains, Inc." **NEW 700**

85 DOUBLE RACING AUTOMOBILE SET (1912-16): Same as 84, but including eight sections A straight track. **1500 2400 1400**

455 ELECTRIC RANGE (1930, 1932-33): Porcelain and steel construction, green legs, cream oven and stove, two stove-top heating elements, two heating units in oven (one for broiling, one for baking), thermometer on oven door, nickel trim, brass plate, decal of chef's face with lettering "LIONEL" above stove elements, four control knobs, master switch, pilot light, five cooking utensils, 25″ wide, 11″ deep, 33″ high. Reader assistance is requested to identify cooking utensils. **250 500 250**

1500 LOCOSCOPE (1939): Small hand-held Hudson type locomotive with viewing lens and slot for film strip of seventy-five pictures, "LIONEL" embossed beneath cab windows; offered only on back page of 1939 catalogue with $1 subscription to *Model Builder Magazine*. Excellent price requires film strip.

(A) Film contains railroad subjects. **50 100 —**
(B) Film depicts 1939 World's Fair. **50 100 —**

A TRACK (1912-16): Straight section for Racing Automobiles, 14″ long; reproduced by Lionel Trains, Inc.

(A) Original Lionel. **2 5 3**
(B) 1991, reproduction by Lionel Trains, Inc., catalogue No. 13807, packaged in bulk, embossed "LTI" or "Lionel Trains, Inc." **— 18 —**

I TRACK (1912-16): Curved section for Racing Automobiles, eight sections to a 30″-diameter circle; reproduced by Lionel Trains, Inc.

(A) Original Lionel. **2 5 3**
(B) 1991, reproduction by Lionel Trains, Inc., catalogue No. 13808, packaged in bulk, embossed "LTI" or "Lionel Trains, Inc." **— 22 —**

L TRACK (1915-16): Similar to I, but forming 36″-diameter circle; reproduced by Lionel Trains, Inc.

(A) Original Lionel. **2 5 3**
(B) 1991, reproduction by Lionel Trains, Inc., catalogue No. 13809, packaged in bulk, embossed "LTI" or "Lionel Trains, Inc." **— 22 —**

O TRACK (1912-14): Similar to L. **2 5 3**

INDEX

Page numbers in italics denote color photographs.